Status and Security in Southeast Asian State Systems

Southeast Asia serves as an excellent case study to discuss major transformations in the relationship amongst states. This book looks at the changing nature of relationships between countries in Southeast Asia, as well as their relationships with other states in Asia and beyond.

A diverse region in many areas, open to outside influence in many fields, but not without dynamics of its own, it has been through centuries the site of states with very differing levels of power and in a variety of forms. It has also been exposed to powerful neighbours, seawards empires and contending world powers. Adopting a historical approach, this book analyses state relations against the background of regional and geopolitical developments from within and without. It discusses how Southeast Asian states of the twenty-first century can best preserve their security in the context of the rise of China, and goes on to look at the extent to which they can preserve their autonomy of action.

Offering a long-term perspective on these issues, this inter-disciplinary study is of interest to scholars and students of Southeast Asian history and politics, world history and international relations.

Nicholas Tarling is a Fellow of the New Zealand Asia Institute at the University of Auckland, New Zealand, and one of the world's leading authorities on the history of Southeast Asia. His publications include *Southeast Asia and the Great Powers* (Routledge, 2010), *Britain and the Neutralisation of Laos* (NUS Press, 2011), and *New Zealand: The Making of an Asia-Pacific Society* (Confucius Institute, 2011).

Routledge Studies in the Modern History of Asia

1 **The Police in Occupation Japan**
Control, corruption and resistance to reform
Christopher Aldous

2 **Chinese Workers**
A new history
Jackie Sheehan

3 **The Aftermath of Partition in South Asia**
Tai Yong Tan and Gyanesh Kudaisya

4 **The Australia–Japan Political Alignment**
1952 to the present
Alan Rix

5 **Japan and Singapore in the World Economy**
Japan's economic advance into Singapore, 1870–1965
Shimizu Hiroshi and Hirakawa Hitoshi

6 **The Triads as Business**
Yiu Kong Chu

7 **Contemporary Taiwanese Cultural Nationalism**
A-chin Hsiau

8 **Religion and Nationalism in India**
The case of the Punjab
Harnik Deol

9 **Japanese Industrialisation**
Historical and cultural perspectives
Ian Inkster

10 **War and Nationalism in China**
1925–45
Hans J. van de Ven

11 **Hong Kong in Transition**
One country, two systems
Edited by Robert Ash, Peter Ferdinand, Brian Hook and Robin Porter

12 **Japan's Postwar Economic Recovery and Anglo-Japanese Relations, 1948–62**
Noriko Yokoi

13 **Japanese Army Stragglers and Memories of the War in Japan, 1950–75**
Beatrice Trefalt

14 **Ending the Vietnam War**
The Vietnamese communists' perspective
Ang Cheng Guan

15 **The Development of the Japanese Nursing Profession**
Adopting and adapting Western influences
Aya Takahashi

16 **Women's Suffrage in Asia**
Gender nationalism and democracy
Louise Edwards and Mina Roces

17 **The Anglo-Japanese Alliance, 1902–22**
Phillips Payson O'Brien

18 **The United States and Cambodia, 1870–1969**
From curiosity to confrontation
Kenton Clymer

19 **Capitalist Restructuring and the Pacific Rim**
Ravi Arvind Palat

20 **The United States and Cambodia, 1969–2000**
A troubled relationship
Kenton Clymer

21 **British Business in Post-Colonial Malaysia, 1957–70**
'Neo-colonialism' or 'disengagement'?
Nicholas J. White

22 **The Rise and Decline of Thai Absolutism**
Kullada Kesboonchoo Mead

23 **Russian Views of Japan, 1792–1913**
An anthology of travel writing
David N. Wells

24 **The Internment of Western Civilians under the Japanese, 1941–45**
A patchwork of internment
Bernice Archer

25 **The British Empire and Tibet**
1900–1922
Wendy Palace

26 **Nationalism in Southeast Asia**
If the people are with us
Nicholas Tarling

27 **Women, Work and the Japanese Economic Miracle**
The case of the cotton textile industry, 1945–75
Helen Macnaughtan

28 **A Colonial Economy in Crisis**
Burma's rice cultivators and the world depression of the 1930s
Ian Brown

29 **A Vietnamese Royal Exile in Japan**
Prince Cuong De (1882–1951)
Tran My-Van

30 **Corruption and Good Governance in Asia**
Nicholas Tarling

31 **US–China Cold War Collaboration, 1971–89**
S. Mahmud Ali

32 **Rural Economic Development in Japan**
From the nineteenth century to the Pacific War
Penelope Francks

33 **Colonial Armies in Southeast Asia**
Edited by Karl Hack and Tobias Rettig

34 **Intra Asian Trade and the World Market**
A. J. H. Latham and Heita Kawakatsu

35 **Japanese–German Relations, 1895–1945**
War, diplomacy and public opinion
Edited by Christian W. Spang and Rolf-Harald Wippich

36 **Britain's Imperial Cornerstone in China**
The Chinese maritime customs service, 1854–1949
Donna Brunero

37 **Colonial Cambodia's 'Bad Frenchmen'**
The rise of French rule and the life of Thomas Caraman, 1840–87
Gregor Muller

38 **Japanese–American Civilian Prisoner Exchanges and Detention Camps, 1941–45**
Bruce Elleman

39 **Regionalism in Southeast Asia**
Nicholas Tarling

40 **Changing Visions of East Asia, 1943–93**
Transformations and continuities
R. B. Smith (Edited by Chad J. Mitcham)

41 **Christian Heretics in Late Imperial China**
Christian inculturation and state control, 1720–1850
Lars P. Laamann

42 **Beijing – A Concise History**
Stephen G. Haw

43 **The Impact of the Russo-Japanese War**
Edited by Rotem Kowner

44 **Business–Government Relations in Prewar Japan**
Peter von Staden

45 **India's Princely States**
People, princes and colonialism
Edited by Waltraud Ernst and Biswamoy Pati

46 **Rethinking Gandhi and Nonviolent Relationality**
Global perspectives
Edited by Debjani Ganguly and John Docker

47 **The Quest for Gentility in China**
Negotiations beyond gender and class
Edited by Daria Berg and Chloë Starr

48 **Forgotten Captives in Japanese Occupied Asia**
Edited by Kevin Blackburn and Karl Hack

49 **Japanese Diplomacy in the 1950s**
From isolation to integration
Edited by Iokibe Makoto, Caroline Rose, Tomaru Junko and John Weste

50 **The Limits of British Colonial Control in South Asia**
Spaces of disorder in the Indian Ocean region
Edited by Ashwini Tambe and Harald Fischer-Tiné

51 **On The Borders of State Power**
Frontiers in the greater Mekong sub-region
Edited by Martin Gainsborough

52 **Pre-Communist Indochina**
R. B. Smith, edited by Beryl Williams

53 **Communist Indochina**
R. B. Smith, edited by Beryl Williams

54 **Port Cities in Asia and Europe**
Edited by Arndt Graf and Chua Beng Huat

55 **Moscow and the Emergence of Communist Power in China, 1925–30**
The Nanchang Rising and the birth of the Red Army
Bruce A. Elleman

56 **Colonialism, Violence and Muslims in Southeast Asia**
The Maria Hertogh controversy and its aftermath
Syed Muhd Khairudin Aljunied

57 **Japanese and Hong Kong Film Industries**
Understanding the origins of East Asian film networks
Kinnia Shuk-ting

58 **Provincial Life and the Military in Imperial Japan**
The phantom samurai
Stewart Lone

59 **Southeast Asia and the Vietnam War**
Ang Cheng Guan

60 **Southeast Asia and the Great Powers**
Nicholas Tarling

61 **The Cold War and National Assertion in Southeast Asia**
Britain, the United States and Burma, 1948–62
Matthew Foley

62 **The International History of East Asia, 1900–968**
Trade, ideology and the quest for order
Edited by Antony Best

63 **Journalism and Politics in Indonesia**
A critical biography of Mochtar Lubis (1922–2004) as editor and author
David T. Hill

64 **Atrocity and American Military Justice in Southeast Asia**
Trial by army
Louise Barnett

65 **The Japanese Occupation of Borneo, 1941–45**
Ooi Keat Gin

66 **National Pasts in Europe and East Asia**
P. W. Preston

67 **Modern China's Ethnic Frontiers**
A journey to the West
Hsiao-ting Lin

68 **New Perspectives on the History and Historiography of Southeast Asia**
Continuing explorations
Michael Aung-Thwin and Kenneth R. Hall

69 **Food Culture in Colonial Asia**
A taste of empire
Cecilia Leong-Salobir

70 **China's Political Economy in Modern Times**
Changes and economic consequences, 1800–2000
Kent Deng

71 **Science, Public Health and the State in Modern Asia**
Edited by Liping Bu, Darwin Stapleton and Ka-che Yip

72 **Russo-Japanese Relations, 1905–17**
From enemies to allies
Peter Berton

73 **Reforming Public Health in Occupied Japan, 1945–52**
Alien prescriptions?
Christopher Aldous and Akihito Suzuki

74 **Trans-Colonial Modernities in South Asia**
Edited by Michael S. Dodson and Brian A. Hatcher

75 **The Evolution of the Japanese Developmental State**
Institutions locked in by ideas
Hironori Sasada

76 **Status and Security in Southeast Asian State Systems**
Nicholas Tarling

Status and Security in Southeast Asian State Systems

Nicholas Tarling

Routledge
Taylor & Francis Group
LONDON AND NEW YORK

First published 2013
by Routledge
2 Park Square, Milton Park, Abingdon, Oxon OX14 4RN

Simultaneously published in the USA and Canada
by Routledge
711 Third Avenue, New York, NY 10017

Routledge is an imprint of the Taylor & Francis Group, an informa business

British Library Cataloguing in Publication Data
A catalogue record for this book is available from the British Library

Library of Congress Cataloging-in-Publication Data
Tarling, Nicholas.
Status and security in Southeast Asian state systems / Nicholas Tarling.
p. cm. – (Routledge studies in the modern history of asia)
Includes bibliographical references and index.
1. Southeast Asia–Foreign relations. 2. Southeast Asia–Politics and government–1945- 3. Security, International–Southeast Asia. I. Title.
DS526.7.T365 2013
355′.033059–dc23 2012025428

ISBN: 978-0-415-53211-2 (hbk)
ISBN: 978-0-203-07959-1 (ebk)

Typeset in Times New Roman
by Cenveo Publisher Services

Contents

Acknowledgments

The author is pleased to acknowledge his debt to many of the historians of Southeast Asia, upon whose works he has drawn. He is grateful, too, for the services of the University of Auckland Library and for the support of the New Zealand Asia Institute. His thanks also extend to Brook Barrington who, amidst a busy career, still finds time to deploy a shrewd mind and sharp eyes when presented with another typescript.

1 Introduction

Reviewing Benno Teschke's *The Myth of 1648*, the historian Theodor K. Rabb commented on the internecine disputes within the discipline of International Relations, IR as it was rendered, mischievously adding that History might be called H. '[O]ne felt one had stumbled across a rerun of the impenetrable revisionism vs anti-revisionism Marxist quarrels of a century ago. Indeed, the book is a distant descendant of the polemical social/political/economic theorizing we associate with the age of Edward Bernstein and Rosa Luxemburg, replete with accusations of "intellectually spurious" work, fallacies and other such sins.'[1]

If a practitioner of H can thus criticize the current practice of IR, it is perhaps risky for another historian to think that he can contribute to the debate within that discipline, and it may be hubris to think that his contribution could be seen as positive. That, perhaps, is especially the case inasmuch as IR has always had a somewhat equivocal relationship with H, and that some of that equivocation is related to the differences between practitioners in the US and practitioners in the UK, the two countries where IR is most studied. The former, more numerous than the latter, have, moreover, taken a view that depreciates the rather more historically informed approach of the latter.

Robert M. Crawford argues that the IR discipline is in crisis. 'A science of IR, or any branch of politics, that concentrates only on how things *are* (or how they appear to be) is not merely one-sided, but misses the whole point of political analysis.' Yet that, he thinks, was what is sure to happen when 'the rich realities of socio-political life are forced through the crude sieve of positivist categories and distinctions'.[2] US practitioners have included Realists, Neorealists and Neoliberals, but they have, Crawford suggests, all diminished the discipline by their adoption of scientistic methods. The British school is less narrowly focused, but open to accusations that it lacks theory and that it is not policy-oriented nor amenable to being so. Indeed it stands more apart from practising politicians or potential statesmen, just as, one might add, the academic and political worlds in general stand more apart in the UK than in the US.

An historian can hardly avoid the temptation to offer what might be called historical explanations for the supposed crisis in the discipline of International Relations. 'International Relations emerged as a discipline in its own right after World War I.'[3] The discipline was 'established with the conviction that war must never happen again'.[4] Born of the wish to prevent another world war, it was, in E.H. Carr's terms, 'markedly and frankly utopian'.[5] The discipline was, as Knutsen adds, 'primarily an Atlantic phenomenon, infused with the political ideals of the Atlantic tradition'.[6] In particular it took up the ideas that President Woodrow Wilson had drawn from the traditions of Benthamite liberalism, repudiating the *realpolitik* that was considered to have been a prime cause of the war. Even the adjective itself – which Jeremy Bentham was the first to use, writing of 'international' law[7] – had a liberal overtone: what it was concerned with was in fact inter-state relations.

'The failure of the League [of Nations] system inevitably gave rise to charges of misplaced idealism and legalism from students of International Relations. The stage was set for power politics and its analysis.'[8] A rebirth of idealist internationalism after the Second World War was only brief, thanks to the tensions of the Cold War. 'Realism' re-emerged, and in a more shallow way than protagonists like Morgenthau, Kennan and Niebuhr envisaged. That was reinforced by attempts to employ quantitative methods in an endeavour to achieve a scientific approach. In this the US took the lead.[9]

So it did in the theorizing that followed. The most famous attempt was Kenneth Waltz's wonderfully articulate and articulated *Theory of International Relations* (1979). States, he argued, are placed within an anarchic international system, equal in status, unlike those in a hierarchical pattern, but quite unequal in capability. Any ordering principle is formed by their self-interested interactions, in particular by their search for security. 'Survival is a prerequisite to achieving any goals that states may have. … The survival motive is taken as the ground of action in a world where the security of states is not assured.'[10] Their sovereignty does not mean they can do as they please. 'The sovereignty of states has never entailed their insulation from the effects of other states' actions. Sovereign states have seldom led free and easy lives. To be sovereign and dependent are not contradictory conditions.'[11]

But could not even Waltz's theory – so well advanced, yet clearly placed in the context of the relationship between the US and the Soviet Union, and suffused by comparison between states and firms – be an illustration of what Crawford calls 'parochialism'? 'In the post-Second World War era, American IR has been … obsessed with itself.' He offers as an example the 'hegemonic stability theory', offered in the 1980s by Kindleberger and Keohane. It is 'a construct that can be applied to any power willing and able to provide the resources for the creation and maintenance of a stable world order, but that has in practice been applied mainly to the case of American leadership after which it is patterned. ... Developments at the level of American IR theory have merely mirrored, and have been inextricably bound up with, an almost evangelical commitment at the political level to the global spread of American economic-cultural values.' As Crawford says, powerful countries have generalized and transplanted their problems and philosophies to other countries 'throughout the ages'.[12]

The historian will be struck by the ways in which some IR experts have been able to reflect on the course of their discipline and the reasons both for the changes within it and for the disputes within it. An historian of Asia cannot help being struck, if not by its concern for the US, then by its focus on the West and on the state system that emerged in the West and is usually described as Westphalian after the treaties that ended the 30 Years War in Europe in 1648. The First World War was, perhaps, not so world-wide as to deprive the originators of the discipline of some justification for their focus, though China, Siam, and of course Japan were at Versailles, and others wanted to be, such as Vietnam and Korea. But the Second World War was certainly world-wide, as was its Cold War successor. Yet for the most part IR focused on the state and 'state actors' as they had at the end of the first war, and looked back at previous theorists of previous periods in what historians would consider a Whig interpretation: what had they 'contributed'? What was the canon of readings?

An historian of Asia cannot be sure that widening the range of IR – both in terms of time and place – would resolve what some of its practitioners see as a crisis in the discipline. But it is possible that a re-focus would be a source of renewed strength. Have there been other systems besides 'anarchy'? What was their nature? And how far did anarchy itself preclude order? Was that merely the result of competition? Some of these questions have been asked and some of them answered, but there is perhaps still room even in those cases for further discussion, particularly, perhaps, one that takes more account of the Southeast Asian region, rarely covered, or even used as a source of example or illustration, in general books that consider theories in IR or indeed in H.

The present study takes on rather an ambitious role. It attempts to discuss the systems of international relations that have applied in the region over several centuries, extending indeed back before the Europeans arrived, let alone developed the state system which the term 'Westphalia' is commonly used to denominate. It uses the term 'international' for 'interstate', and accepts a wide interpretation of the term 'state'. '[H]ow can one talk about a state's formation without taking for granted what a state is – the criteria usually prescribed by social scientists, not by the early Southeast Asian peoples themselves?' Thongchai asks.[13] 'State', Martin Stuart-Fox echoes, connotes centralized administration and defined territory.[14] Not necessarily, so far as this book is concerned: it recognizes that there are different kinds of states. Even in late medieval Europe the Latin word 'status' and its vernacular equivalents estat, stato, estado, state, were mainly used with reference to the standing of the rulers: only in the sixteenth century did Machiavelli talk of the state as an independent agent.[15]

The book, too, focuses on the different kinds of interstate relations that necessarily exist. In early times those were generally hierarchical in form, as Thongchai says,[16] though, paradoxically, it can hardly be said that there was a single hierarchy. The Europeans introduced, or, one might better say, improvised new forms of relationship, especially in the nineteenth century, but it was only in the twentieth century that Westphalia-type states emerged from the curious collection of colonial states and protectorates that they set up in the previous centuries. The book risks, though it seeks to avoid, a Whig interpretation of its own, since in some sense it is the story of the emergence of the Westphalia state in the region.

No doubt the book reflects the changes in world politics and inter-state relationships in the period of its preparation. Not for the first time, it may be, theory will be catching up with reality, but may also be a contributor to future reality. The two have always had a mutual relationship of a somewhat equivocal nature. Writing of nineteenth-century positivism in international law, C.H. Alexandrowicz thought it would be 'difficult to state with precision to what extent the new Europe-centred school of thought came in the wake of events and to what extent it was instrumental in shaping them. But it would also be difficult to ignore the obvious interconnection between the change of legal doctrine and the course of history leading to nineteenth-century colonialism.'[17] Nothing so encompassing is intended by or to be expected of the present work, But possibly it may offer a modest but helpful contribution not only to IR as a discipline but also to international relations as a practice. Policy-driven research and writing have not always been useful even to the discipline. The book is not policy-driven. But it may be useful for practitioners as well as theorists to be aware of a longer history and a larger area than that of the Atlantic and the twentieth century. A wider study of IR – mixed indeed with more H – could lead to a wider understanding of purpose and practice in international relations and the study of them.

It may also be useful to consider that there have been systems of international relations other than 'Westphalia', not only for purposes of comparison that theorists might value, but also for the way in which they have inflected and may still inflect the deployment of Westphalian concepts themselves. And such 'contributions' are still being made. IR theory – whether for the sake of its discipline or for the sake of the usefulness the pursuit of which has sometimes misled it – must surely take account of ASEAN and 'the ASEAN way' just as it has to consider such interstate constructs as the EC. Must it not also reckon with the 'rise' of China? Is that to be considered only in the terms of a 'hegemony' such as IR realists discuss or also in terms of a 'hierarchy' such as it to a greater or lesser extent once exercised in Southeast Asia? And must it not also reckon with Islam, not only, or not so much, in terms of 'civilizational' divide or terrorist threat, as in terms of political theory and practice developed over a long period of contact with the Europeans before, during and after the colonial phase in Southeast Asia as elsewhere?

'Hierarchy' is a descriptor of one system of international relations – though used more by Waltz in respect of internal relations – while 'anarchy' is often used to describe the Westphalian alternative. A system, this book assumes, should be seen not only as a collection of institutions. It comprises codes of practice as well as laws, conventions as well as prescriptions, words as well as deeds. It shapes the behaviour of states but is also shaped by them. Yet at the same time it offers a degree of regularity and predictability that allows those who guide the policies of states within a system to calculate the possible outcome of those they adopt or to react against those that others have adopted.

In this the book differs from Hedley Bull and Adam Watson, in essence adopting their definition of 'society' for its definition of 'system'. 'By an international society we mean a group of states (or, more generally, a group of independent political communities) which not merely form a system, in the sense that the behaviour of each is a necessary factor in the calculations of the others, but also have established by dialogue and consent rules and institutions for the conduct of their relations, and recognize their common interest in maintaining these arrangements. Such was the international system that emerged in Europe in early modern times. ... Such an international society also ... is the worldwide system of today.'[18] Bull and Watson slip into stating or assuming states are 'independent'. But a system – perhaps even a 'society'? – does not have to assume that and in practice may accept degrees of independence. So it seems possible to compare it with another system that in a sense does the reverse, accepting dependence but allowing its modification. It is difficult to call that a 'society' perhaps, but if they are both termed a 'system', they can more readily be compared.

Both systems have to deal with two fundamental issues in interstate relationships. One is the disparity of power among its component states. A hierarchical system, one that is based on inequality of status, handles that by an explicit recognition of disparity that is also mutual: if the lesser know their place, they may be able to preserve or even enhance it. The characteristic relationship in such a system may be a lord/vassal or patron/client relationship, and/or the rendering and reception of tribute, always with the assumption that there is an element of obligation on the part of the superior as well as the inferior, that submission is counterparted by protection. The system is known to the history of Europe itself, of India and of Southeast Asia and, in an extreme form, of China.

The equivalent in the modern system, anarchy, is far less specific, but it is surely there. States are theoretically equal in their sovereignty, but they are grossly unequal in power – or capability, to use Waltz's term – so that some have indeed been termed 'super-powers' or 'hegemons'. The system works only because in practice the powerful moderate the exercise of their power, and the weaker their aspirations to equality. A range of supplementary options may help: the making of alliances, the pursuit of 'balance of power' and the creation of international and regional organizations. But the system is poorly described as 'anarchy', if that brings to mind an image of complete disorder or chaos. States come to develop the kind of rules and understandings that encouraged Bull and Watson to talk of 'society' rather than mere 'system'. '[I]f anarchy means complete disorder, this is not a true description of international relations', as Martin Wight wrote. 'There is cooperation in international affairs as well as conflict. … It can scarcely be denied there is a system of states, and to admit that there is a system comes halfway to admitting that there is a society.'[19]

Both hierarchy and anarchy are closely related to matters of allegiance or control. In earlier times – and not only in Southeast Asia – the state did not have the power that the modern state has and seeks. It might be content with a diminished allegiance at least outside its core and with indefinite frontiers. It might control its people loosely, exercising symbolic rather than actual control, its officers exemplifying rather than enforcing appropriate behaviour. It might allow 'foreigners' more or less to rule themselves, rather than attempting to assimilate them, or even use them as an instrument of control over 'natives'. The modern state looks for more: it seeks definite frontiers, within which citizens or subjects owe it and it alone services and taxes and are subject to ever closer invigilation, and 'minorities' have such rights as an entity ruled by or based on a 'majority' sees fit to allow them.

In both systems what we may call 'diplomacy' is at work. In our system we are aware of the functions of permanent ambassadors, the use of 'summits', the manipulation of the media, the pursuit of intelligence: we know of the processes, even though we may in practice know little of their content. There has been something of a tendency not to think of the ancient systems in a similar way, but rather to assume that they were a kind of semi-celestial clockwork. Related is what Jan Wisseman-Christie has described as Clifford Geertz's concept of 'statecraft-as-a-thespian art'.[20] 'Court ceremonialism was the driving force of court politics', he suggested; 'and mass ritual was not a device to shore up the state, but rather the state … was a device for the enactment of mass ritual. Power served pomp, not pomp power.'[21]

Yet surely such systems were operated by men with schemes and ambitions and, symbolic though they might be, were also subject to manipulation. They not only worked; they might be worked. The Balinese king was not simply an icon, as H. Schulte Noordholt points out, but 'a charismatic leader of flesh and blood who had to overcome constant threats to his position'.[22] The idea that spectacle was not for the state but what the state was for would have seemed odd to Elizabeth I and Louis XIV, but odd, too, to the courtiers of Sultan Agung of Mataram, who, as Merle Ricklefs says, 'thought that the state was for getting rich and powerful while avoiding enemy plots and treasons'.[23] And intelligence, though less easy to gather, was even so essential.

Tensions come with change, often leading to conflict, even wars, big or small. Change is the second problem that systems face. In any one phase a system is likely to reflect a particular distribution of power among states. Yet that surely changes over time. The sources of such change may be geographical, demographic, technological, religious, economic. They may also be political, ideological and personal. A system must provide for and allow or adapt to a measure of change. Again 'hierarchy' and 'anarchy' did that in different ways. Vassal states turned from old lords to new or insured with more than one. Independent states became conquerors or fell to conquerors, perhaps in both cases seeking allies.

'Every discipline … needs a set of cutoff points for attention; otherwise there is no way to handle the material. … Accepting conventional time brackets does have its costs, however, because *where* one chooses to pick up the threads of the narrative introduces its own biases and blind spots.'[24] Historians distrust other historians, as well as practitioners of other disciplines, when they divide up time and label their periodizations. Do the dates really mark 'turning points' or are they arbitrarily imposed upon a continuity? Can an era effectively be labelled as one of 'violence' or an age one of 'imperialism' without degrading a story that can meaningfully be told only in all its 'detailed glory'?[25] The answer, of course, is one of convenience. It is impossible to compose a book without a theme or analyse a situation without an assumption, even if it does not take on the force of a Whig interpretation.

If we accept that international order in modern times can, with due reservation, be described, as by students of IR, in terms of 'anarchy', we may ask whether it was preceded – as might be inferred – by a different order, sustained by 'hierarchy'? And if there is such a shift, can it be marked off by dates, even if they are striking or symbolic?

Dealing with similar problems, the systems were in some ways similar, less distinctive than a schematic approach suggests, less cut-and-dried. Nor are the chronological divisions so sharp as dates or labellings imply. Even in Europe hierarchy did not prevail throughout the period of hierarchy, nor did it promptly disappear in the period of anarchy. Nor, on the other hand, did 'anarchy' emerge full-blown as Minerva from the mind of Jupiter. It came to prevail in Europe only over two centuries and more. The Westphalia system was certainly not definitively established with the treaty of 1648 that names it.

Nor should we merely look for a temporal division, since that would once more place IR within a narrow focus. Indeed it would risk passing over what was seen in Europe as 'the greatest event in the history of the world, apart from the Incarnation and Death of Him who created it',[26] and certainly also changed the stance that other parts of the world adopted. However we may now describe the 'voyages of discovery' – those of the Portuguese and the

Spanish, and then of the other Europeans, French, English, Dutch – we should certainly recognize their unprecedented nature. It was a step towards a single world. Marx saw the nineteenth century – when bourgeois society encompassed the world – as a second sixteenth.[27]

That took place well before the treaty of Westphalia. Arguably its initial outcome so altered the distribution of power in Europe – in particular by boosting Spain with Latin American silver – that it contributed to the religion-informed inter-state conflict that Westphalia was to be designed to limit. Meanwhile in the absence of a world-wide system the Europeans improvised. Was conquest justified? Could one deal with the Mughal emperor or the Sultan of Aceh as with other potentates outside 'Christendom'? What relations, if any, could be entered with fabulously populous China? And how should Europeans – increasingly divided among more or less independent states – deal with one another in the non-European world?

The treaty of Westphalia did not resolve the issue. Designed to limit war in Europe by stressing state sovereignty, secularizing interstate politics, and constraining intervention, it did not constrain the companies to which several European states had delegated their sovereign powers in Asia. Those built up forms of empire that comprised both exercises of what the Europeans regarded as sovereignty and also collections of treaty relationships of which their interpretations might differ from those of their partner. In general, however, they were cautious over handling the major states they faced. James I had himself to send an envoy to the Great Mogul, and the East India Company's trade to depend on a firman, a grant not a treaty.[28] The envoys of the Dutch Company (VOC) made no difficulty over kow-towing to the Chinese emperor.[29]

Increasingly it seems possible to find a useful chronological divider that suits both developments in Europe and in its relations with Asia. Indeed it points to further connexions between them. It centres on the late eighteenth and early nineteenth centuries. In Europe, on the one hand, the Westphalia system was consolidated both by the development of its interstate politics in the eighteenth century and then by the challenge presented by Napoleon's failed attempt to build a European empire.

The mid-century international lawyer Emer de Vattel insisted that each European state was independent of the others. But he also insisted that 'Europe forms a political system in which the nations … are bound together by their relations and their various interests into a single body. … no longer … a heap of detached parts … a sort of republic, whose members … unite for the maintenance of order and the preservation of liberty.'[30] Napoleon was an interlude, not to be repeated. Indeed his wars were brought to an end by a Congress at Vienna and the subsequent conduct of European international relations is sometimes labelled the 'Congress system'. This inclusiveness, however, was combined with exclusiveness. Only 'recognized' states were part of it.

The war terminated the long Anglo-French rivalry of the eighteenth century in favour of Britain, and it also boosted the industrial revolution already under way, making Britain the first industrial power. But even before the war Britain had been making itself the leading commercial power, and to that end seeking 'free trade', by which was then meant a trade carried on without the inhibition of monopoly companies. London might become the 'Emporium of the Asiatic Trade to the western world', as an enthusiast put it in 1786.[31] Even before the French revolution, Britain had decided on a mission to China. The Emperor was to be reassured lest he was apprehensive about the conquests the Company had made in India.[32] Henry Dundas of the India Board looked for 'a treaty of friendship and alliance'. '[O]ur views are purely commercial.'[33] Yet surely the virtual collapse of the Mogul empire was another factor in the change of attitude towards the major Asian states. Not all Britons had after all shared the Enlightenment's admiration of the Chinese empire. Writing after a visit to Canton in the 1740s, George Anson thought it doomed 'not only to the attempts of any potent State but to the ravages of every petty Invader'.[34]

Trade, too, came to seem a right to be asserted not only against a domestic monopoly, but also against an obstructive foreign state. Frustrated on visiting Bangkok in 1822, John Crawfurd nevertheless concluded that 'national' treatment was the most that could be demanded. 'If the subjects of a free and civilized government resort to a barbarous and despotic country, there is no remedy but submission to its laws, however absurd or arbitrary, so impossible is it in all respects to reconcile the fair and equal commerce of nations and opposite states of civilization with the freedom of conduct which must be supposed vested in every independent government, whatever its nature.'[35] 'There had never been a rule of international law in Europe permitting one state to force another to respect commerce within the territories of the second state', as Rubin comments.[36] But the success of the industrial revolution – coupled, no doubt, with the growth of positivism – changed the attitude the Europeans adopted to non-European states.

China was in the event forced to open up its trade, but it did not fully enter the Family of Nations, concluding what came to be seen as an 'unequal' treaty. Now it was Japan's turn to abandon the 'seclusion' it had adopted in the seventeenth century towards all the powers with an exception to prove the rule in the VOC. '[T]he compulsory exclusion of the Japanese', declared the *Edinburgh Review* in 1850, 'is a wrong not only to themselves, but to the civilised world'.[37]

'[A]fter the 1820s – after the aspiration of the Holy Alliance to restore the European dynastic system and the revolt of Spain's colonies in Latin America had called forth the Monroe doctrine and foundered on the opposition of Great Britain – the European outlook upon the extra-European areas', as Hinsley writes, 'rapidly became one which instinctively applied the concept of the sovereign state and the notion of international sovereignty to conditions in which these ideas remained alien ideas.'[38]

The changes of attitude caught Asian states at different stages and so had different outcomes. States that were sufficiently independent were admitted to the family of nations pledged to the Westphalia principles on the conditional basis of 'unequal treaties'. Those less independent tended to lose what independence they had, both because of their political weakness and because of collaboration and rivalry among the European powers. Westphalia was far from universal. Instead the European empires applied some of its principles and improvised others. Britain's primacy – the result of its security in Europe, its naval pre-eminence after the defeat of France, its industrial revolution, its empire in India – was not expressed in territorial empire. Its preference was indeed rather for trading opportunity than imperial responsibility. The result of these two factors was to produce a diverse and fragmented system. Even though it can be argued that the British had a vision of a world of states, that was a long way off.

European powers built colonies and protectorates that both borrowed from and displaced the political structures of the past and projected some features of the European system and not others. Though many have talked of 'colonialism', few scholars have attempted to analyse that peculiar, if not indeed paradoxical structure, the colonial state, including its protectorate variants: its Westphalian concepts of allegiance and frontier stopping short of sovereignty, and its inability to conduct its own foreign policy. It can only be seen, at the risk of a Whig interpretation that presumes that the end product is a world of states, as another transitional order. The colonial state could not play a full part in the changes that economic globalization was bringing about within and among states: certainly it could not readily industrialize, in the way that, behind protective barriers, Germany and the US were to industrialize. But what was to replace it? The extension of Westphalia was not necessarily perhaps the only option. Old empires might be replaced by new.

What made it the only option was its self-modification. The second economic globalization was associated with the industrial revolution, and that with the predominance of Britain, the first industrial power. But the French revolution, the other major change that had occurred in late eighteenth/early nineteenth century Europe, had stimulated, both by its own ideology and by the reaction to it, the concept of nationhood. The republic set up there differed greatly from Vattel's. It became associated with the concept of the independent state so that 'state' and 'nation' assumed a synonymity that has become regular usage. The struggle against Napoleonic empire stimulated the connexion in Germany and in Spain. It also inspired the struggle against the Habsburg, Romanov and Ottoman empires. The ideas associated with nationhood were transmitted to other parts of the world, where educated elites gave them their own special meanings and applied them in their own particular contexts. The combination produced nationalist movements directed against the European empires and seeking to compete with the alien governments in the task of modernization, though whether they would remain within the colonial frontiers was open to question.

The struggle among empires contributed to the advance of these ideas. In the First World War the German, Habsburg, Russian and Ottoman empires disintegrated, and new states and 'nation states' replaced them. US participation helped to endorse the concept, though in the event it did not join the League of Nations the victorious powers created. In part that was designed to compete with another alternative, advanced as a result of the Bolshevik revolution in Russia. That indeed appeared to envisage a different kind of post-imperial world order. But it had quickly to compromise with the nationalism it faced, and the Soviet regime retained an ambivalent relationship with nationhood and the nation state, both at home and abroad, manipulating it but arguably finally defeated by it.

Inter-war German nationalism took another stance. It reverted to empire-building but in a new form. Germany would not only dominate Europe by reducing the independence of other states, absorbing them, or destroying them in favour of 'protectorates'. It would also become a settler empire, displacing the inferior peoples of Eastern Europe as the American settlers had displaced the native Americans and, when they failed to defeat the Soviet regime, stepping up a final solution for the Jews.

Such a project offered little or nothing to other peoples, and in the event only catastrophe to the Germans themselves. But the resultant conflict led to a Second World War that in effect meant that the old European empires could not survive. The Japanese had stepped in in Southeast Asia, and the British survived the German onslaught only with the help of the United States. And that help was combined with the belief that European empire should be replaced by nation states. The ideas of Westphalia-Versailles were reinforced. With the decolonization that followed the end of the Second World War it could be said that 'anarchy' extended across the world and the colonial phase could be seen and presented as one of transition, during which the Europeans had operated two different systems.

The old empires had, however, been succeeded not only by a world of states, but also by a 'Cold War' between the two super-powers whose emergence the Germans had at once both feared and precipitated. Their rivalry was presented in ideological terms: Communism and Freedom. But neither ideology replaced that of the nation state. Instead the conflict took place within its bounds. The rivals upheld it against each other's interference. They sought to manipulate the regimes of the new states, to install puppets, to use local parties to keep them in line, and to buy their allegiance with aid. They did not overthrow the states themselves nor challenge their frontiers. Other states reacted in a variety of ways, accommodating the super-powers, playing them off, trying to modify their antagonism, asserting their own neutrality or non-alignment, making alliances, realizing that puppets could sometimes string their masters along and satellites move out of orbit. It was a period of local conflicts, though they should not be seen as merely proxy wars.

Only with the collapse of the Soviet Union could it be said that both forms of the second globalization – that of 'free trade' and that of the Westphalia state – had been achieved. But that was not after all the end of history. The system still has to accommodate the unequal distribution of power among states – more extreme than ever – and its changing distribution. But no alternative is in sight that seems likely to be any better than world-wide Westphalia.

The purpose of this book is not to write a world history, a task no octogenarian should in any case start. Its focus is on Southeast Asia. But tackling the issues that the concepts of state and system raise with a regional approach, and including Southeast Asia as a region, may be welcome strategies, and, it may be hoped, profitable ones, both for the study of international relations in general, and for that of Southeast Asia in particular.

In the past neither public nor scholarly debate was ready to identify Southeast Asia as a region, and even in recent works of generalization or popularization it tends to be by-passed. When it was distinguished in the past, it was often labelled in a misleading way: it was 'Further India', the Nanyang, the Nan-yo. Public events – the Second World War in particular – led to the wider adoption of a more neutral geographical labelling, and it was filled out by both political and academic activities. Histories of 'Southeast Asia' appeared in the 1950s (magisterially led by D.G.E. Hall's) and the Association of South East Asian Nations (ASEAN) – its leaders conscious of the past as well as the present – was inaugurated in 1967. It was a diverse region, but that was no longer a reason for not seeing it as a region either for action or for study. Rather the reverse.

Students of the region, as well as statesmen, both sought commonalities, moreover, and it may be that it still retains, albeit in modified form, practices inherited from a past that temporally is after all not so distant, even if in the interim the region has been the scene of unprecedented change. One feature of the last 150–200 years is its shift from demographic immaturity: perhaps there were only 30 million people in Southeast Asia in 1830. Now there are 600 million. Certainly in the more remote past what counted among the state-builders of Southeast Asia had been men rather than land, and the attitudes that established arguably help to account for the contemporary strength of patron–client relationships, vastly changed though the context is.

'[T]he South-East Asia diplomatic system', writes Kobkua Suwannathat-Pian, 'aimed not to regulate the relations between sovereign states of equal status but rather to emphasize the unequal, hierarchical nature of the political units involved. … Within this political system, tributary relations were an effective means of regulating interactions in order to minimize clashes, rivalries and wars, and to ensure that relative peace and order would prevail in the region.' Tributary systems 'regulated' relations between major power-centres and smaller states, but 'there was no acceptable formula for friendly or enduring relations between any two power-centres.' The relations between equal states 'tended to perpetuate rivalry, suspicion, and resentment which eventually led to open hostility and warfare.'[39]

It was the product of this mix, neither a simple hierarchy nor a complete anarchy, with which Europeans came into contact from the early sixteenth century, adding elements of a third system at least in the archipelago. Again, it overlapped, rather than displaced. It was shaped by what they encountered there, as well as by their own motives, preconceptions and rivalries. To a limited extent in turn it helped to shape, albeit indirectly, their own emerging international system, ultimately to become the world system of our day. But further patterns meanwhile supervened: the colonial states and protectorates of the European empires, the puppet states of the Japanese empire, the satellites and neutrals of the Cold War phase.

Now Southeast Asia has a novel kind of regionalism in which its states – emerging from the colonial pattern, largely with colonial frontiers, despite the implications of self-determination, and very disparate in size and power and indeed in ideology – sustain their sovereignty with an anxiety intensified by their colonial experience, but try to ensure their security by limiting their intra-regional disputes and restricting the intervention of outside powers. The 'ASEAN way' insists on a Westphalia-type sovereignty but also in practice qualifies its full exertion. 'Anarchy' prevails in an orderly manner, shaped by the treaties, laws and conventions that international relations have developed and are developing, but also by those further complementary codes and practices that ASEAN has created and sought to spread.

It also limits the possibility that the great power to the north as it 'rises' will do more to assert an apical role. Traditionally that neighbour saw itself, and was often seen, as in a hierarchical relationship with Southeast Asia. That world-view was difficult to sustain as the world expanded beyond the limits known to the Chinese. Tied as it was to the nature of the Chinese state itself, and to the ideology that sustained it, it was, however, hard to adapt. The famous voyages of the Ming admiral Zheng He may have been attempts to extend 'hierarchy' beyond the region within which it had developed. They were abandoned. And then the world further expanded. The new dynasty reacted in the 'company' phase by attempts at compromise, isolated as far as possible from a domestic ideology that it was determined to retain. Foreigners were allowed limited access, and subjects allowed limited travel. And Nerchinsk was the first and only treaty, not to be seen as a precedent by maritime states, since the Russians might be regarded as another Siberian tribe. The Emperor declared adhesion to Confucian orthodoxy, as C.P. Fitzgerald put it. 'But Chinese historians, and, one must suppose, contemporaries also, were perfectly well aware that this was often a polite fiction.'[40]

In the colonial phase the dynasty again compromised, accepting extraterritorial jurisdiction and making the so-called unequal treaties at a time when even equal treaties would have marked a defeat. Would they be accompanied by the 'reforms' for which the British hoped? Or would the empire break up as they feared? And what would become of the countries with which it had been in a hierarchical relationship? They now became defensive outworks of a state threatened by the advance of other empires, European, and later Japanese. Vietnam was the focus of a war with France, Korea and Manchuria of wars with Japan, and Taiwan was lost. The failure of the Manchu government to defend these territories, and to modernize their relationship with China's government, helped to bring about its fall. Its opponents were moved by the 'humiliation' it involved.

Post-imperial China sought to utilize the principles that Versailles amplified and generalized, but with only limited success. Nor did the League provide a defence against Japanese aggression in Manchuria. Some of the unequal treaties were, however, undone, and the Second World War led the Allies to end extraterritoriality and treat China at least rhetorically as a major power. In the first part of the Cold War phase the new People's Republic, not recognized by the US, was denied the seat at the United Nations (UN) that now marked international recognition. It asserted all the more determinedly that it was ready to abide by the principles that the UN endorsed. These were set out as the five principles of co-existence in an agreement concluded between Prime Minister Nehru of India and Foreign Minister Zhou Enlai in April 1954.

With this the PRC (People's Republic of China) appeared once more to endorse Westphalia/Versailles. The agreement was reached, however, only after the absorption of Tibet. In other words China was drawing the frontiers of itself as a nation state so as to exclude some of the old dependencies but not others. They excluded Korea and Vietnam, but included Tibet, Manchuria, and Taiwan. Not surprisingly, however, the five principles of co-existence are a key part of ASEAN/PRC rhetoric. Have they ruled out any attempt to hierarchy? Is it only a question of hegemony? Students both of IR and H have something to reflect about.

Maybe, too, Southeast Asia has an importance beyond itself. Tony Day has developed a case, surely rightly, 'for claiming that "Southeast Asia" and its history in the fullest, deepest historical sense are an important heuristic framework for comparative analysis in our global age even as the region is being critically examined and reconfigured'. What kind of meaning does 'Southeast Asian' have in front of 'state'? 'My own understanding of the derivativeness and hybridity of Southeast Asian states', Day writes, 'is that these qualities define them. ... Foreignness haunts the formation of Southeast Asian states. ... But ... the incoherence, arbitrariness and artificiality ... in Southeast Asian state formations are not criteria that define their historical uniqueness. These characteristics make them like any other state formation, once we start thinking of all states as culturally constructed repertoires of practices reticulating out into the world at large, saved only from total dissolution into the multiplicity of power networks that constitute them by the magical and illusory boundaries that define their "statehood".'[41]

Many observers stress the 'diversity' of the region. Day prefers to apply the adjective 'incongruous', recalling 'its long history as a transcultural cross-roads'. Its states still tend to behave as self-styled unique centres, reducing the possibility of accepting one another on equal terms and developing closer relations. But incongruities have co-existed and also merged.[42] The 'ASEAN Way' is unique. Can it apply elsewhere? Is 'ASEAN centrality' a possibility?

2 Traditional hierarchy

In the world that preceded the globalization of the sixteenth century the links among the centres of power were naturally slight, indirect or non-existent. Ideas of empire, though they might be couched in world-wide terms, were, in our perception, regional in scope. Indeed their world-wide aspirations could hardly have existed had they known that their range was limited. The world was the world known to contemporaries, rather than the world known to us, or even the expanded but still incomplete world found by the European 'discoverers' of the sixteenth century. Systems would adjust as the situation changed, though the concepts would themselves also be a source of change.

Even in the centuries that preceded the first globalization, there had, of course, been many changes within Southeast Asia and in its relations with its neighbours. Those have been the more difficult to describe and analyse because of the lack of evidence and because of the partial nature of what there is. Archaeology has been a main source, but what is preserved especially in a tropical environment is limited, and inscriptions are difficult to puzzle out. Written evidence is largely confined to Chinese sources. Invaluable as they are, official reports were in officialese, in an idiom, as Hermann Kulke puts it, 'deeply pervaded by the Chinese conception of their own centralized State'.[1]

One of the main controversies that has been difficult for scholars to resolve has focused on the relationship between Southeast Asia and its major neighbours, China and India. Only a limited part of the region might be described as Sinicized, the part we know as northern Vietnam. But much of it could be described – as by Georges Coedès[2] – as Indianized. But how had that come about? And to what extent? It was a question that was at the core of J.C. van Leur's discussion, developed before the Pacific war, but becoming better known only in the post-war period with the publication of *Indonesian Trade and Society* (The Hague, Bandung: van Hoeve, 1955), and being the more welcome given the post-colonial context in which it was now read. Was the creation of Southeast Asian states a matter of Indian colonization or of Southeast Asian borrowing? What role did China and the Chinese play?

Kulke suggests that there were three phases or levels in state formation in Southeast Asia: the local, the regional, and the 'imperial'. 'Very generally speaking, the first step always had to be the successful establishment and consolidation of a solid local power within a limited territory.' This he characterizes as 'chieftaincy'. Next might come the conquest of one or more neighbouring nuclear areas, incorporated not by annihilation nor by administrative unification, but by the establishment of more or less regular tributary patterns. These were the somewhat precarious 'early kingdoms'. From the early ninth century a small number of what Kulke calls 'imperial' kingdoms emerged, beginning with Angkor, which unified two or even several core areas of former early kingdoms.[3]

The categorization involves another distinction. States might be built on two bases, more or less exclusively, or in sometimes uneasy combination. One kind of state was predominantly agrarian, its wealth and stability built upon rice cultivation, found on the mainland, in Angkor, in Pagan and its successors in Burma, and in the Thai states, such as Sukhothai and Ayudhya, and also in Java, the site of a succession of states climaxing with Majapahit and Mataram. The other kind of state found its main base in trade, within the region and outside. Such states were characteristic of the Malay peninsula and the outer islands of the archipelago, though there were states and cities on the mainland and in Java that sustained a role in regional and supra-regional trade, Champa included. It was along the sea-routes that the main contacts with India and China were made. Their role in state-making can be assessed only by reference to chronology.

'The Southeast Asian trading communities were probably already in direct contact with the regions both east of the Malay Peninsula and west of the Bay of Bengal and the Indian Ocean long before Chinese, Indian or Arab sources began recording their activities.'[4] 'In fact, there is much to suggest that the emergence of long-distance trade between Southeast Asia and adjacent regions was but a natural course of development, particularly for those Southeast Asian centres which had had experience of intra-regional trade during prehistoric times.'[5] Collecting centres and entrepots developed on the Peninsula. Long distance trade, Leong Sau Heng suggests, assumed a greater importance in the first millennium CE, and became 'truly international. … No longer can we view this development as extraneous, arising from the arrival in the Peninsula of foreign merchants, particularly from the Indian sub-continent.'[6]

The issue clearly relates to the question of Indianization and its role in the creation of states. Evidence for the existence of states on the mainland suggests that they emerged during the period of trade contact with South and East Asia, Jan Wisseman Christie writes in what is the most persuasive analysis of the processes involved. 'There is thus no reason to believe … that they owed nothing to older states of neighbouring regions, though this is not to say that [they] were either colonial or even clearly imitative in character. … These inland, agrarian states possessed economic infrastructures and spatial organizations broadly similar to those of the early states in South Asia. How many of these parallels were the consequence of independent responses to broadly similar environmental conditions, and how many of conscious imitation, will possibly never be clear in the absence of written remains.'[7]

The coastal trading states, however, developed under very different conditions. Discussing them, Wisseman Christie draws upon archaeological evidence but also upon historical evidence, since, in her view, the Malay states of the Peninsula, Sumatra and Borneo retained their basic character through many changes of context: there is, to use her term, a 'classic type', evidenced in early nineteenth-century Palembang.[8] The states were coastal and riparian. The rulers attracted the allegiance and cooperation of their peoples, the rakyat, by 'a combination of religio-political and economic means', the latter commonly in the form of patronage and the redistribution of status-enhancing imports.[9] The exports included forest exotics, metals and semi-precious stones, secured from the interior.

In that respect Christie draws a distinction between the states of the Peninsula and those of Sumatra and Borneo. In the former the rakyat might be directly involved in securing alluvial tin. In the latter the coastal state would have to deal with upriver clients who were not part of the state, hunter-gatherers or organized settlers too distant or militaristic to be absorbed into the state and able to channel their products through more than one river system. The 'gatekeeper' states often found it impossible 'to compel interior populations to trade exclusively with them', and they competed with one another. 'Competition leading to the forceful imposition of some sort of trading monopoly was the inevitable consequence.' It produced trading 'empires' like Sri Vijaya and Brunei, 'powerful, but relatively unstable'.[10]

The original form of the Malay state, Christie suggests, originated in the easier conditions of the Peninsula, and was followed and modified in the different conditions of Sumatra and Borneo. 'What, then, did the earliest coastal states owe to Indian political traditions?' Possibly very little, 'apart from the general stimulus which contact with sophisticated political systems might be expected to create'. 'It seems likely that borrowings from the Indian cultural and political traditions were grafted on to already relatively sophisticated local systems.' Perhaps that was the result of 'the pressures which the sudden growth in the Chinese trade in the fourth and fifth centuries A.D. must have placed upon the still small polities of the Melaka Straits.' China was the principal market for forest products, and 'was the ultimate source of many of the goods which Southeast Asians used in their India trade'. The boom partly resulted from the impact of Buddhism on China, 'stimulating pilgrimages and intellectual traffic through the southern seas between them'.[11]

Sri Vijaya – whose existence was rediscovered by Coedès only in 1918 – established its control over the polities of the Peninsula and Sumatra during the seventh century, using an armed force substantially made up of orang laut, sea-people, the Celates of the later Portuguese account by Tomé Pires, and enlisted through winning over and rewarding their leaders, the datus. It thus made itself an entrepot for the traffic of maritime Southeast Asia with its larger neighbours, making other entrepots and feeder points subordinate.[12] Once its dominance was asserted, it provided security against piracy, having absorbed potential pirates and put down opponents who resorted to piracy. It was also, as the Chinese pilgrim I Ching noted, a centre of Buddhist learning.[13]

In general, perhaps, states emerged from the binding together of leaders and followers. In Central Asian culture the ideal was of a heroic lord and his comitatus, 'a war band of friends sworn to defend him to the death', lavishly rewarded for their loyalty.[14] In what became Poland, Norman Davies tells us, '[p]rinces described their realm not in terms of acreage but in terms of the people who obeyed their orders, or sought their protection'.[15] It is easy to make a connexion with the 'men of prowess' who feature in Oliver Wolters' persuasive accounts of the emergence of early Southeast Asian states. 'A political system cohered only in the sense that it was a projection of the leader's personal influence', he wrote, 'backed by the personal loyalty and ubiquity of the leader's representatives. Only short-term goals were plausible.' There were no prolonged periods of strong centralized government. Nor were there borders in the modern sense, 'only porous peripheries'. The region, he suggests, was balkanized, but without ethnic-grounded Balkan wrath. Populations might be transferred, slaves captured. 'Otherwise ecological factors kept ethnic groups in habitation zones where they could live comfortably.' But 'peripheries were indispensable to the center's status. A ruler's prestige depended on his claim to be the overlord of a multi-ethnic polity.'[16]

Intelligence and diplomacy were essential. An overlord had to be able to bring his rivals under his personal influence 'and accommodate them within a network of loyalties to himself. … Administrative power as distinct from sacral authority depended on the management of personal relationships, exercised through the royal prerogative of investiture', the same skill as attributed to earlier 'men of prowess'. He had to attract loyal subordinates and preserve their loyalty. '[A]dministrative power as distinct from divine authority had … to be shared.'[17]

It was the divine authority that Indianization provided. 'Borrowings' from India – further developed on the ground – were designed to strengthen rulers and empire-builders in face of difficult conditions and intractable subordinates. The relationship between the ruler and his people was thus 'based on the concept of the king as a supernatural being, to whom were ascribed supernatural powers *(daulat)* and who was looked upon as the incarnation of a particular deity'.[18]

What were the relations among these states? They were bound to reflect the nature of the states. How were they described? How should we describe them? Students of Asia and of Southeast Asia in the period before the arrival of the Europeans have rightly sought to describe the relations among states in terms of hierarchy. But the word is best used in the plural. There were hierarchies, not a single hierarchy. And if there is more than one hierarchy in a region, clearly hierarchy will not in itself be an adequate descriptor.

The object of contemporaries was to work within a system and find, if not define, their place in it; ours is to describe and understand. The practice and the precept had to take account of both the limited capacities of all states and the differential level of power they nevertheless enjoyed. Even strong rulers in powerful states might be content with an acknowledgment of allegiance rather than direct rule. It might be possible for a smaller state to acquire autonomy as well as sustain security by a discreet acknowledgment of the superior claims of its neighbour. It might even be possible, if risky, to take out insurance with another powerful neighbour or even to shift allegiance at a chosen moment. In such a way the system would provide what a working system has to provide, both a degree of stability and a facility for change according to changing circumstances.

Authorities in the field such as Wolters and Stanley Tambiah have utilized the concept of the mandala from ancient Indian political traditions and have turned to modern metaphor in their attempts to describe the relationships that thus prevailed among Southeast Asian states.

Aware of the 'Indianization' of the Southeast Asian state, Tambiah analysed Kautilya's *Arthashastra*, the only complete work of the brahmanic politico-economic literature to be preserved, made notorious for its alleged Machiavellianism by Max Weber.[19] It deals inter alia with the maintenance of 'state sovereignty' and the conduct of diplomacy, making alliances, making war, in a system in which 'circles of kings' formed enemies and allies in actuality or in potentia.

He also analysed the Buddhist texts. In them dharma, righteousness, is an absolute imperative. Its symbol in political life was the wheel, cakka, not the sceptre, danda. In his past lives the Buddha admitted that, as a wheel-turning raja, he used violence. 'The Cakkavarti is depicted as a cosmocrator whose conquest proceeded through the continents at each of the four cardinal points, and whose rule radiated out from a central position either identified or closely associated with the central cosmic mountain of the Indian traditions, Mount Meru.' The cakkavatti grants their domains back to the conquered kings when they submit to the basic moral precepts of Buddhism: 'in a sense the king *must* let the conquered rulers keep their thrones, since only as a king of kings is he a world monarch.' The Emperor Asoka embraced the model, and he was in turn the model for many Southeast Asian Buddhist monarchs.[20]

Before he turns to them Tambiah describes the empire of their exemplar. Asoka's Mauryan state 'was not so much a bureaucratized centralized imperial monarchy as a kind of galaxy-type structure with lesser political replicas revolving around the central entity and in perpetual motion of fission or incorporation. Indeed, it is clear that this is what the much-cited *cakkavatti* model represented: that a king as a wheel-rolling world ruler by definition required lesser kings under him who in turn encompassed still lesser rulers, that the raja of rajas was more a presiding apical ordinator than a totalitarian authority between whom and the people nothing intervened except his own agencies and agents of control.' The model was 'a closer representation of actual facts than has usually been imagined by virtue of misreading the rhetoric'.[21]

It was the concept of mandala, Tambiah tells us, that led him to invent the label 'galactic polities'. In a common Indo-Tibetan tradition, mandala was composed of a core, manda, and an enclosing element, -la, and it was applied to designs, diagrams and cosmological schemes. Representing a cosmic harmony, it was a pattern for the state. 'In the center was the king's capital and the region of its direct control, which was surrounded by a circle of provinces ruled by princes or governors appointed by the king, and these again were surrounded by more or less independent "tributary" polities.' The capital itself was a mandala, with the palace at the centre, surrounded by three circles of earthen ramparts, four gateways at the cardinal points. Each lesser unit replicates the larger, and is more or less autonomous, 'held in orbit and within the sphere of influence of the center'. At the margin, however, are 'similar competing central principalities and their satellites'. The system is 'a hierarchy of central points continually subject to the dynamics of pulsation and changing spheres of influence'. Territorial jurisdiction was not characterized by fixed boundaries but by fluidity. Behind its cosmology and the 'ritually inflated notions we see the dynamics of polities that were modulated by pulsating alliances, shifting territorial control, and frequent rebellions and succession disputes'.[22]

The modern literature on these polities has tended not to adopt Tambiah's celestial metaphor. Nor indeed does it turn to Vic Lieberman's preferred 'solar polity', though he considers it more accurate: 'provincial "planets" revolved around a sun whose "gravitational pull" diminished with distance. Insofar as each planet had its own satellite moons, its gravitational system replicated in decreasing scale the structure of the solar system as a whole.'[23] Searching for other metaphors has not led to borrowing the one Davies applied to early Poland, though it seems not inapt. 'Political power radiated from a few centres of authority, whose spheres of influence constantly waxed and waned, and very frequently overlapped. These centres can best be likened to magnets, and the people living in between them, to iron filings pulled hither and thither by fluctuating and conflicting magnetic fields.'[24] A further metaphor is adduced by Leonard Andaya. 'The relationship between center and periphery is often explained through an analogy with the beam of an upturned lamp. When cast on a flat surface, the beam is most intense at the center and becomes progressively weaker towards the edges. … To carry the analogy a step further, if two lamps are placed close to each other, their beams overlap at the edges, just as the authority of two competing centers may overlap at their peripheries.'[25]

For the most part modern historians prefer Wolters' use of 'mandala' – Stuart-Fox would like to use it in place of 'state' – and indeed an inscription discovered at Sabokingking near Palembang utilized the term, John de Casparis suggested, for a province, or what I Ching called a kuo.[26] 'The map of earlier Southeast Asia which evolved from the prehistoric networks of small settlements and reveals itself in historical records was a patchwork of often overlapping *mandalas*, or circles of kings. In each of these *mandalas*, one king, identified with divine and "universal" authority, claimed personal hegemony over the other rulers in his *mandala* who in theory were his obedient allies and vassals.' Wolters also borrowed a modern metaphor from music. '*Mandalas* would expand and contract in concertina-like fashion. Each one contained several tributary rulers, some of whom would repudiate their vassal status when the opportunity arose and try to build up their own networks of vassals.'[27]

Perhaps exaggerating his case, Wolters suggested that Naresvara [Naresuen] of late sixteenth-century Ayudhya was following Kautilyan practice when he offered to embarrass the rear of Japan when it was at odds with China over Korea. He was thinking in terms of circles of states, successively made up of friends and enemies: 'in the rear of the conqueror there happen to be situated a rearward enemy, a rearward friend, an ally of the rearward enemy, and an ally of the rearward friend.' 'The mandala conception was an ancient and familiar one in Southeast Asia, except among the semi-sinicized Vietnamese.' The Sanskrit literature was 'the matrix that provided the courtly minds of Southeast Asia with their windows on the "civilized" world'. It was 'perhaps … India's greatest gift to Southeast Asia'.[28]

Exaggeration or not though this interpretation may be, the concept of the mandala, however it was perceived at the time, serves a useful purpose for historians and for those who read their works. We need not substitute the word mandala for the word state in order to recognize that the states of early Southeast Asia were not the centralized bureaucratic states of modern times. Nor do we need the various metaphors that have been advanced as options in order to recognize that such mandala states had very different concepts of inter-state relations from those that prevail among the states of theoretically equal status with which we are familiar. Hierarchy was indeed a feature. Yet even that was qualified by the discontinuity of practice, and within Southeast Asia no single hierarchy prevailed for a long period or over a wide area.

Metaphors, moreover, may be too mechanical and misleading: they may override the historian's concern with specificity. We must be as cautious over Wolters as Ricklefs is over Geertz. Writing of Java, for example, Wisseman Christie finds that the early states were neither as centralized and monolithic as the 'oriental despotisms' of Wittfogel, nor as 'fragile' and 'fissiparous' as Geertz's negara. The meaning of the word mandala, though used in eleventh-century inscriptions, she finds at best unclear. States may have treated each other as equals. Certainly they were 'more cohesive and integrated than predicted by the "segmentary state", "galactic polity", and *mandala* models'.[29] Wisseman Christie also points to the risk that such models – as well as the 'backward extrapolation' of ethnographic data – downplay the possibility of change, except that from the outside, and imply an old-fashioned assumption of stasis or circularity in the history of the Southeast Asian state. In any case, example needs to be added to metaphor.

Mandala/realms had a monarchy that could activate its segments, which were related to the monarchy and its capital in various ways according to closeness or distance, 'whether in terms of geographical space, kinship, marriage, power or ritual ties, or perhaps ethnicity. Those closer would follow the centre more tightly, those farther away less so.'[30] 'Bureaucratic apparatuses were mostly Indianized fiction', writes Renée Hagesteijn: 'a ruler was dependent on patron-client relations with "lesser" political leaders.'[31] At the centre the supraregional leader had direct relations with the headman. Regional leaders were clients, offered protection, honours, gifts. On the periphery control was 'almost lacking'.[32]

Such statements echo Wolters. Was Angkor like that? In the Angkor court, as Ian Mabbett writes, there was a 'web of obligation and influence. … Power was … something that arose from relationships and needed to be negotiated'.[33] Yet, at the same time, the founder of the state, Yasovarman I, was 'the supreme master of the earth, which had for its limits the barbarians, the ocean, China and Champa.'[34] Michael Coe suggests that the mandala model applies to the mainland pre-802 CE, but is less applicable afterwards: 'for most of the time during the next five centuries, in spite of sporadic revolts and foreign invasions that could have occurred in any empire, the Angkor state – that is, the king – had complete control over all Khmer territory. This was enforced out to Cambodia's frontiers not only by his army and his judicial system, but by his roving inspectors (the *tamrvach*) and by periodic census-taking.'[35] Ian Harris offers a different view. 'Angkor … – the capital city synonymous with the kingdom itself – was the "royal heart" of the polity and it is difficult to visualize the polity as having a bounded space, for its potency manifested itself at a maximum at the centre, the seat of the king.'[36]

Lan Xang, the fourteenth-century creation of the legendary Fa Ngum, was, Stuart-Fox is clear, a collection of *meuang*, four of them at the core. They were held together by the ceremonial payment of tribute in person every third year, together with military backing sustained by wealth drawn from trade and tribute, and religious sanction.[37]

Champa itself has been seen as a somewhat exceptional version or variant, 'a land in what many scholars have come to call the "Mandala system" (whereby a polity's power radiated outward from its centre, growing weaker on the periphery) had a more even balance among its segments (that is, the centre did not grow increasingly more dominant over the centuries), and leadership in the form of the "men of prowess" remained important (i.e., the administrative development was relatively low).' Champa, Whitmore tells us, was less focused than Angkor, Pagan and Thang Long, the political, ritual and economic centres were separate, and the major segments retained more or a balance among themselves. The ruler's task was to defend the realm. He was the 'protector' of the negara.[38]

What was true of the mainland was true also of the archipelago. In Java, at least in the later centuries, the capital was 'the magical centre of the realm', as Soemarsaid Moertono put it, 'but also, from the point of view of state politics, the central region was preponderantly important. … [T]he core region was relatively closely knit through the use of a remuneration system of appanages, while the outer regions were more loosely administered.' In the empire of Majapahit, as described in the *Nagarakrtagama*, there were three regions: Java at the centre, the islands outside it, and countries beyond, like Champa and Cambodia. Later Mataram was composed of the core, nagaragung, the outer provinces, mantjanegara and pasisir, and the lands across the sea, tanah sabring. Territorial jurisdiction was 'characterized by a fluidity or flexibility of boundary dependent on the diminishing or increasing power of the center'.[39]

The prince controlled the crown lands round the kraton, nagaragung. Elsewhere governors ruled, paying homage and tribute, supplying labour and military support when needed, watched over by spies and inspection tours, occasionally punished by military expeditions. The distinction between 'international' and internal relations was, as Wertheim puts it, fluid: it was a sliding scale.[40]

'Whatever system was applied – whether the landed nobility were retained as vassals, members of the royal family were established as local administrators, or the territory was put in charge of officials – the ties which held the various parts of the realm together were always comparatively loose', B. Schrieke wrote of Mataram. Majapahit must have been similar, he assumed: vassal states would have submitted with reluctance, and would have 'made whatever use they could of shifts in the balance of power within the archipelago to promote their independence'.[41]

If, as Wisseman Christie suggests, Palembang was a state so durable that its early nineteenth-century characteristics are a guide to the past, despite her doubts about 'backward extrapolation', the same is true, it seems, of neighbouring Jambi, described by Locher Scholten. Malay states, she writes, did not have precise borders or a powerful central authority, their central government had no monopoly of force, their rulers no well-defined constitutional powers, there was no trace of popular sovereignty. The raja was a symbol of unity and prosperity. The 'state', kerajaan, was life under a raja, who offered protection and, for his immediate followers, the promise of after-life. Government was left to the *pangeran ratu*, ruling in cooperation with ministers and advisory council. But the sultan was to the fore in war and foreign relations, symbol of state unity. 'Appanage holders and "officials" circled round their sovereign and patron-client relations of their own, which conferred power and influence. The sultan's strength was derived from the size and power of his retinue, not the size of his territory. People … were the primary measure of his power. Resources to win loyalty came from duties on imports and exports and from trade monopolies', not, as in Java, from taxes on agriculture.[42]

Indirect successor of Sri Vijaya, Melaka was the last of the empires in the Straits before the Europeans arrived. It followed a not unusual pattern. The realm was made up of three concentric circles, a directly ruled inner circle, a middle circle ruled by mandarins and mendelika appointed by the ruler, and an outer circle of tributaries, vassals, and allied kingdoms. The sultanate was supported by tribute and by trade and, like Sri Vijaya, could recruit the orang laut. Melaka provided in return protection, a market, a share in prosperity. But centripetal tendencies were offset by centrifugal: vassals sought independence, the orang laut had a propensity for piracy, lesser trading centres were jealous of the entrepot.[43]

Paradoxically it was perhaps just because these structures were structurally so flimsy that, once destroyed, they could be rebuilt. The dynasty that ruled Melaka was able to build a new empire at Johor after the Portuguese conquest in 1511. Certainly Malay states other than Palembang and Jambi endured into the nineteenth century, Sulu for instance. Some European observers – such as Raffles and Robert Farquhar – then assumed that they had decayed and had to be reformed. But that, it has been argued, was a misinterpretation, mistakenly taken up by some later historians. 'Government to them [Farquhar and Raffles] was *synonymous* with strong central authority. When they found this relatively lacking at Jolo, they called weakness and decline what was in fact the normal working order of a political process alien to them.'[44]

If Wolters is right, international relations among early Southeast Asian states was a form of inter-entity politics that welcomed, utilized and adapted the tradition and practice India had developed. India itself, however, was an exemplar, not an active part of the system. Though there were Cola raids early in the eleventh century – 'little more than a pirate venture, bursting on a port, burning, looting, and then sailing away'[45] – no Indian empire laid a larger claim over the Indianized states of Southeast Asia: the sub-continent was perhaps more than challenge enough for its political contenders. But, given their geographical position, it was not surprising to find that Southeast Asian states, largely Indianized though they were, might see their neighbour to the north, the Chinese empire, which had met the extreme challenge of political unification far from easily but more consistently than Indian empires, as the apex of a hierarchy that included them. It was a question of power, but also of accommodation and mutual advantage. Though their political systems were Indianized, traditional Southeast Asian states fitted into a hierarchical pattern dominated by their northern neighbour, the Chinese empire. It was a framework for managing inequality.[46]

China had regional dominance which it conceived of as world dominance: it was built on and maintained by an ideology that identified the Chinese state with 'civilization'. Others, semi-civilized, might have their place but in an appropriate subordination. Beyond were the non-civilized, the barbarians. China thus developed a view of the 'world' as it 'knew' it. Its concept of hierarchy was not the same as that associated with the mandala system: there was one hierarchy, not several; there were no further circles of power whatever Naresuen might imply. Outside countries, if in contact, were tributaries, and, though policies varied more than the pattern suggested, Chinese regimes felt free to regulate trade as well as tribute, to prescribe that it be conducted only in that context, even to cut it off.[47]

Southeast Asia included both tributaries and barbarians. There two systems thus overlapped, one a collection of local hierarchies – mandala, concertinas – the other seeing itself as a world system built on a conceived civilizational difference.

What or who drew the 'line' between China and region and when? The creation of a Vietnamese state was crucial. That was in part the work of the Chinese themselves, but they lost control and accepted instead the formality of suzerainty. Conquered by the Han in the first century, the Red River area had become the site of a relatively stable polity, built up by Chinese frontier administrators and leading local clans, sensitive to dynastic interests but ready also to take advantage of dynastic weakness. As part of its frontier reorganization, the Tang dynasty set up the Protectorate of An-nam, Pacified South, in 679 CE. In its later years the Tang was able to drive back a ninth-century invasion from the kingdom of Nanzhao in Yunnan. That, as Keith Taylor puts it, 'affirmed Vietnam's long-standing ties to Chinese civilization'. Yet the Tang were now too weak to dominate Vietnam itself, and the regime that emerged from the post-invasion reconstruction was 'the first of a number of transitional regimes that finally led to the establishment of an independent Vietnamese monarchy'.[48] But though Dinh Bo Linh called himself emperor, he managed to come to terms with the new Song dynasty, which had threatened the autonomy Vietnam had enjoyed during the decline of the Tang.[49]

In the late thirteenth century the Tran dynasty succeeded in defeating to the north the armies of the Mongol (Yuan) dynasty, coupling their success with the payment of tribute, and also to the south the armies of Champa. Following the collapse of the Tran in the late fourteenth century, Ho Quy Ly, the chief minister, proclaimed himself ruler in 1400, only to provoke the intervention of the new Ming Dynasty. Posing as restorers of the Tran, the Ming endeavoured in the event to restore the province of Giao. That endeavour was abandoned in the 1420s in the face of Vietnamese resistance.

Not altogether paradoxically, a state that drew at least some of its strength from its Sinicization effectively resisted China, and sustained its independence, modified and made more or less acceptable to China by acknowledgment of its suzerainty. Had their neighbour deployed all its force, the Vietnamese realized, they could not have survived. But the Chinese understood that for whatever they coveted in Vietnam the Vietnamese would have exacted too high a price. 'The Vietnamese people … clearly understood China's awesome might. Realism dictated that they downgrade their victories and simultaneously whitewash Chinese retreats.'[50] There was an element of make-believe on both sides, but make-believe is part of any inter-state system.

The other 'frontier' was established by the Mongol dynasty's conquest of Yunnan. Its neighbours included the Burmese, the Tai of Sukhotai and Lan Na, and the Lao of Luang Prabang [Meoung Sua]. 'Under threat of military invasion, all were brought within the Chinese tributary system, thus initiating lasting diplomatic and political relations.'[51] Kublai Khan sought tribute from Pagan in 1271, and when it was denied, sent a punitive force from Tali in 1277, and another in 1283. A new kingdom in Burma defeated the Mongol invasion of 1301 but offered tribute.

In the early fifteenth century, the new Ming dynasty not only tried to re-establish control over the Vietnamese kingdom, it also was responsible for the remarkable series of voyages mostly led by Zheng-he. The founder of the dynasty had been more laid back. 'Those countries of the overseas barbarians which cause us trouble must be fought, but otherwise we must not take the initiative in attacking them', T'ai-tsu, the Hong-wu emperor, told his officials in 1371. 'The men of old had a saying: having too large a land is not a means of bringing about peace. … Our opinion is that these barbarous countries are small ones. They are separated from us by mountains and seas, and they are far way in a corner. If they cause us no trouble, we shall certainly not attack them. … Only the *Hu* and *Jung* barbarians in the north-west have … been a trouble to China.'[52] But between 1405 and 1433, in some seven voyages, Zheng-he visited Champa, Java, Sumatra, India and Sri Lanka, and even Arabia and East Africa, and called at Melaka several times.

The importance of the relations between contemporary China and Southeast Asia has renewed interest in these extraordinary ventures, but nowhere in the Ming records is the purpose of the voyages stated. The immediate achievement was to bring large numbers of new countries into the tributary system. 'Could it not be', Wang Gungwu asks, 'that the expeditions were the logical outcome of an effort to extend that system and make it truly the machinery of a world order?'[53] The Yongle emperor's personal aggrandisement may have played a part, Stuart-Fox suggests, a view Geoff Wade endorses: a usurper, he needed to 'bolster his political legitimacy by ensuring that a steady stream of foreign ambassadors came to pay him homage in his new capital at Beijing'. Possibly, too, he needed to compensate for the closure of land routes by controlling maritime routes, so as to meet the demand for foreign products. The main purpose of the voyages was, however, 'to enforce acceptance of the Chinese world order'. '[R]itualised submission' would suffice.[54] The scale of the fleets was intended to bring that about without the actual use of force, 'to coerce through fear',[55] to 'overawe',[56] and so create 'a Pax Ming'.[57] Force was used only where the threat of it failed to sustain the world order. The enterprises were indeed in Julia Lovell's view 'as much an exercise in imperial Chinese self-love as a pragmatic, entrepreneurial colonial initiative'.[58]

Under Mongol and Ming both the spasmodic assertions of control and the maintenance of tributary patterns of trade were designed to mark the influence of China in Southeast Asia, partly for domestic purposes, partly in order to sustain order and check the over-mighty. A tribute mission was, for a Southeast Asian state, a means of avoiding something worse – pre-empting a more forceful deployment of China's power – but it also had a more positive aspect. 'The emperors thought that they were manipulating their vassals by techniques of indirect control; the vassals were manipulating the China trade … to amass wealth as a means of asserting their authority.'[59]

Wolters connected the rise of Sri Vijaya with this pattern. He pictures Kan-t'o-li, ruler of a proto-Sri Vijaya, sending missions to China, establishing his ability to supply archipelagic goods there, receiving a seal of office or imperial presents as a token of standing. 'His privileged status in China, with its commercial implications, could then be dangled as a bait to attract roaming Malay shippers to his ports.'[60] It was another means of building an empire, though exposed to the possibility that rivals or dependencies would emulate it.

Sri Vijaya itself sent a number of missions to the Tang court in the seventh and eighth centuries. The object of such missions on behalf of Malay polities was to establish, 'in the eyes of the Chinese courts, their political hegemony over the respective subregions', or to reaffirm 'their economic position in the eyes of new Chinese dynasties establishing their rule in southern China'.[61] Initially insistent on the tribute pattern of trade, the Song dynasty modified it late in the eleventh century, allowing Chinese private traders into Southeast Asia to the disadvantage of Sri Vijaya and Malay shipping. 'Tribute missions lost their economic function and instead came to be viewed as manifestations of the Song dynastic rule's imperial virtue, as laid out in Confucian precepts, and treated as affirmations of a foreign state's status by the Song court',[62] the more important because of its defeat at the hands of the Jurchens early in the twelfth century.

The Yuan dynasty's policy towards private trade fluctuated.[63] So did that of the Ming, though on a more long-term basis. The projection of its power into Southeast Asia and the Indian ocean in the early fifteenth century was 'immediately followed first by a turning inward by the Chinese court, away from the outside world, and then by the banning of Chinese maritime shipping, trade, and foreign travel by Chinese citizens from the 1470s on', a ban was lifted only in 1567.[64] The number of missions was limited, the burgeoning trade of the fifteenth century left in the hands of smugglers.[65]

For the Chinese there had been, Wolters suggests, another consideration. Supporting a strong maritime kingdom in the Straits vicinity would also check the piratical potential of the Malays.[66] Indeed Wolters came to the conclusion that the missions had political as well as commercial aims on the Malay side, too. 'Missions would be sent to enhance and verify the prestige of rulers.' They were more 'frequent when the rulers had particular reasons for reaffirming their reputation as overlords'.[67] Four of the early missions to Yung-le sent by newly-rising Melaka were royal visits, and the Brunei monarch flattered him in the same way.[68] In 1405 the emperor granted Melaka an inscription after 'the envoys said that their king admired righteousness and wished to like one of China's prefectures and annually offer tribute'.[69]

The relationship could indeed serve the purposes of Southeast Asian rulers in ways other than commercial. 'Vassalage' might assist one kingdom to maintain itself over against another. It became part of the region's inter-entity diplomacy. A fourteenth-century king of Burma, Mingyi Swasawke, was recognized as 'Governor of Burma', and the two powers cooperated to some extent against the Shans. The Thai state of Sukhotai sent missions to Beijing in the Mongol period, and the Thais had the support of China as a splinter movement in the Cambodian empire. Champa's Che Bong Nga took advantage of the accession of the Ming: a change of dynasty offered the chance of recognition. Generally the Chinese sought fragmentation, as well as submissiveness. Ayudhya expanded when the Mongols were in decline, but it sought to cultivate good relations with the Ming. So did the ruler of Melaka, anxious over the advance of the Thais, though the ruler of Brunei was the first southern ruler to journey personally to Nanjing. The Ming government admonished Vietnam for invading the Lao state of Lan Xang in 1479, but did not send in troops, as it requested. Instead it sent envoys to both courts 'to "instruct" them how to maintain good relations and to care for their people'.[70]

The apical power, it would seem, exerted itself spasmodically and made no attempts to Sinicize. Within the region a whole orchestra of concertinas played. There was, it might almost be said, an anarchy of hierarchies. Like other systems, they brought a measure of order. But they clearly required diplomacy, the exercise of wit and intelligence, and the deployment of a range of resources, ritual, intermarriage, patronage, as well as force. The relationship with China was part of a different pattern of hierarchy, but it was inter-related. '[S]ubmission to China was valued in South East Asia because it implied equality among the South East Asian rulers.'[71]

Two systems overlapped. That was particularly obvious in the case of Vietnam, more Sinicized than its regional neighbours. It accepted it was a tributary of China, and also adopted a tribute system its respect of its neighbours, though it was 'a pale shadow' of the tribute system of its own great neighbour. 'While the Vietnamese had copied the tributary diplomacy framework of the Chinese in dealing with their neighbours, the very states that they had demanded tribute from were used to operating in a non-Sinicized diplomacy framework'.[72] 'Finding a framework for diplomatic relations which would accommodate the cultural differences between the tensely balanced "Indianized" world of Bangkok and the "sinicized" world of Hué was never easy', as Woodside remarks.[73] Make-believe again came into play.

The old systems were fit for purpose, since they reflected realities. How would they cope with or adapt to new realities? The first globalization brought new crops to Asia that were to transform agriculture, new trade routes, different attitudes to religion, state and society. In what ways would they affect inter-state relations in Southeast Asia?

3 Conquests and contracts

The first globalization brought major changes to Southeast Asia as to other parts of the world: the 'discovery' of America brought new crops, new wealth, new perspectives, new links and new conflicts. In respect of the nature of states and their inter-relationships, there was much less novelty, though it may be suggested that elements of a third system were introduced, and that what transpired there, a focus of intra-European competition, affected the development of European international law. It was, however, only later that the full implications of what took place became apparent.

The first globalization was a novelty for the Europeans as well as for those they encountered. It opened up contacts between European states and regions of which there had been only limited knowledge and with which there had been only limited contact. It also opened up contacts with a whole continent that had been assumed not to exist, a 'New World'. How were they to be fitted into the current 'world view' of the Europeans? In what ways would it need to be modified? And how would they deal with the rivalries among themselves that the overseas ventures expanded?

The Europeans of the time conceived of their sub-continent as Christendom. That was indeed a collection of states, even to some extent of nations, but they were in the making, and indeed the overseas ventures resulted from and contributed to the process. But the sub-continent was also the site of the Holy Roman Empire and its much damaged super-ordinate claims, and, at least at the pre-Reformation outset of the ventures, of the overall claims of the Papacy in Rome.

The initial ventures were those of the two Iberian states, Spain and Portugal, though they utilized the knowledge and skills of the Genoese, the antagonists of the Venetians who controlled the links with the European trade with Asia across the Middle East. To limit the conflict between them, they appealed to the Pope to adjudicate and divide the newly uncovered world. The Bull *Inter Caetera* of 1493 was followed by the negotiation between them of the treaty of Tordesillas the following year:[1] it fixed an Atlantic line, but could not fix a Pacific one. When they uncovered the New World, they had to decide how to treat realms and peoples who had not had the chance to receive the Christian message. It could justify conquest, but it could also limit the insatiable appetites of the conquistadors and their royal masters for the abundant wealth the uncoverers had also happened upon.

Did the Bull merely separate the rivals or also grant a title? Medieval canon lawyers differed over the treatment of infidel rulers: did they have a right of dominion or was it of itself invalid? The conquering Spaniards used the Bull as a gift, crazy as Atahuallpa thought it.[2] But they nevertheless debated the justice of what was being done in Mexico and Peru. Christian powers could make war on infidels only to spread the faith, not for wealth or dominion, argued the Dominican Marias de Paz at the University of Salamanca in 1512.[3] Another Dominican, Bartolomé de Las Casas, argued for peaceful conversion. 'All the peoples on earth are men.' No nation existed that could not be 'attracted and converted to all political virtues and to all the humanity of domestic, political and rational men.'[4] Could those who resisted be treated as making unjust war and be enslaved? Las Casas denied it: it was absurd that the infidels should lose life and land because they did not submit themselves 'to the dominion of a king whom they never saw and whom they never heard of … whose messengers and men were so cruel and so debarred from all pity and such horrible tyrants'.[5] Infidels should retain estates, dignities and jurisdictions, for they were rational beings. 'Natural law is common to all men everywhere.'[6]

What, as Donelan says, was 'the most enduring work to come out of the controversy'[7] was the lecture *De Indis* given in January 1539 by the Dominican Francisco de Vitoria, professor of theology at Salamanca. He argued that the Pope's grant had no temporal value. Nor was the Holy Roman Emperor lord of the world. So the refusal of the 'Indians' to recognize their dominance was not a ground for war on them. What then were lawful titles?[8] He rejected as reasons for a take-over not only the idea of a papal gift, but also the right of discovery and the refusal to accept the Christian faith. But drawing on and adapting an ancient Greek and Roman idea, that of the Stoics, he put forward the view that all men are bound by a moral law and as part of it a ius gentium, a law of nations. Men had the right to trade, travel and settle across the world, a ius communicationis. They had no right to force the adoption of the Christian faith by war, threats or torture.[9] They had, however, the right to spread the faith peacefully, 'with sufficient propriety and piety', and, if prevented, could wage war, with moderation.[10] They could not punish the Indians for offences against the natural law, but they could defend innocents who were being killed. They could assist allies in a just war. Possibly a primitive people could be taken over for its own good.[11]

The influence of this doctrine on Western practice was limited, Hedley Bull points out. Though it might provide some defence for the rights of Amerindians, or later African slaves or aborigines, it could work the other way. Asserted unilaterally, it 'provided a rationale for forcing non-European peoples into commercial and diplomatic intercourse against their will'.

The ius commercialis Vitoria invoked in the West Indies would be invoked in the East Asia of the nineteenth century.[12] Indeed the arguments developed by the Dominicans and others in respect of the novel circumstances in the Americas influenced the rationales advanced in respect of European activities in Asia, though the circumstances was far less novel.

The ventures of the sixteenth and seventeenth centuries were partly inspired by the search for wealth and security on the part of the emerging states of Europe, and their initial results, creating new distributions of power, prompted ventures on the part of non-Iberian powers. Some of them were or came to be Protestant, so that religious differences intensified commercial and political competition. Another source of inspiration for Spain and Portugal had, however, been a continuation of the crusades of medieval Christendom. The Iberian kingdoms had only recently pushed the Muslim rulers out of the Peninsula. Their further ventures were designed to undermine Muslim dominance in the Middle East, confirmed as it had been by the destruction of Byzantium in 1453. The Genoese were the more ready to take part because their Venetian rivals had proved ready to trade with the Muslims and dominated the important trade in spices that crossed the Arabian peninsula.

'Religious rhetoric provided the terms by which the claims of sixteenth-century monarchs were articulated', Palmira Brummett argues. ' … Divine mission was combined with imperial ambition to legitimize the conquests of expansionist powers.'[13] But that applied within the Muslim world as well as outside it. The Ottomans who had taken Constantinople used the failure of the Mamluk sultans in Egypt to secure the hajj routes as a justification for seizing their territories, while Shah Ismail of Safavid Iran [the 'Grand Sophie'] used the language of jihad against his Ottoman antagonists. But, as Brummett has it, the 'language of divine favour notwithstanding, political expediency and commercial imperialism provided the incentives for the military and diplomatic actions which circumscribed the power struggles for the Euro-Asian world'.[14]

Perhaps that oversimplifies the position, obscuring the role of rationale and rhetoric, and downplaying the mixing of motives. But if the Muslims fought among themselves, they both fought and came to terms with Christian states. Conceptually the world was divided into two spheres, Dar ul-Islam, where Islamic law prevailed, and Dar ul-Harb, the abode of war where infidels lived, and against whom jihad is legitimate if not mandatory. In practice the barriers were 'not impenetrable'.[15] The Ottomans dealt with non-Muslim states, though not seeing them as equal. Peace treaties between Muslim and non-Muslim states were acceptable, but only if limited in duration to ten years or, in Ottoman practice, the life of a Sultan.[16]

Threatened in Europe, the Venetians, who had a resident bailo or envoy in Istanbul, came to terms with their Ottoman opponents in a treaty of 1503, losing some territory and paying an indemnity that the Ottomans regarded as tribute, though the Venetians did not.[17] The Portuguese had meanwhile rounded the Cape and their subsequent successes against the Mamluks in the Indian Ocean and Sultan Selim's seizure of Cairo [1517] confirmed the Ottoman–Venetian connexion. Under Suleiman the Magnificent, the Ottomans launched an attack on Portuguese Diu in 1538–39 in vain. But the opening of the Cape route by the Portuguese did not dislodge the overland trade, which Venice and the Sublime Porte had a common interest in preserving.

The Ottoman Empire did not focus only on the Arabian peninsula and Iran: it aspired to extend in Europe, too. The struggle between the Valois and the Habsburg for the Holy Roman Empire gave Suleiman an opportunity. While Charles V fought Francis I, he seized Hungary. The French wanted more help, and their ambassador Jean de la Forêt made an agreement with the Ottomans in 1536. The written document, modelled on concessions granted to the Venetians and Genoese in the previous century, termed capitulations because set out in chapters, focused on commercial privileges, the military and political being only oral. For the Sultan it was a unilateral grant rather than a treaty, applying only in the Sultan's lifetime. A formal alliance could not be made with an infidel.[18]

The word 'capitulations' conveys to us a suggestion of inferiority on the part of the Ottomans. The reverse was in fact the case. All the word then implied was that the document proceeded by chapters. The meaning is retained for us in our word 'recapitulation', which conveys no sense of inferiority or superiority. What was conveyed at the time was a permission to trade that was exceptional. Capitulations in a wider sense had long existed. 'It was one of the oldest customs in most Asian countries to grant substantial concessions to settlements of foreign merchants. Such settlements or factories were allowed to govern themselves by their own laws and subjects.' Muslims so resided in Hindu lands. Capitulations were grants, acts of generosity, revocable, not derogatory of sovereignty, though '[r]evocability and equality gradually gave way to irrevocability and inequality'.[19] Over time – by the nineteenth century – the meaning of the word had indeed changed, reflecting and boosting a change in the relative position of the partners: 'the capitulations came to confer privileges greatly in excess of those originally granted'.[20] They were indeed a precedent for the 'unequal' treaties. Extraterritoriality and the exercise of consular jurisdiction – one of the aspects of the capitulations – became a badge of inferiority, of a semi-civilized status. The Ottoman Empire was admitted to 'Europe' only at the peace of Paris in 1856.

The Portuguese were themselves ready to deal with non-Christian monarchs, as Brummett points out. Affonso d'Albuquerque, their leader, was ready to negotiate with Ismail of Iran and sent him an ambassador, Ruy Gomez, in 1510–11. King Manuel's armada, he said, could help him against the Mamluk Sultan, and 'give you great help by sea against the Turk and you with your great forces and cavalry by land can combine to inflict troublous injuries upon them'.[21] But their readiness to deal with great kings, Muslim or not – they tried to emphasize that the Grand Sophie was almost a Christian – on an apparently equal diplomatic basis was combined with a policy of extraordinary violence directed against less significant realms. Possibly that is partly explained by the anti-Muslim ideology that Brummett plays down. And it was certainly evoked in 1511 in their successful attack on Melaka, scarcely indeed a minor realm compared with some of the coastal states they dealt with in India.

'The Portuguese probably could have traded peacefully in the Indian Ocean as one among many participants in Asian trade and obtained spices for the Cape traffic at reasonable rates', James C. Boyajian suggests,[22] perhaps influenced too much by his evidence that private Portuguese traders were to do rather well up to the 1620s. 'But King Manuel's captains and viceroys chose to establish the Portuguese military presence in Asia and to exclude the Arabs and Gujaratis of India's western coast and the Venetians from the spice trade to the Levant and Europe.' To attain their monopoly and interdict the trade of others, they destroyed their opponents' fleets and extended the system of fortresses and trading posts [feitoria] they had used in the advance down the West African coast.[23] Was that in part the result of their crusading zeal?

The impact of the Portuguese irruption was considerable, especially at first. For a time the Middle East supply route was disrupted, and the great spice merchants of Europe, the Fuggers, the Affaitati, turned to Lisbon for their supplies. The effect diminished over time. The Portuguese failed to dominate the trade, let alone sustain a domination. Their venture relocated the trading centres of Asia, but did not displace them. From the start, indeed, they realized that their activities, including the costs of their feitoria and their shipping, would have to be funded in part not simply by attacking Muslim vessels, but by permitting through licence [cartaz] and taxing Asian traders, 'an imposed protection regime', and that could only facilitate the revival of the overland trade and in fact undermine the factory system.[24] The King had sought to be a great merchant, drawing such a profit from a royal monopoly of spices that it could fund his realm's adventures in Africa and sustain its independence in Europe. But the royal trade fell away, not only in face of the Asian competition stirred by Muslim reaction, but also in face of the private trade allowed to the Portuguese in Asia. That indeed was to display a capacity of survival into the seventeenth century and beyond, as stressed by Boyajian, even though the Inquisition struck at New Christians [converted Jews] as well as Muslims.

The Portuguese described their venture in Asia as the Estado da India. In fact there was no 'state', but rather a collection of fortified posts, linked by maritime forces. It has been possible to over-estimate the impact of the Portuguese and consider the sixteenth as a 'Portuguese century'. In fact they were not predominant. But it has also been possible to under-estimate their impact. In Southeast Asia, after all, they captured Melaka in 1511,

Sri Vijaya's successor as the main entrepot of the region, linked with the Chinese traders and seeing itself and seen by the Chinese as a tributary, and that produced a redistribution of power in the maritime world, as well as spurring the reactive advance of Islam.

It cannot be argued, however, that the venture introduced either into Asia or into Europe a new concept or concepts of inter-state relations, nor even the kind of debates that the Spanish venture in the Americas provoked. The Portuguese accepted the existence of other states in a pragmatic way, dealing with them as allies or opponents, with a mixture of religious ideology and secular opportunism that, at least until the Counter-Reformation and the advent of the Inquisition, was not far from the mixture that also marked the relations of the Venetians with the states of the Middle East. A minor European state was after all hardly in a position to define a new relationship between the sub-continent and Asian states. '[T]he Asian powers concerned recognized the Portuguese as members of their system without seriously modifying their concepts and their practices to suit the newcomers.'[25]

The Portuguese establishment at Melaka was again a novelty that did not mark a structural change in the nature of inter-state relations. The destruction of the entrepot led to the creation of other substantial centres with a similar function, Johore and Aceh among them. But they were still constructed on the model which Wisseman Christie recognized as so persistent, with the difference that they adopted, in reaction to the Portuguese incursion the Muslim version of the state structure that Melaka had already adopted, though that did not prevent their allying with the Portuguese in pursuit of their own commercial and political rivalry.

Melaka itself was structurally novel, it might be said, in a negative sense. It could call on the resources of the Estado elsewhere in Asia, such as they were. But it was without the underpinnings of the traditional entrepot. It could not utilize familial or religious links with the Malay states. King Manoel wanted to be 'declared suzerain over as many rulers as possible in Asia', seeking 'a widespread rather than a deep influence', but the Portuguese in Melaka failed to persuade the Sultan to return as a vassal.[26] Novelties were to emerge as a result of divisions among the European states, and in the much longer term as a result of the Westphalia concept prompted by the religious wars in Europe.

The struggles among the European states were intensified both by the acquisition of American wealth – despite the treaty of Câteau Cambrésis of 1559 that allowed armed conflicts in the New World to continue 'on the understanding that they would not disturb the peace of Europe'[27] – and by the Spanish-led Counter-Reformation. That affected the Estado's treatment of the New Christians,[28] but also promoted, through the activities of the new Society of Jesus, a new kind of contact with China. Its greatest impact was, however, an indirect one, the result of the conflict between the Spanish monarch Philip II and his subjects in the Low Countries. He and his governor the Duke of Alva were determined to establish royal authority and quell 'outbursts of iconoclastic religious violence'. Many of the merchants of Antwerp, the principal outlet of the spices imported via the Cape, deserted the town in 1577 and again in 1587, the Catholics, including the Portuguese, settling in Cologne, the Protestants in Holland and Zeeland, nucleus of a rebellious Dutch Republic.[29]

For Portugal neutrality might have been the best policy, but it was not available. Now Amsterdam inherited much of the merchant community that had marketed its spices, while Baltic grain was brought to it by the powerful merchant navy that was now in the hands of the rebels. They, on the other hand, depended on Iberian and especially Portuguese salt for their fisheries, and on silver, brought from America, for their grain purchases. Silver, essential for the purchase of pepper and other spices in Asia, had come from central Europe, but now came from Spanish America. The pursuit of a Portuguese policy independent of Spain's was, however, ruled out on other grounds. King Sebastiao had led a disastrous Portuguese attack on Muslim Morocco in 1578, and the last king of the Avis dynasty died in 1580. Philip II asserted his claims. For 60 years the monarchies were united, and Portugal's empire was opened up not only to the Spaniards – who had in 1571 in any case already secured a new base in Manila, through which silver was traded across the Pacific for Chinese goods – but to the attacks of their enemies, in particular the English and, then much more powerful, the rebels of the Dutch Republic.

For them indeed the war of independence in Europe was connected with their pursuit of trade in Asia. It thus introduced a new phase of violence in Asia, but also the beginnings of a new kind of rationale for European activity which might be considered in some measure as a new system of international relations. The wealth Spain had acquired by discovery funded its campaign to dominate Europe and advance the Counter-Reformation. Incidentally it also made the Dutch wealthy and facilitated their challenge. Inadvertently the Spanish theorists of empire also helped the Dutch to rationalize their activities. Such a rationale could, of course, no longer be secured by an appeal to the Pope. But the principles outlined by Vitoria could be turned to account and alleged to be part of 'international law'.

The early Dutch ventures were conducted by what were later termed the voorcompagnien, ventures to Asia funded by leading merchants [bewindhebbers] and other investors [participants]. But in 1602, as a result of political intervention by the chief minister, Johan Oldenbarnevelt, they were replaced by a single United Dutch East India Company (VOC), granted a charter [octrooi] conferring a 21-year monopoly of the Dutch trade east of the Cape. The early companies engaged in occasional attacks on the Portuguese, but did not embark on large-scale campaigns. The VOC did. Its advocates 'envisioned establishing outposts in the manner of the Estado da India, seizing them, if necessary, from the Portuguese. Indeed, one purpose of fusing [the] resources of the several companies was to engage directly the hostile power of the Portuguese and Spaniards in Asia.'[30] Monopoly, not competition, was the aim. Only that, it was argued, would produce the profits that would justify a costly enterprise. In fact the profits in the early years were small and dividends limited. '[M]any stockholders … felt that its founders had duped them into financing an expensive war against Spain and Portugal in Asia, not a business enterprise.'[31] The private Portuguese trade withered, however, because the King lost the naval struggle.

The VOC's activities both gave rise to and were justified by concepts of international relations offered by a man whose opinion it commissioned, Hugo Grotius, who has long been feted as a legal scholar, but not always rightly interpreted. The Estates of Holland asked him to write a history of the Dutch revolt against Spain in 1601. In 1604 the Amsterdam directors of the Company asked him to write an apologia for their privateering campaign in the East Indies following the spectacular capture of a Portuguese merchantman, the *Santa Catarina*, in the Singapore Straits in February 1603. In the absence of Portuguese sources on the Luso-Asian trading regime, his work, as Peter Borschberg has persuasively argued, drew upon Vitoria and the Dominicans: he 'transposed the principles from the Americas to the Asian scenario', though the two, as he was aware, were very different, 'especially with regard to the principles historically associated with the idea of discovery, the treatment of (and treaties with) native rulers, and the conduct of trade and missionisation'.[32]

As is the way with contractors, he told those who paid him what they wanted to hear. The twelfth chapter of the work was published in April 1609 as *Mare Liberum.* Grotius invoked natural law. That both justified free navigation and trade in monsoon Asia and permitted men to avenge the misdeeds of other men. Indeed he alleged the Dutch were liberating the natives from Portuguese tyranny.[33] When it came to dealing with the English – who had chartered their own East India Company in 1600, but were then much weaker rivals of the Dutch – natural law was invoked to rather different purpose. The VOC proceeded by making 'contracts' with the native princes, requiring the delivery of spices and other products. The Portuguese had done the same, but the Dutch contracts differed by providing for the exclusion of rivals. Pacta sunt servanda, Grotius argued in his contribution to the Anglo-Dutch colonial conferences of 1613 and 1615: contracts are to be honoured, even though the English argued that contracts made under duress could be broken, and, as he knew, the native rulers who entered them had rarely done so of their free will. They had been relieved of Portuguese tyranny, but they were, he insisted, in no position to make contracts with the English.[34] Grotius' arguments undermined Iberian claims to the extra-European world, but were flexible enough to justify the VOC's attempt to monopolize the spice trade in the East Indies.

In the longer term, his arguments were helpful to the English in other parts of the world. Grotius had found himself on the wrong side in the politics of the Republic: the Stadtholder of Holland, Maurice of Nassau, sided with the orthodox Calvinists against the [Arminian] Remonstrants, Oldenbarnevelt was executed, and his client, Grotius, banished for life. The enforced leisure produced his most famous work, *De Jure Belli ac Pacis*, published in Paris in 1625. That influenced John Locke, who wrote 'Of Property' as the fifth chapter of the *Fundamental Constitutions of Carolina.* As M.J. van Ittersum suggests, 'Grotius' notion of divisible sovereignty, his theory of subjective rights and his account of the origins of private property were perfectly suited to justify the establishment of British colonies on the eastern seaboard of North America and the English East India Company's dual role as trader and ruler in Bengal'.[35]

By contrast, as she adds, Grotius's arguments were less attractive in those parts of Europe that were not engaged in colonial enterprises or were themselves battlegrounds for the most powerful rulers on the European continent. Samuel Pufendorf, who held a new chair at Heidelberg, argued that Indians enjoyed absolute property rights, not to be taken away because they were perceived as lazy natives. Nor, on the other hand, were the Dutch, the Swedes, the French and the Danes justified in intervening in what became a 30 years war on the pretext of relieving the Holy Roman Empire from Habsburg 'tyranny'. More significantly still, Pufendorf rejected the notion of divisible sovereignty, and interpreted the treaty of Westphalia that ended the war in 1648 as providing 'an iron-clad guarantee for the freedom and independence' of the electoral princes, though in theory they still owed fealty to the Emperor.[36]

The treaty of Westphalia – the delegates had assembled in Osnabrück and Münster – was designed to bring peace and stability to Europe by establishing the sovereignty even of minor states over against the power of the Holy Roman Emperor and the religious ideology he promoted. The signatories were to be 'free perpetually … to make alliances with strangers for their preservation and safety'. Under Article 17 of the treaty of Osnabrück signatories were bound to uphold the dispositions of the peace 'without distinction of religion'. 'Reason of state' prevailed, in the form of 'interests', 'depriving the notion of its religious garb'.[37]

This was a step towards ending the 'wars of religion' in Europe, and towards limiting the aspirations of the Holy Roman Emperor. It was also a step in the creation of what is called the Westphalia system. Further steps were taken in the eighteenth century in face of the attempts of France to dominate the Continent, renewed by its 'Sun King', Louis XIV. Much of the apparatus associated with the Westphalia was developed. The struggle for power, as Paul W. Schroeder argues, was accompanied by a struggle for order, dictated by the search for security and survival.[38] Diplomatic rules, conventions and norms were adopted, permanent diplomatic missions set up, diplomats trained, espionage promoted. Alliances were no longer used only for war: they would help maintain the balance of power. The idea of a European family of states emerged: congresses were held at Cambrai and Soissons.

It was, however, the attempt to create another all-European hegemony that firmly established the 'Westphalia system'. That attempt was again made by France, now backed by a new ideology, that of the Revolution of 1789. Yet again – though with a different ideology – one power sought to bring Europe under its domination, either direct or through the creation of dependent states. The Holy Roman Empire was brought to an end in 1805. Napoleon became Emperor of the French but aspired to dominate all Europe. He was welcomed by some, opposed by others, finally defeated by a combination of European states.

The legal positivism of German counter-revolutionaries like A.H.L. Heeren, C.W. Koch and F. Schoell argued that the treaty of 1648 had inaugurated a European state system, regulated by treaties, and that Europe was 'a constellation of mutually tolerant and fully sovereign entities which did not brook interference in their own domestic affairs'. Napoleon had destroyed the system, Heeren argued.[39] Its object, argued Koch and Schoell, had been 'to maintain public order, to protect the weak against the strong, to put obstacles in the way of the ambitious projects of conquerors, and to prevent dissensions that might lead to the calamities of war',[40] though it had not, of course, saved Poland from the partitions of the late eighteenth century.

Southeast Asia had followed a different trajectory, as the differences between Grotius and Pufendorf suggested. There the maritime region at least could be regarded as entering a new system that might be called the contractual phase, that of the seventeenth and eighteenth centuries. To some extent the local rulers tried to fit it into existing patterns, though the contracts sought to reduce their ability to turn to others, European or otherwise. Family links were, of course, ruled out, so that the traditional exchange of gifts assumed additional importance in the conduct of diplomacy, more, as Barbara Andaya points out, than the Dutch recognized.[41] For the Dutch and the English Companies the prime purpose of treaties was to facilitate and control trade. For the rulers the most important clause was the initial statement of friendship. The contract had in a measure made the parties kin and established a framework for their relationship.[42]

If there were constraints on the rulers, there might also be advantages. Grotius attributed to them a range of sovereign rights 'largely alien to their own political culture'.[43] In turn, as Borschberg argues, they jockeyed to improve their standing, entering relations with the VOC for that purpose, rather than with a view to making an irrevocable contract.[44] Compare their diplomatic use of tribute to China in earlier times.

Leonard Andaya points out that the European requirements for the delivery of cloves boosted the build-up of the sultanates of Ternate and Tidor. The sultans were treated as European monarchs, treaties were made with them, duties paid into their treasuries, arms sold to them. 'Treaties became a useful vehicle for clever monarchs to call legitimately on the

Europeans to accomplish political goals, such as maintaining order on their borders or suppressing rebels.' The Ternate rulers became even by the late sixteenth century 'much more like the image the Europeans projected of kings'.[45] In the late seventeenth century Ternate became a vassal [leen] of the VOC by right of conquest, but in Ternatan terms child of the Company father. Tidor, not formally a vassal, saw the VOC as 'a large tree under which the Tidorese have for many years found security'.[46]

Indeed in some cases at least a treaty was seen as more than a statement of friendship: though the Dutch might be interested in securing a product, the ruler was seeking their protection. Such was the case on the Peninsula with Sultan Muzafar of Perak and the treaty with the VOC he made in 1746. As Governor Albinus of Melaka pointed out, 'the king's aims seems to be the obtaining of protection against the Bugis of Selangor by the building of a fort and a new alliance'.[47] The treaty was seen by the Malay party as a 'grand alliance' with the most important European power. 'Centuries before, Malay overlords had looked to China with hopes of beneficial results, and Sultan Muzafar approached the VOC with the same expectations.'[48] The *Misa Melayu* speaks of the Company as coming 'to guard Kuala Perak' against the Bugis. Neither party, Barbara Andaya observes, 'saw Perak as anything other than a sovereign state'. Twenty years later, Governor Schippers urged that a new Resident should try to dissipate the idea that the Dutch were trying to dominate the government. 'It is well known how obsessive these people are concerning that point.'[49]

'[W]ho are the friends of the Company?' Sultan Iskandar wrote to Governor Boelen in 1760. 'They are likewise my friends. Who are its enemies? They are also my enemies. … the country of Perak and Melaka are truly and sincerely one. I have not forgotten our contract, which we made in former days, and I will not deviate from it, as long as the sun and the moon shine and as long as egrets are white and crows black.'[50] But he insisted on his 'sovereign status', though, Barbara Andaya suggests, 'it is obvious that there is only a fine line dividing an independence maintained solely by an alliance with a stronger state from vassalage pure and simple'.[51]

In the Malay world there were – as indeed there had been in the case of the Ottoman Empire – different understandings of what a treaty was, as Leonard Andaya says. The Malays emphasized trust, friendship and cooperation: trade was a mark of friendship. The Dutch – like the Portuguese – saw them as binding contracts, not to be seen as null and void when the signatory ruler died.[52] Written agreements were 'but one, and the more minor, dimension in the relations between the Dutch and Johor' in the early seventeenth century. ' … Of greater importance was the unwritten code of conduct between these two sovereign powers.' They had a mutual concern for peace in the Straits. The Dutch, the dominant Laxamana believed, 'were the best guarantors of Johor's prosperity and security'.[53]

Thus, as Peter Borschberg has pointed out, the VOC 'behaved increasingly like an Asian patron state that engaged its allies and treaty partners as dependents or client polities'. A semi-tributary relationship evolved.[54] Reinhout Vos has indeed questioned the practice of presenting the VOC's eighteenth-century history as one of decline. The system it operated in the Straits – purchasing tin by exclusive contracts and controlling strategic rivers – 'worked very well'. The Company was a large bureaucracy which could not compete in 'a purely commercial way with cheaper and faster traders. But it was in fact precisely this characteristic, the role of a permanent political power, slow but remarkably consistent in its policy, which made the Company most attractive as a political ally for Malay kingdoms.' The VOC was 'specialised ... in cultivating political alliances with the Malay courts'. In return it secured commercial privileges: low-price tin and pepper. The decline of the VOC's maritime power did not destroy the system. Merely having power at its disposal was 'adequate political assurance for the allied kingdom'. What counted with the Malay ally was 'reliability': Batavia, the VOC capital, would back up the local residency in the Straits.[55]

The contract with Palembang of 1755 gave the VOC the exclusive right to buy tin and pepper. The VOC promised to 'maintain the Sultan in the peaceful possession of his states and to let him enjoy all the rights and prerogatives attached to his Crown; and to do all that is suitable to contribute to the growth and prosperity of his states and subjects'.[56] 'I cannot understand why kings who are allies of the Company quarrel with it', declared Sultan Mahmud Badaruddin of Palembang, 'while experience shows us that they always succumb and the Company triumphs. I fire pepper and tin at the Company, and it bombards me with good Spanish rials.'[57]

Was the Sultan's satisfaction justified? The Company, he noted, always triumphed. It had permanency, as Vos puts it, reliability: Batavia was a central authority that offered local backing. Amidst the continuities the VOC had brought a change to the archipelago, as Dianne Lewis has pointed out. Van Leur, she argues, downplayed the effect of the European incursions. Trade had been 'splintered' by the Portuguese, and the Dutch occupation of Melaka in 1641 'inhibited the growth of any centralized Malay power'. Sri Vijaya and Melaka depended on their freedom as trade centres as much as on sea-power. A foreign port in the Straits, protected by a foreign power (Batavia), operated against 'all the Malay rulers who sought to assert their power over more than a small portion of the Malay world'. Because of the presence of a Dutch port in their midst the Malay rulers were to face the new world of the late eighteenth/early nineteenth centuries in disunity.[58] The old dynamics of the Malay world had been stultified. Nor did the Chinese sustain their old interest in the strong state in the Straits.

What the reformers such as Stamford Raffles identified was a Malay system in decline. They were partly correct. They attributed much of the decline to the Dutch, and again were partly correct. But they were not allowed to determine the policy the newly dominant Britain adopted. Its European and commercial priorities prevailed, and the Dutch were not dislodged. Instead, the position of the Malay rulers – in the Straits and elsewhere, too – further deteriorated. The contractual system – which they had been able to see as an often comfortable kind of semi-dependent alliance – became an uncomfortable dependency.

If the contractual system is to be regarded as a third 'system' of international relations in Southeast Asia, it must be stressed that it was divisive, in the sense that nothing like it applied on the mainland. In mainland Southeast Asia the Europeans had little impact in the early modern period. There was no contractual phase. What marks its history – masterfully charted by Vic Lieberman – is the disintegration and reintegration of the three main polities, Burman, Thai and Vietnamese. There was another difference. Though Chinese intervention was to cease in the archipelago, it did not cease on the mainland. The apical power continued to be part of Southeast Asian history, playing a negative role in the maritime area, a more active one on the mainland, in both cases significant.

According to Tomé Pires, the Portuguese were aware of Melaka's political and economic relationship with China, but did not expect a military reaction to their conquest.[59] 'The reason why these two powers did not clash is based upon China's highly divergent view from those of the Portuguese on the ordering of state relations and the role of maritime trade.' The conquest, Souza suggests, 'disturbed China's "world order"'. It was 'a new barbarian problem'. Ming officials 'in all probability ... had to determine the exact nature of China's relationship with the Malacca sultanate'.[60] In fact the Shih-tsung emperor agreed in 1521 that the Thai and other barbarian kings should be ordered to expel the Portuguese from Melaka on behalf of the Sultan.[61] That, of course, did not happen.

At Canton Ming officials 'ordered the exclusion of the Portuguese and implemented a ban on all dealings by the inhabitants of China with the barbarian devils'.[62] Melaka had to conduct its trade with China through visiting junks, but Portuguese lancados based on the Fukien coast participated in the piracy and smuggling encouraged by Ming policies of restriction coupled with unsatisfied demand. But as the problem of wako/wo-kou 'piracy' developed – more Chinese than Japanese – and Ming forces began to attack the pirate bases, the Portuguese, 'confronted with the difficulty of finding holes in the "Chinese wall" wide enough to slip through', and anxious not to be 'confused with "true" smugglers',[63] sought to legitimize themselves at least with the local officials, and were allowed to base themselves at Macau in the early 1550s. But that hardly represented a structural change in international relations, nor was it seen as such: instead a concession or compromise, winked at or ignored.

The collapse of the Ming and the emergence of the Manchu [Ching] dynasty might perhaps have resulted in another assertion of the Chinese world-order, but it did not do so. The reasons are not found only in the entrenchment of the Europeans in maritime Southeast Asia, but also in the attitude of the Manchus. An alien dynasty, it clung all the more closely to what it perceived as the Chinese tradition, lest it lost the allegiance of the Chinese gentry on whom it so largely relied, and even when the practices that enjoined could not be followed and were subjected to compromise, as with the dealings with the Russian empire at Nerchinsk, the principles were not openly disavowed. The Chinese world-order must appear to be maintained, even or all the more if in practice it was not. The Manchus' interest, indeed, focused on the north and west, not on the south. There indeed their achievements were stunning, involving the incorporation of Manchuria, Mongolia, Xinjian and Tibet.

In 1647, however, the Manchu court did issue an edict inviting Southeast Asian states to become tributaries of the new regime, and the Shun-chin emperor accepted that 'earnest and respectful' vassal states should be able to conduct trade 'accompanying the tribute presentation'.[64] Trade was seen 'within the framework of politics', while for tributaries such as Ayudhya it was an end in itself. Even at times of imperial prohibition, local Chinese officials had an interest in allowing it to continue. There was 'an apparent gap between word and action, policy and practice, underlying the Chinese official stand on foreign trade and the maritime ban'. Corruption and bribery played their part. '[T]he Confucianized Manchu rulers clung to the myths of the tributary system, pretending that foreign trade could be safely and effectively contained within such a context in spite of the obvious prostitution of this system in later periods.'[65]

On the mainland the Manchus intervened somewhat in the old manner, seeking to check over-ambitious states and maintain stability abroad as well as to sustain prestige at home. Son of Alaung-hpaya, creator of the new Konbaung dynasty in Burma, Hsinbiyushin set out to conquer the neighbouring Thai state, Ayudhya, and sacked it in 1767. In preparation he had conquered the Lao states of Chiengmai and Vientiane. The incursion 'caused such a ferment among the states bordering on Yunnan that the Chinese were forced to intervene'. A series of invasions in 1766–69 in fact forced the Burmese to relinquish their attack on the Thais. Some Shan states, alarmed by Hsinbiyushin's ambitions, appealed to China. The Yunnan viceroy attacked Kengtung, 'the largest and most easterly of the Shan states subject to Burma'. His failure was followed by Chinese invasions along the Bhamo route, intended to punish Burma. They, too, failed. In 1770 a peace treaty was concluded, though it was never ratified by Hsinbiyushin. The Chinese agreed to withdraw, trade would be restored, decennial missions were to be exchanged.[66]

China was an important factor in the restoration of the Thai state after the destruction of Ayudhya. Taksin recognized the importance of the China trade and sent a substantial embassy to the Chien-lung emperor. He was not recognized, but Rama I, the founder of the Bangkok dynasty, achieved that objective. At the same time he expanded the tribute trade well beyond the emperor's wishes. Again Beijing preferred to ignore what it could not prevent.[67] What the Thai king sent was not what he exacted from his own tributaries among the Malay states. He offered gifts. They had to send the bunga mas, the gold and silver flowers, in return receiving the protection due to a tributary.[68]

In Vietnam the Manchu emperor responded to the appeal of the legitimate Le monarch against the Tay-son rebels, and an army crossed into Vietnam. That, the Grand Council thought, was sufficient, and ordered its withdrawal. The commander left it too late and was routed.[69] The Tay-son themselves were broken by Nguyen Anh in the 1790s. When he took Hanoi in 1802 and proclaimed himself emperor, he sent an embassy to Beijing seeking formal investiture. This was granted in 1803 on condition that tribute was sent every two years and homage paid every four.[70]

Tribute missions were also received from maritime states not under European control. The sultanate of Sulu revived its earlier tribute trade. Seven tribute missions were recorded in the years 1726–54, and its dependent territories in northern Borneo were an important source of goods in demand in China.[71] But, like the Ming, the Manchu did not intervene among the barbarians further south. They were anxious to keep them at arm's length, and not to become involved in risky conflict.

They were concerned about the activities of the Chinese in the Nanyang, but endeavoured to deal with them by edict from China. In 1712 the emperor tried to put a stop to long-standing emigration southwards: an edict prohibited trade to Nanyang and requested governments in the region to repatriate Chinese for execution on their own soil. The Manchu dynasty was indeed weakest in the southern provinces from which most of the migrants originated, and the overseas Chinese were and remained hotbeds of anti-Manchu feeling, their secret societies anti-Manchu in origin. The edict was, of course, inoperative, another illustration of the unreality mixed with the reality of Manchu attitudes to the outside world.

China's policies had involved no urge to incorporate parts of the Southeast Asian region, even, for most of the time, Vietnam, once it had gained independence, but rather a desire to avoid over-mighty neighbours, dividing them but not ruling them, averting any challenge on the 'frontiers' of civilization. Occasionally a display of power had reasserted China's view of the world more generally, usually being associated with legitimising a new regime at home. But, if at times it felt forced to intervene, that was not the result of a reaction to the intervention of other powers from outside the region. In any case the Europeans had indeed not effectively penetrated the mainland states, which were obviously more important to the Chinese empire than the maritime states so far as security was concerned.

The other striking feature of the traditional relationship was the disjunction between the trading interests of the Chinese merchants and the political attitudes of the Chinese regimes. Though Southeast Asia, especially the maritime region, was a source of goods in demand in China, there were no attempts to back up private Chinese traders in or trading with Southeast

Asia: even piracy was dealt with as a matter of maintaining order not protecting local Chinese interests.[72] There was no clearly established role for private trade in the tributary system, where trade was handled as a matter of political recognition and reward and was subject to arbitrary interruption. Southeast Asia, again, was a field of migration, temporary or not, but with that, too, the Ching regime certainly had no sympathy. With some justice the Manchus indeed saw overseas Chinese as a source of subversion.

'A dwarf is as much a man as a giant', Vattel had declared; 'a small republic is no less sovereign than the most powerful kingdom.' International law was based on a respect for difference among states: 'the difference of religion is absolutely foreign to them'. All have 'a right to be governed as they think proper, and ... no state has the smallest right to interfere in the government of another. Of all the rights that can belong to a nation, sovereignty is, doubtless, the most precious', though it could be overridden in the case of 'intolerable persecution' and 'evident tyranny'.[73]

At the end of the eighteenth century and the beginning of the nineteenth, the Westphalia system was asserted and with the defeat of Napoleon accepted in Europe. '[With states and nations] the union of all depends on the independence of each', the historian Leopold von Ranke wrote in 1833. ' ... A decisive positive dominance of one over the others would lead to the others' ruin. A merging of all would destroy the essence of each. Out of separate and independent development will emerge true harmony.'[74] But, though independent states had emerged outside Europe that were accepted as equal with the European states – the US, Haiti, Liberia – and more of them were added when the Latin American colonies, prompted by Napoleon's displacing the Spanish monarch, turned to revolution – it was far from clear how or indeed whether the system would generally extend beyond Europe.

At the same time, indeed, states outside Europe that had been treated as independent began in the eyes of the Europeans to lose their full status, even if they did not lose their independence through conquest or disintegration. A further process was also at work from the late eighteenth century. The mercantilist attitudes of the sixteenth century had persisted, though the implementation of the policies they inspired was regularized. But another concept was put forward, notably by Adam Smith, whose *The Wealth of Nations* was published in the very year that the American colonies proclaimed their independence. If government 'interventions' and impediments were removed, trade would expand. There was no need for territorial control, merely for fair opportunity. Initially the concept was particularly advantageous to Great Britain. Not only had it engaged successfully in the 'commercial revolution' of the eighteenth century. It became the first industrial nation in the nineteenth.

The initial advantage Britain enjoyed would not last forever, since others, too, would industrialize. But it was accompanied by a range of policies, not only affecting those in the family of nations, but those outside it. Sustaining a balance of power in Europe that the overthrow of France had created, and preserving the naval predominance that the defeat of the French navy had secured, Britain had an unusual degree of predominance among the European powers. It thus played a major role in determining the new relationship with the outside world. But its predominance was not expressed in territorial dominance or formal political control. Instead a whole variety of connexions was created and indeed improvised, including those that were considered to be within the 'empire', but also those outside, and those in the empires of others. Why? Because it recognized it was a small state, on the periphery of Europe, with predominantly economic rather than imperial interests in the rest of the world.

What it did not produce was the immediate or indeed early extension to the rest of the world of the Westphalia system. Rather it was another set of relationships built upon or replacing the relationships between Europe and the outside world already developed alongside the Westphalia system in Europe. Historians might term it a 'transitional' phase. To some extent it was seen as that by contemporaries. Even though the transition might take a long time, it was possible that the world would become a world of states, though for the time being it was a world of empires.

What kind of states would they be? That was also worked out during the 'transitional' phase. It was, however, much influenced by what had happened in France and in reaction to the revolution there. Proclaiming Liberty, Equality and Fraternity, the Revolution sought to overthrow privilege and to transform social relationships. But it also stressed a new form of community, that of the Nation, and was indeed obsessed with the need to focus loyalty on that intangible and impersonal object rather than on the monarchy, to make people citizens not subjects. Language, education, architecture, music, museums, were called on to perform this function as well as the restructuring of government. Other countries were to follow in imitation or in reaction. Nation and state became closely connected, both in thought and action. Where they could be identified – and the French themselves had had great difficulty – connecting them was a source of major political strife within Europe and within the 'multi-national' states of Europe. Towards the end of the century the idea was taken up outside Europe. Should not the states that would succeed the empires be 'nation states'?

One reason it was taken up was the presentation of example and the need – which the Germans had felt when contending with the French revolutionaries and Napoleon – to fight back with the weapons that subdued you. Another was social change, partly set in motion by the policies of the imperial powers themselves, as well as the economic change they had introduced. Yet a third was the association of nationalism with development, in particular with the urge to adopt industrialization, even though France itself, though inventive, was in fact slow to industrialize. A common language, a common education system, literacy, were adjuncts of the nation state that would also serve industry, and overall the 'modernization' for which new national elites yearned. The entities that the imperialists had improvised could produce change, but not that change.

4 European empires

In the nineteenth century, the Westphalia system, having emerged more belatedly than some have argued, did not yet apply outside Europe. What appeared as a result of the growth of European wealth, power and technological advance, was a world of empires, though that included states, mostly in the Americas, that had recently become independent, or that had retained an earlier independence now accepted on a conditional basis. It was a world indeed of improvisation as well as of change and adjustment. An international system emerged, together with a body of international law that both accepted and guided what had been or could be done. It included understandings about overseas occupation that went far beyond Tordesillas, covering a world undergoing what some, like Karl Marx, saw as a second globalization, marked also by expanded international trade and improved communication by rail, steamship, telegraph and canal-building. The Berlin conference of 1884–85, for example, created an obligation to establish authority in occupied regions on the coast of Africa.[1]

The European enterprise, like that of the conquistadors and the companies, was indeed shaped not only by rivalry but also by commonality. But, by contrast to the earlier period, those features were in turn shaped by the albeit temporary dominance of one power, Great Britain, its attitude to the international system, and the policies and attitudes to international law it adopted. The defeated Napoleon was amazed. 'Castlereagh had the continent at his disposal. … The peace he has made is the sort of peace he would have made if he had been beaten.'[2] It did not attempt, outside Europe any more than within, to turn its de facto dominance into territorial control, and its industrial success and initial primacy prompted it to abandon the remnants of mercantilism and to favour a concept of free trade that included but went beyond the free access of which Smith had written. Other European empires could exist, preferably also avoiding protectionism and providing opportunity and security for foreign trade. Non-European states could survive if they adopted enough of European practice to provide for a foreign commerce from which it was assumed with some justice that the British would be the first to benefit. The emerging – or, as it turned out to be, the transitional – state system was deeply affected by the priorities

Britain adopted and enjoined and by the reactions to its predominance and its policies on the part of other states in and beyond Europe.

In Europe, states retaining or gaining independence characteristically sought to industrialize, and, like the US, adopted protectionist measures in order to counteract Britain's pre-eminence. Some Asian states survived, but could take part in the emerging international system only by accepting extra-territoriality, a development of the 'capitulations' through which the Ottoman Empire had earlier come to terms with European traders, and that inhibited their economic development. Yet other states lost their independence, unable or in no position to make the necessary adjustment. They did not, however, all become 'colonies', a term originally implying the settlement of foreign people that now came also to apply to territories overseas that became formal possessions of European sovereigns. Other forms of relationship were developed, in particular the protectorate, another word whose changing meanings and implications reflected changing usage. The inter-relationships among states and political entities in the second globalization was, as in the first, marked by innovation and improvisation. The roles and functions of those involved also changed. A 'Resident' had wider powers than an 'Ambassador', though the words had originally covered similar functions. The role of 'Consul' tended to shift with the advance of the term 'protectorate'. What a 'High Commissioner' was depended on usage and circumstance.

It was primarily perhaps a British improvisation, and indeed some of the other shifts in meaning reflected British practice. In turn that reflected both the predominance of the British and the way they preferred to use it. They sought to limit their territorial responsibility, both because of their own preferences as a commercial power, and because of their wish to avoid unnecessarily provoking other powers. Though the European states had much in common, their own societies differed, as did their strategic position, their interests, their perceptions and their articulation of purpose. But others besides Britain came to contribute to, as well as to share, the repertoire of practice and precedent that framed Europe's relationships with the non-European world. So, of course, did the reactions they met among non-European powers, positive or negative or indeed creative. The repertoire expanded and modified the repertoire already developed. Not only were there 'unequal treaties', colonies and protectorates. Attempts were made – by the Germans as well as the British – to revive the chartered company, though the Dutch had terminated the VOC in 1799 and the British the EIC (East India Company) after the Mutiny of 1857. There were even states created by individual entrepreneurs. James Brooke of Sarawak had imitators. Leopold II – at one time interested in taking over his raj[3] – later invented a fraud called the Congo Free State.

The legal position of such territories mattered not so much because it defined what their rulers could do as because what they did could become a question taken up at home in the metropolis or by another 'imperial' power.

But a broadbrush description might qualify them all as 'colonial states'. That phenomenon should be compared with the 'normal' state of the nineteenth century, and with the 'modern' state of the twentieth, if the 'transition' to a Westphalia world is to be understood. In what ways did it resemble and in what differ? It was, says Anne Phillips, the 'facsimile of a state'. It was 'no simple extension of the metropolitan political system to overseas possessions' says Jurgen Osterhammel, 'but a political form in itself'.[4]

In some ways it is easier to say what it was not than what it was, to point to the ways in which it 'fell short' of the norm. Its nature, as Yao Jen-to says, has not been much discussed. It had features of a 'modern state', partly the result of its being thrust into a globalizing system in a multi-empire world. Thus it had, or was expected to have, 'recognized' frontiers, accepted by other states. Within those it was expected to have exclusive jurisdiction over its subjects. But it was deficient in other respects. Did it have their loyalty? On what grounds could it call for it? The state did not conduct foreign policy: that was the task, not indeed of its immediate rulers, but of foreign offices in metropolitan capitals. It had in fact no international relations since it was not sovereign. Nor did it defend itself. That was predominantly the task of imperial troops and navies, within the larger framework of the naval predominance of British sea-power. In protectorates, if not in colonies, it might expect to control its domestic policy, but even that was seldom fully the case in practice. In turn it did not determine the degree to which it might modernize or industrialize. That became a core concern for the new elite elements that the rulers bred up, sometimes in spite of themselves, and who were to seize upon, even in states given frontiers out of the convenience of European powers, the powerful concept of the nation that became attached to the state in the course of nineteenth-century European history.

The 'colonial state' in that context was something of a paradox, a contradiction in terms. That was what Sir Andrew Cohen recognized when he became Governor of Uganda after the Second World War. 'When governor of Uganda, he actually tried to manufacture nationalism where there wasn't any before', as Ronald Robinson put it. 'Thought you had to have a national will for national economic and social development and that a colony could never have one. He deliberately set out to nationalize and democratize what he thought was an antiquated and ineffectual nineteenth-century structure of alien colonial rule.'[5]

The 'colony' possessed some features common in the European state system, such as fixed frontiers – by contrast to the flexibility common in earlier Southeast Asia – but did not possess the sovereignty that was its essential feature. That lay in the metropolis. In theory, the 'protectorate' did not convey sovereignty to the protecting power, though the practice diverged. Neither colony nor protectorate had the power to defend itself or determine its course of development. Both had some of the attributes of modernity, but neither could not fully modernize nor mobilize the talents of those they ruled. Their continuance came into question when the internal role of the state expanded. Their attempts to change the status of its subjects brought their own status into question. W. Gifford Palgrave, once a British consul in the Philippines, and earlier a well-known Arabist, praised the benefits of the clerical government that sustained Spanish rule in the Philippines: 'a Philippine hamlet feels and knows little of the vexations inseparable from direct and foreign official administration; and if under such a rule "progress", as we love to term it, be rare, disaffection and want are rarer still.'[6] But if officials and friars did not disturb the status quo, educated Filipinos did.

While Britain's prime concern was commercial exchange with other countries rather than territorial dominion over them, India was an exception to the rule. In the late eighteenth and early nineteenth centuries the EIC built up an Indian empire based on a mixture of direct control and 'subsidiary treaties' with native princes. By 1818 it claimed 'paramountcy', a term that suggested overall dominance and the right to intervene in any state but took no particular theoretical or constitutional form. At mid-century it displaced the Mughal emperor. In 1878 Queen Victoria became absentee Empress. India was not insulated from Britain nor its policies. It provided a market, it provided bases, it provided soldiers, it offered careers. But it did require a rather different approach to foreign policy. That had to focus on the security of this extraordinary dominion. It must not be challenged within the sub-continent, nor on its frontiers. 'Believing their hold on India itself to be precarious, Indian policy-makers suffered from a nightmare of foreign invasion leading to internal revolt.'[7] The dictates of such a 'continental' policy were rather at odds with Britain's normal priorities, those of a commercial and industrial power.

Of that the British were aware. It was a kind of warning not only to others but to the British themselves. China, *The Times* insisted, must not become another India.[8] Indeed the British were determined to avoid the break-up of China, though often accused of wanting it. What they wanted was for it to transform itself. The 'unequal treaties', inaugurated by their victory over the Manchus in the war of 1840–42, were intended to be an interim measure. The new pattern of international relations was applied in a form suited to what Lord Palmerston called 'imperfectly civilized States'.[9] The Chinese were participants in the Westphalia system, but not full participants. And yet, on the other hand, their apical position did not at once or entirely disappear. Indeed they fought to sustain it.

Even in their struggle to retain their apical role, however, the Chinese were changing it, and accepting that theirs was a state among states. The transformation begun by defeat in the war of 1840–42 was long drawn out. Only step by step did the Manchu dynasty assume a role in the Western state-system, accepting the terms set out in the so-called 'unequal treaties'.

In 1843 it ceded Hong Kong island as a base for British traders; opened so-called treaty ports; accepted consular jurisdiction; but it did not agree to the exchange of ambassadors. That came only in the treaties of 1858 and 1860, which also removed the restrictions on migration, travel in the interior and missions. As the empire thus changed its status among states, its periphery came into question. Were the states that had accepted a tributary status under the Confucian system to become dependencies of China in the style of western protectorates and colonies? Or were they to gain independence or, more likely, fall under the control of other powers?

Increasingly they were seen as buffer states and their defensive role was stressed. 'The border provinces are China's gates: the tributary states are China's walls. We build the walls to protect the gates, and protect the gates to secure the house.'[10] A document of 1882 described Tonkin as a 'Barrier of the Middle Empire, a small nation which serves to protect the provinces of Yunnan and Kwangsi. … .Although [it is] situated outside the Empire, we cannot abandon it.'[11]

The partially modernized regime enjoyed some success until the 1890s. Some of the outer satellites fell away. But when in his struggle with the French in Tonkin, the Vietnamese emperor appealed to his Chinese suzerain, Chinese troops were sent across the border to help. In May 1884 the Chinese government acknowledged the French protectorate. It renewed the war when it realized it had lost its traditional suzerainty in the 'Barrier', but Admiral Courbet bombarded Foochow, and it had to accept a new treaty in April 1885. The Chinese were unhappy with the British annexation of Upper Burma in 1886. 'If we annex Burmah at the expense of quarrel with China, our commercial interest will profit very little, and ultimate results may be disastrous', as Lord Randolph Churchill, the Secretary of State for India, put it.[12] Britain's policy, however, was to uphold the integrity of China, rather than see it break up, and in an Anglo-Chinese convention of July 1886 it was agreed that Burma would continue to send a mission to China every ten years on the basis of equality, the British having satisfied themselves that, according to a treaty of 1769, Burma's position was that of a friend rather than a tributary.[13]

Major changes had indeed been taking place in Southeast Asia. There, though it is often neglected in general books on both H and IR, many of the improvisations involved in the relating the Europeans and non-Europeans in the second phase of globalization were illustrated if not invented. Only Siam/Thailand concluded 'unequal treaties' of the Chinese kind. In a long process, the nineteenth century saw the rest of Southeast Asia incorporated into European empires, despite or because of Britain's overall predominance. A fourth pattern of relationships thus displaced the earlier patterns, but it utilized elements of them, adopted new versions of shared sovereignty, such as protectorates and protected states, revived the ruling company, and illustrated the paradoxes of the colonial state.

Burma, annexed by the British in three steps after three wars, was an exception to their rules, or, it might better be said, it exemplified their 'Indian' policy rather than their more normal policy on a world of states. It was viewed less from the point of view of its commercial opportunities – even after it came to be perceived as a back door to trade with China – than for its relationship to British dominion on the sub-continent of India. No foreign power could be allowed to establish itself on the confines of that dominion. No regime in Burma could be allowed to set a precedent of defiance to the Indian princes over whom Britain was 'paramount'. Such views could allow Burma its independence, but it had to be a qualified independence. That was a position its monarchs – unwilling to abandon the traditions of Southeast Asian monarchy or a recently renewed identification of monarch and cakkavartin – proved unable to accept. More than any other factor, that difference underlay the extension of conquest from India to Burma.

The Konbaung dynasty had reincorporated Pegu and destroyed Ayudhya. Bodawpaya [r.1782–1819] began to think of himself as the most powerful monarch in the world, not only making Siam his tributary, but then turning to the west, possessing himself of the British colonies and attacking the Great Mogul.[14] Michael Symes, reporting on the mission the Company's Governor-General sent to Ava in 1795, warned of the 'characteristic pride and unbounded arrogance' of the Burmese. They had 'an extravagant notion of their own power'.[15] It seems, a later envoy observed in 1809, that King Bodawpaya 'will treat with no power on earth as an equal, but he graciously receives under his protection China, Ceylon, Assam, and the British Empire in India. He will grant a boon, but he will not make a treaty.'[16] But, as the two powers acquired common boundaries, there were border issues with which their divergent attitudes made it difficult to deal.

Governor-General Lord Amherst went to war with King Bagyidaw in March 1824. The object was to put Burma in its place by demonstrating the power of British India, 'to produce such an impression of the power and resources of the British Empire in India as will deter the Court of Ava from any attempt to again to disturb the friendly relations which may be re-established by the result of the present contest'.[17] Annexations followed under the treaty of Yandabo not because they were the object of the expedition, but because it had taken so much time and labour and loss of life to demonstrate the power of British India. Without the new terms, 'success would not have been manifest … and the powers of India might have been tempted to believe that the British Government had at last encountered an enemy whom it had failed to humble'.[18]

The loss of Tenasserim, Arakan and Assam did not, however, make it easy to develop a positive relationship. A brilliant Resident at Ava, Henry Burney, tried, but found Bagyidaw 'most unwilling to admit the British Government as equal to his in pride and strength'.[19] The presence of a Resident he saw as 'a proof of our supremacy and a badge of his servility and vassalage'.[20] Indeed the word 'Resident' was a British Indian usage, implying a relationship short of that between fully independent states. Bodawpaya's successor, Tharrawaddy, claimed that the treaty was made with his predecessor, not with him and so he was 'determined to have nothing to say to it'. 'I will not send an embassy to Bengal; if I send one it shall be to the King of England.' The Governor-General was 'an officer who receives pay and is not a King'.[21] He thus invoked the notion that treaties endured only for the lifetime of the signatories. He also tried to avoid the subordination implied in dealing with a Governor-General, at least claiming equality with the British king. Burney finally left the capital, and his successor was withdrawn.

In the second war, status and standing were again an issue, and perhaps more crucially. 'While I should be reluctant to believe that our empire in India has no stay but by the sword alone, it is vain to doubt that our hold must rest mainly upon the might of the conqueror, and must be maintained by that power', Governor-General Lord Dalhousie argued. 'The Government of India cannot, consistently with its own safety, appear for one day in an attitude of inferiority, or hope to maintain peace and submission among the numberless princes and peoples embraced within the vast circuit of the empire, if for one day it gave countenance to a doubt of the absolute superiority of its arms, and of its continued resolution to assert it.'[22] This time the war was marked by prompt victory. Dalhousie argued against trying to negotiate a treaty. That would be a difficult task, perhaps requiring further military action. The only alternative was simple acquisition. That he limited to Pegu.

The new king of what remained of Burma, Mindon, accepted the need to develop relations with British India. Complimentary missions were exchanged with Calcutta, then the Indian capital, and new commercial treaties allowed trade up the Irrawaddy so as to provide access to Yunnan. His attempts to pursue a foreign policy based on equality in sovereignty – in emulation of his neighbour, Siam – were more risky. A mission to Europe in 1872–73 concluded a treaty with France, but, following an intervention by the British ambassador in Paris, it was not ratified. The Government in London also received the mission. The Government of India had warned of the implications of so doing: it would complicate its dealing with the Mandalay government; it would be a precedent for other powers. In the event the mission was given a merely ceremonial reception. And it was introduced to the Queen – to whom it brought a letter addressed by Mindon to his 'Royal Sister' – by the Secretary of State for India, not the Foreign Secretary. 'It was as if the Government here was willing to consider questions of relations with Burmah', commented the US ambassador in London, 'as belonging to the policy which controls in regard to the eastern possessions of Great Britain, and not to the treatment which is to be given to an independent power.'[23]

Riskily, Mindon's successor, Thibaw sent a new mission to France in 1883. The 1873 treaty was ratified. The British ambassador was told of supplementary negotiations, which were not of a political or military nature. But Jules Ferry sent a secret note offering to supply arms once the French had established their control in Tonkin.[24] Furthermore a French consul in Mandalay tried to build up French interests. The aim, the British Viceroy, Lord Dufferin, was told, was not to add Burma to the dominions France was building up in Southeast Asia, but to enable it to put pressure on Britain and secure concessions in Siam and Laos.[25] But, if so, it was Burma that paid for this diplomatic ploy.

The main cause of the third Burma war was indeed once more strategic. 'It is French intrigue which has forced us to go to Burmah', Churchill wrote to Lord Dufferin; 'but for that element we might have treated Theebaw with severe neglect.'[26] The war was short. Theebaw was sent into exile, and his kingdom annexed. That was a practice with more precedent in British policy in India than in British policy in Southeast Asia. But then the relationship with Burma was always seen in an Indian context, and it continued to be so.

In maritime Southeast Asia, Britain's policy was less inflected by concern about India, and more typical of that of a commercial state than a continental. More powerful than before, it was more ready to question the Dutch position, invoking the concept of free access that it was seeking to apply elsewhere. There were, however, political limitations: a friendly Dutch regime was an important support for Britain's security in Europe. It was cautious, therefore, about taking up a challenge to the entrenched Dutch system of treaties and alliances with Malay and Indonesian rulers. There were, however, many parts of the archipelago that could be considered to be free of such contractual relationships.

The war of the American Revolution had come to include a fourth Anglo-Dutch war. In the peace treaty, the Directors of the EIC suggested demanding 'liberty to navigate and trade to the islands in the Eastern seas without any molestation'. Instructing the negotiator, Lord Grantham explained that 'the Dutch had hitherto kept themselves Masters of the Navigation of the Eastern Seas. … It will be necessary that the liberty of navigating those Seas should be asked for, and granted.'[27] The EIC insisted that it had no intention of trading with any Dutch establishments, but argued that free navigation would not only guarantee the passage of its ships to China, but also permit 'an uncontrouled Trade to any of the islands situated in those Seas, not possessed by the Dutch'.[28] That was unsatisfactory to the Dutch, but they had to sign the treaty, with its objectionable Article 6, in 1784.

The pro-French Patriots were overthrown in 1787,[29] French influence in the Republic destroyed, and negotiations for a new Anglo-Dutch alliance begun. Article 6 was one of the obstacles to its conclusion. The Board of Control, set up to give the Government control over the EIC's growing Indian empire, planned a new deal with the Dutch in Asia as well as Europe. In the archipelago, it proposed, Britain should guarantee the VOC's spice monopoly by dropping its claim to navigate east of Sumatra and undertaking to make no settlement there unless a third party did. But it would secure an entrepot at Riau to attract Indonesian traders from the archipelago, and it would not drop its rights elsewhere.

A long series of negotiations followed, of which this issue was one focus. Faced by Dutch opposition, Lord Auckland, the ambassador, proposed admitting that the right of navigation did not convey the right to trade, but that was found quite inadmissible in London: it would be 'inconsistent with our General Right by the Law of Nations, to navigate and trade to any places, as well in the Eastern Seas as elsewhere, not occupied by the Dutch or any other nation'.[30] 'The jealousies and apprehensions of the Dutch relative to the Navigation of the Eastern Seas … rest on the ground they dare not avow', Henry Dundas wrote. 'I mean their consciousness of the radical and internal weakness of the sovereignty they claim in the Eastern Isles, and they are afraid that the communication we may have with the Natives would lay the foundation for their total shaking off of the miserable dependence in which they are held by the Dutch.'[31] But no treaty had been made by the time the armies of the French Revolution penetrated the United Provinces, and the Patriots set up a Batavian Republic.

During the Revolutionary war the British occupied Melaka and the Dutch settlements in Maluku and elsewhere. In the succeeding Napoleonic war they occupied Java itself, now the core of the Dutch empire. In the peace negotiations, however, Britain's policy was again dominated by European considerations: a new kingdom of the Netherlands was a factor in the balance of power that was being reconstructed; and it would be strengthened by securing the Dutch empire in the East. The convention of 1814 did not even cover the cession of an entrepot in the Straits, such as Dundas and his colleagues had sought before the wars. Stamford Raffles, who had governed Java during the interregnum, believed the policy was mistaken.

Even before the conquest, he had argued that the British should adopt 'a bolder policy'. The Dutch claims to 'territorial right in the Eastern Isles, in which all the nations of Europe have so long and so blindly acquiesced, will be found to be very much inferior to what is generally supposed, unless, perhaps, in the Isle of Java itself', and it might be 'our soundest policy to form the most intimate connections, by treaty, with those which have indisputable pretensions to independence'. Those would be retained if Java were returned at the end of the war. The rulers might recognize the Governor-General as Batara or Protector, the ancient title of the emperor of Majapahit, he suggested, and 'this would give a general right of superintendence over, and interference with, all the Malay states, which might be acted upon when circumstances should render it necessary; and might be so limited by treaty as to remove all occasion of suspicion from the native powers'.[32]

As Lt-Governor of Java he made a number of treaties with Indonesian rulers, which he saw, not as 'interfering with the authority of any of the sovereigns of those islands', but as a means of 'restoring it by restoring to them the right of levying duties and thus placing at their disposal the means of maintaining a salutary and restraining authority over their subjects', and so suppressing the piracy that interfered with a regular trade.[33] But maintaining such treaties was seen by his superiors as inconsistent with Dutch empire in the Eastern Seas. 'We have viewed with considerable anxiety the engagements proposed to be entered into … with Petty States in the Eastern Seas. … We are decidedly of opinion, that such engagements are impolitic and injudicious; that they are calculated to involve the British Government in the internal concerns of those States, and the perpetual contests which they are carrying on with each other.'[34]

Back in the Archipelago as Lt Governor of the old Company's possession on Benkulen in remote western Sumatra, Raffles took steps to counter the Dutch. He made a treaty with Menangkabau and imagined restoring its authority, once, he argued, widely respected by other princes. 'Sumatra, under British influence, [might] again rise into great political importance.'[35] Early in 1819 he visited Aceh, never indeed under Dutch control, and concluded a commercial treaty that also allowed for stationing a British agent in the sultanate. For that, however, he had the authority of his superiors in Bengal, who had accepted his argument that the Dutch by renewing their treaties were not only threatening British trade in the archipelago but also the security of the route to China. Under the instructions he secured, he also proceeded to make a British settlement at Singapore, another part, with Riau, of the empire of Johore.

Only some of the Raffles argument was accepted in London. There was no wish to challenge the basic decision that the Dutch should predominate in the Archipelago. But how were British interests to be provided for? The Dutch wanted to avoid an inquest into their title deeds. Instead a new deal was made, the Treaty of 17 March 1824, the last to be made in the name of the Most Holy and Undivided Trinity. It provided for British trade with Dutch possessions and for trade with states in treaty relationships with the Dutch. It also provided that the Dutch would acquire Benkulen, transfer Melaka, and drop their opposition to the British settlement on Singapore. The two parties were respectively to abstain from political connexions with the states of the Peninsula and Sumatra, with a reservation, in respect of the recency of Raffles' treaty, over Aceh. A notional line was thus drawn through the Malay world, even through the empire of Johor. The Dutch and the British were, as Canning put it, 'exclusive Lords of the East', though it was desirable not to provoke other powers by too openly proclaiming it.[36]

Other powers were indeed in general to respect the unspoken lordship. The result was, of course, felt largely by the Indonesian states. Whatever the theoretical status of their treaties and contracts, their position in practice deteriorated: they had no political contact with other powers. That is a point which struck the great scholar of Indonesian legal history, G.J. Resink, who published a number of essays that challenged the notion that the Dutch had ruled Indonesia for three hundred years by exposing the legal position between the Dutch and the native princes in many parts of the archipelago even in the nineteenth century. '[T]he far-flung archipelago', he declared, 'was divided by a cleavage in international law that was a great deal longer, and cut a great deal deeper, than the international boundaries with Britain on Borneo and with Portugal on Timor'. In 1854 the Minister of the Colonies had accepted that there were 'independent Indies princes', if 'very few', in the Netherlands Indies. In a law on import and export duties of 1873, the Crown and the States General distinguished between 'Netherlands Indies possessions' and 'native States of the Eastern Archipelago in amity with the Netherlands Government'. The Supreme Court at Batavia [Jakarta] distinguished in 1880 between the 'Netherlands Indies state' and the 'Netherlands Indies Archipelago'.[37] As late as 1879, the Batavia Court of Justice saw a Controleur [sub-Resident] in Jambi as a political agent accredited to the Sultan.[38]

The history of international law in the Indies did not end till about 1910, Resink maintained. Up to that time, a small Netherlands Indies, though part of the Dutch state when seen from the Netherlands, was, 'when approached from the view of its position in Indonesia and in international law and legal practice acting alongside and on a level with the native states of the eastern Archipelago in friendship with the Dutch Government.'[39] Netherlands India was a 'dust cloud of sovereignties', he suggested. But, writing to Locher Scholten, he admitted that '[v]assals enjoyed sovereignty beneath the glass dome of Dutch authority'.[40]

Indeed their legal position did not necessarily represent the actual position. The position of Indonesian rulers had continued to deteriorate, their sovereignty becoming ever less complete, even disappearing over time. The 'permanency' and the reliability that had been seen by the Sultan of Perak in the eighteenth century as an advantage was long-term a disadvantage: what had been a source of security became a source of dependency. Divisible sovereignty had provided 'a convenient tool for gradually eroding sovereign rights', as Borschberg puts it. By the early twentieth century the Dutch government 'had effectively acquired and exercised many, if not all, the rights of sovereignty, leaving Asian rulers with little more than an empty titular shell'.[41]

In 1911 the young Hendrik Colijn had sharply shaped the question Resink was to raise: 'either these political contracts should be considered as agreements between equal parties, looked upon as treaties in the international-legal sense, or else we have to do with *political manifestos* in which the Netherlands Indies authorities declare that once certain conditions are met they are willing to refrain from intervention in the internal affairs of a given region'. At the outset of 'our appearance in the Indies', the former was their nature. There followed a period in which VOC and princes concluded contracts on the basis of equality, 'and this is followed by an era in which the contracts are characterized by the fact that the Company is manifestly the superior power and that it also exercises authority here and there, albeit on the basis of *agreement*'. The evolution proceeded through the eighteenth and nineteenth centuries. 'First the native states came into the position of vassal states with extensive powers on the part of the vassals and little influence on the part of the liege lords, and finally … we have arrived at the period in which these political agreements, even though the form does not still everywhere correspond to the actual situation, are really nothing but *instruments of investiture*', and native 'self-governors' became 'organs of the State administration'.[42]

What is striking about the process is not that it took place but that it took place over a long period, and that what might be termed shared sovereignty took so long to erode. The reason is in part to be found in the policy of the British. The region had become interesting to them because of its position vis-à-vis the empire they had created in India – itself based on divided sovereignty, defended by Sir Henry Maine over against the positivist John Austin[43] – and the trade they built up with China. Even the provision of strategic support for those interests, however, should not damage their security in Europe, one aspect of which was the preservation of the Netherlands from any dominant continental power. The British thus determined that the Dutch should preserve an empire in the archipelago, though not on the peninsula, and that they would contend only for a share in the commerce of the Indies, rather than set themselves up as political rivals, Britain engaging, as Lord Castlereagh put it, in 'a fair and friendly competition, without the establishment of any other preponderating military or political authority … to counterbalance that, which the Dutch now and long have exercised'.[44] The compromise was represented by the treaty of 1824.

For the greater part of the century, the Dutch were thus able to take their time in extending their power in the archipelago. Occasional alarms over the impact of private adventurers, such as Brooke, led to assertions of Dutch control or at least the making of new treaties. But only when Britain's primacy declined, and other powers became more assertive, particularly after the Berlin conference of 1884–5, did it become more urgent to reduce the status and powers of the native rulers. Paper claims were no longer enough. The long war that followed the attempt to establish control on Aceh after 1873 prompted the invention of the 'short contract'. That was also used in other parts of the archipelago,[45] though a large part of the empire was still made up of 'self-administering' territories at the time of the First World War. The 'contractual' pattern of relations – what Michael Leifer called 'a colonial international system'[46] – thus lasted a long while, merging only gradually into the different pattern of the colonial state, Netherlands India.

The conquest of Upper Burma did not necessarily mean it would be annexed. Churchill and Dufferin had considered whether it might become a 'protected state'. The Viceroy argued that it would be cheaper. A protected state would also be better able to ignore the tribal depredations on Burma's ill-defined northern frontier and to ease any tension with China. Then he had second thoughts. A 'semi-protected state' would still need Indian troops, while the ruler might be 'obstructive', even 'disloyal', and drag India into wars with neighbouring powers. A 'fully-protected' state – in which a British Resident had full control of foreign affairs and some control of internal affairs – the Viceroy ruled out only reluctantly, since it might have helped to restore order more quickly: there were, he maintained, no trustworthy princes.[47] Annexation was decided upon, though a long period of 'pacification' proved necessary.

These concepts did not merely reflect British practice in India: the concept of the protected state had developed throughout the nineteenth century as one of the improvisations in the relationships between European states and the outside world prompted by the putative extension of the Westphalia system and the globalization of trade. The French, whose expansion in what they called Indo-China had proved so disastrous for Burma, had proceeded by first establishing a 'colony' in southern Vietnam which they called, after a name Europeans commonly gave to the lands the Nguyen family had ruled before the Tay-son rebellion, Cochin China. But in the early 1870s they were talking of 'protection' as a means of fending off other powers from the rest of Vietnam, and in the 1880s, as they extended their empire, they found further advantages in 'protection'.

In central Vietnam, which they called 'Annam' after the old Chinese name for Vietnam, they retained a Nguyen monarch and ruled theoretically in his name. In the north, which they called Tonkin, their rule was more direct, though nominally a protectorate. 'If we want to act as protectors, and use the King as an intermediary between his subjects and ourselves, it is evidently necessary that this intermediary have some authority', Paul Bert argued. 'And as he lacks this authority by original vice, it is incumbent upon us to give it to him by dint of attention and respect.'[48] In fact, as Bruce Lockhart points out, the protected monarch was never given the power that would in fact have made him useful. Perhaps the French, he suggests, over-emphasized the 'moral' and 'spiritual' nature of his power because of its consonance with orthodox Confucian views. They ignored the non-Confucian tradition of Vietnam, in which the ruler was a protector figure, hero, 'part rebel, part guardian of agricultural fertility, and part cultural innovator', more Southeast Asian than Sinic.[49] They also, of course, downplayed the unity of Vietnam that the Nguyen had restored. Along with the protected states of Cambodia and Laos, the three parts [pays] of Vietnam were thrust into a 'federation' of 'French Indo-China' in 1887.

Raffles had used the word 'Protector' as a word for his historicist version of a new Majapahit. Perhaps he had the traditional English usage in mind: it was a kind of substitute for a monarch, most famously in Cromwell's time. A more relevant usage grew up with the expansion of European relationships with the outer world in the nineteenth century, coupled, as it was, with the anxiety of the predominant power, Britain, to limit or evade its governmental responsibilities. Officials in London gradually formulated the 'amorphous, elastic concept of the "protectorate"'.[50] Cost was not the only factor. Britain sought to avoid alienating other European powers by claiming too much too openly.

Like the shift in the meaning and implication between 'capitulations' and 'unequal treaties', the concept of 'protection' initially developed through the relationship with an Ottoman Empire not before 1856 regarded as part of Europe. In 1825 the jurisdiction of the old Levant Company – designed to 'protect' British subjects – had been vested in British consuls.[51] The Foreign Jurisdiction Act of 1843 was framed to end doubts about the application of British law to cases involving British subjects in the Ottoman Empire, and make lawful Crown power and jurisdiction in the Levant and on the China coast 'in the same and as ample a manner' as if acquired in ceded or conquered territory.[52]

The Act came, however, to be used for other ends, for example to provide for the extension of jurisdiction from the settlements on the Gold Coast and in Sierra Leone. Officials on the ground moved less cautiously. 'Protectorate' began to imply a more direct administration, while in London protectorates might be seen as a way of staking and withdrawing a claim, more easily than if a colony or sovereign possession were at stake. There was a larger shift: it was no longer a matter of 'protecting' British subjects, but of 'protecting' other territories, states and peoples. 'Annexation', Lord Selborne argued in a rather tautological statement of 1885, 'is the direct assumption of territorial sovereignty. Protectorate is the recognition of the right of the aborigine, or other actual inhabitants, to their own country, with no further assumption of territorial rights than is necessary to maintain the permanent authority and discharge the duties, of the Protecting Power'.[53]

That distinction was not always easy to draw, and was becoming harder as European contacts expanded. How, the Germans asked, would their citizens obtain justice in British protectorates?[54] The Germans took a different line in the colonial acquisitions Bismarck made in the 1880s. The German emperor acquired 'suzerainty' and in return offered protection, and companies, set up to run the territory on the cheap – 'Direct colonies we cannot administer. We can only support companies'[55] – were given all the rights acquired from the chiefs, in effect full sovereign rights. In German protectorates all persons were thus subject to German jurisdiction.[56]

The UK considered that protectorates were places where there was neither British nor German sovereignty: no power could exercise jurisdiction over subjects of another unless within its limits. This Westphalia argument had a practical side. If every protectorate became an annexation, Britain would, as Selborne argued, acquire immense obligations.[57] But it also faced the exceptional case of India where the Viceroy had de facto jurisdiction over everyone. A bill was prepared to make it clear that the courts there could exercise jurisdiction over British subjects and others. But Lord Chancellor Halsbury ruled it out. 'Protectorate and the right it confers rests upon Convention', he wrote. 'The extent of obligation imposed on the protecting power varies according to its policy and convenience. Once the extent of those obligations entered international law, the elasticity would be at an end.' It was 'a convenient middle state between annexation and mere alliance so long as it is allowed to remain mere convention … '[58]

The consolidated Foreign Jurisdiction Act of 1890 [4.8.1890 53 and 54 Vic cap 37] retained Britain's narrow conception of the limited administrative responsibilities in a Protectorate. But increasingly practice diverged from precept. Some argued, too, that the Berlin agreement called for more effective administration, and that the 1889 Brussels conference on slavery for more responsible government.[59]

Probably influenced by William Hall's *International Law* (3rd edition, 1890) John Bramston at the Colonial Office in London alluded to the obligations those meetings put on protecting powers. He argued, too, that a protecting power was obliged to protect the subjects of other powers.[60] 'When Great Britain or any other European Power assumes the protectorate of an uncivilized African territory, it necessarily excludes other Powers from holding relations, except through itself, with the rulers of the protected territory, and so far it assumes a portion of what may be called the external sovereignty of those rulers.' The Protecting Power was responsible to other powers for the safety of their nationals, for they could not appoint Consuls. '[T]he native ruler surrenders to the protecting power so much sovereignty as is necessary for giving effect to the protection granted.' This was the nature of what Newbury calls 'the new colonial protectorates'.[61] The Government's Law Officers thought Bramston's views 'sound at the present day' and drew support from Hall's *A Treatise on the Foreign Powers and Jurisdiction of the British Crown* [Clarendon Press, 1894].[62] Ross Johnston refers to 'jurisdictional imperialism'.[63] Certainly the appearance of other powers, as well as their subjects, prompted Britain to reduce the flexibility that Halsbury had wanted to retain.

Maritime Southeast Asia illustrated several of the expedients that Britain adopted and perhaps helped to develop them. At the same time their application helped to shape its history. The fact that 'British Malaya' and 'British Borneo' approached the character of 'colonial states' – though by a route that differed from Netherlands India and French Indo-China – does not exclude some differences in status and structure that were crucial to the post-colonial states that ultimately emerged. That is particularly obvious in the case of Malaya/Malaysia.

At a time when they were still at odds with the Patriot-dominated Dutch Republic, but unwilling completely to break with it, the British had acquired Penang from the Sultan of Kedah in 1786. '[S]upposing that commerce alone first brought an English settlement to this island', W.A. Clubley, a member of the Penang Council argued in 1823 after the Thais had invaded their tributary, 'it must be remembered that the same duties which on a larger scale have fallen to the other Presidencies in India have in a more contracted sphere now devolved on us. … We ought to hold in our hands the scales of justice, to protect the weaker powers against the usurpations of the stronger, to mediate between them all on every occasion when our interference can be effectual, and even at times to exhibit a tone of superiority to check the extravagant pretensions of the different states.' There was an opportunity 'to establish for ourselves a paramount influence over the Malay states'.[64] But no such Indian-style policy was approved by the superior authorities in India.

Their attitude did not change, even though circumstances changed, with the departure of the Dutch from Melaka under the treaty of 1824 and the war with Ava. Nor did the treaty of 1824, excluding the Dutch, mean that the British would control the Peninsula, though in practice it curtailed the relations its Malay rulers might have with other European powers. The local British authorities did not, however, abandon the idea that they should exercise a positive influence over those rulers, though, given the attitude of their superiors, they had to adopt indirect means.

One was to work with the ruler of peninsular Johore, who lived in Singapore and collaborated against orang-laut piracy. But the policy ran into trouble when civil war developed in Pahang and the rulers of Johore and Trengganu intervened on opposing sides. In 1861 Governor Cavenagh sanctioned a treaty between the ruler of Johore and the challenged ruler of Pahang. It might, he suggested, be the prelude to 'other similar engagements, equally recognizing our paramount authority, and thus enabling us, without any undue grasping after power, to imperceptibly extend our influence over the surrounding chiefs and to exercise over their activities that legitimate control which our position demands'.[65] No such authority was secured. But though Cavenagh was driven to bombard Trengganu, the Trengganu-backed claimant was victorious in Pahang, and peace returned to the east coast. Cavenagh found his powers inadequate to deal with changes on the west coast, too, and there the superior authorities were at last to change their policy in the 1870s.

More weakly organized than Johore or Trengganu, the west coast states, particularly Perak, were subject to greater economic and demographic change. Invited by provincial chiefs, Chinese miners were moving into the states in response to a widening world market for tin. Their rivalries had implications for the Chinese in Penang itself, and the wealth they produced for the chiefs imbalanced the distribution of power among them and conduced to civil war. Cavenagh was provided with further arguments for stepping up British intervention on the Peninsula.

'Putting aside the question of commercial benefits to be derived from the maintenance of tranquillity and order, it may be a matter for consideration whether, from our position as the paramount power, … we have not already in a great measure incurred responsibilities which it might be difficult to throw off', he suggested in 1863. The policy the Governors had been pursuing, he was in effect arguing, should be regularized. At present, 'chiefs are emboldened to disregard the advice and admonition of the local authorities under the impression that, as they are acting on their own judgment, and not in accordance with any general line of policy prescribed for their guidance, it is quite possible that their decisions may be reversed, an impression, perhaps, not infrequently created by the tenor of communications received from European firms with which they have commercial dealings.'[66] But the Indian government was still not prepared for a change of policy, which might involve interfering in the domestic as well as external affairs of the states and be 'looked on with jealousy by the Government of Siam'.[67] It should be left for the Colonial Office to consider when it took over the Straits Settlements in 1867.

In the event the CO made no initial attempt to revise British policy. But in the course of 1873, as C.D. Cowan puts it, officials at the Colonial Office and the Secretary of State, Lord Kimberley, 'swung round to the view that some sort of action was in fact necessary in Malaya'.[68] The viceroy of Selangor asked if the British or any other power would interfere so as to provide security for property and investment. That raised the possibility of foreign intervention. Sir Robert Herbert, the Permanent Secretary, suggested that it might be well for Britain to consolidate its position on the peninsula without incurring major risks or responsibilities. Kimberley agreed. 'It would be impossible for us to consent to any European Power assuming the Protectorate of any State in the Malayan Peninsula'.[69] By the time he received a petition from the Chinese merchants in the colony late in August 1873, Kimberley had decided that 'the interests of the British Settlements require that we shall exert our influence to put an end to the state of anarchy and disorder which prevails in several of the States'.[70] The CO thus undertook its belated review of British policy amidst apprehensions about other powers.

The new Governor, Sir Andrew Clarke, was instructed to report in respect of each state 'what mode of proceeding should in his opinion be adopted with a view to restore peace and order, to secure protection to British subjects who may trade with the States, or embark in commercial undertaking in the native territories, and generally to promote the improvement and good Govt. of the native States with which we are connected.' He should consider 'whether these ends would be promoted by the appointment of a British agent … to reside at the seat of Govt. of any of the States not under Siam.'[71] Kimberley justified his instructions to Clarke in a letter to the prime minister, Gladstone. 'We are the paramount power on the Peninsula up to the limit of the States, tributary to Siam, and looking to the vicinity of India and our whole position in the East I apprehend that it would be a serious matter if any other European Power were to obtain a footing in the Peninsula.'[72]

To provide against foreign intervention did not seem to require Britain to go very far. No doubt that was another reason why it went as far as it did. Kimberley suggested the appointment of a resident agent. That was far from annexation. Such a step would have been hard to propose, let alone adopt, but it did not in any case seem necessary. The assumption was that the formal giving of advice would be sufficient, and it was sufficiency that was Britain's concern. It grew out of earlier experience with the peninsular rulers, in particular with Johore, but the information the Colonial Office received tended to support the notion. After a visit to Langat in 1871, C. J. Irving declared that the viceroy, a brother of the Sultan of Kedah, had 'European ideas about his government', was ready to establish regular systems of justice and revenue, and to employ for this purpose European officers selected by the Straits government. 'Johore, with not a tithe of the resources of Selangor, has become a thriving and opulent state, – and why? Simply because the East Indian Government selected the most intelligent of the Native Chiefs, the present Maharajah, and supported him by their advice and influence.'[73] The idea a Resident was familiar from Indian experience. Somewhat ironically, it was the Colonial Office that adopted it.

Famously Clarke reported after he had acted, rather than before, even though the telgraph had reached the Straits. The treaties he made obliged the rulers to accept a Resident and to take his advice on all matters save custom and religion. But what was informally possible in the case of Johore did not work in the case of Perak. The first Resident, J.W.W. Birch, was murdered, and an Indian punitive expedition brought in. After that, advice was likely to be accepted. Indeed it made possible the myth that the British advised while the Sultan ruled. But it was a myth that a strictly legal view supported. The treaties did not convey sovereignty. Indeed in some respects the Sultan was stronger than before, certainly vis-à-vis his ministers and his nobles.

In theory the ruler invited the British Government to send Residents. The formidable ruler of Pahang, victor in the civil war, failed to offer the invitation Governor Weld looked for in the 1880s, but he and his chiefs gave out a number of concessions. The Straits authorities apprehended trouble between the people of Pahang and the concessionaires, not always men 'of the best class'.[74] They were also concerned that the irregular terms of the concessions would retard the development of the state. The attitude of the Colonial Office was affected by the activities of Germany in Africa and New Guinea 1883–84. Bramston raised the question of extending Britain's protection to all the Malay states. 'In these days when our rights and quasi-rights are strictly questioned and boldly encroached upon',

Herbert wrote, 'there must be danger in leaving this protectorate unconsolidated.' The Office swung round to Weld's view that Britain must gain an irrefutable right to 'protect' Pahang owing to the 'possible interference in its affairs of another European Power'.[75]

In January 1887 Weld sent Hugh Clifford to Pekan to get a letter from Sultan Ahmad asking for an 'agreement or convention of amity' on the lines of the treaty Johore had made in December 1885. That would secure Britain's control over Pahang's foreign relations and the appointment of a British Agent with consular powers. Clifford found discontent among Malay chiefs and Chinese miners and among the Europeans as well. At first the ruler rejected Clifford's proposal, but on 10 April he handed him a letter asking for a treaty that would put Pahang 'on the same footing' as Johore.[76]

Sultan Abu-bakar had evaded Weld's attempt to impose a Resident on Johore and gone to London. There he had negotiated a treaty with the Colonial Office, giving Britain control of foreign relations, preventing concessions to non-British Europeans without British consent, and providing for the appointment of an agent with functions similar to those of a consular officer.[77] The treaty left Abu-bakar independent in internal affairs, and that no doubt encouraged Ahmad to follow his example and advice.

Appointed Agent, Clifford found himself, however, with very little influence over the Sultan. The new Governor, Sir C. Smith, again took up the idea of a Resident, particularly as the number of companies being floated suggested the need for a proper administrative framework. The stabbing of a Chinese shopkeeper provided an excuse to act. Governor Smith visited Pekan in June 1888, along with F.A. Swettenham, the Resident of Selangor, and W.A. Pickering, the Protector of Chinese, and demanded that the Sultan accept a Resident. The Sultan 'should … be *made* to introduce reforms into his country'. The Colonial Office accepted the idea with reluctance. 'I do not like this', Meade wrote, 'but our hands are forced and on the whole I think there is less danger in advancing than in disavowing the Governor's action.'[78] Once more, however, the Sultan of Johore was called in, and violence was avoided. The Sultan asked for a Resident.

The intervention in Pahang led to the creation of the Federated Malay States (FMS). The reason was not its success, but its relative failure. Though the old Sultan more or less retired, he sympathized with chiefs who had lost power and perquisites and resisted the new system. Disturbances began with the revolt of the Orang Kaya of Semantan in December 1891, and in 1892 the British obtained military assistance from Perak and Selangor. At the same time, Pahang, relatively inaccessible, without alluvial tin, and burdened with concessions, did not prosper: by 1891 it had a substantial debt to the Straits and dealing with the disturbances increased it.[79]

C.P. Lucas of the Colonial Office corresponded with Swettenham, who later claimed that he put forward a scheme for 'some kind of combination … of the four states … a form of federation'.[80] The idea was not entirely new. The potential advantages of administration and financial coordination were already recognized, and there had been talk of a Resident-General as early as 1880. In his last memorandum before retirement, written in 1889, Hugh Low, long-term Resident of Perak, had urged that the states should be confederated so that 'the policy in all should be uniform', and the surplus of one lent to assist the others.[81] He repeated the notion when Lucas consulted him in 1892.

Lucas prepared a scheme for Smith's comments. There were, he said, two governing principles. The Governor's authority must be unimpaired: 'the prospect of an uniform British policy in the Malay Indies, including Borneo as well as the Malay Peninsula, will most be furthered in future years, as communication by land and sea become quicker and more constant, by entrusting the Governor at the central point with powers of general supervision and control.' A Resident-General, subordinate to him, would be the chief British officer of a united or federated protectorate. The second condition was that the scheme must not be uncongenial to the Malay communities and their rulers. Annexation was out of the question, 'at all events at the present time', but a confederation might be acceptable. 'One strong reason for raising the general question of the status of these States at the present moment is that possibly, in their confederation, might be found the best solution of the Pahang difficulty.'[82]

The new Governor, Sir Charles Mitchell, supported the scheme for 'Federal Union of the Protected States', and proposed that Swettenham should be sent round to secure the agreement of the Sultans.[83] He appears to have drafted the document they were to sign. It extended the powers of advice, now stopping short only at Islam, and so removing the exception in respect of Malay custom in the treaties Clarke had made; yet at the same time it declared that nothing was intended to curtail the powers of the rulers nor alter their relations with the empire. Nor was the agreement federal in nature. Union, federation and confederation had all been terms officials had bandied about. The outcome mixed them, but least of all was the federal component. Certainly the result had no sovereignty. Nor did the British. It remained with the individual rulers. The aim of this state-building was greater 'uniformity, efficiency and economy',[84] and the route was the one likely to cause the least difficulty. Chamberlain, now at the Colonial Office, approved what had been done in December 1895, and Swettenham became the first Resident-General.

The legal position had not changed when the British sought to create a new state, the Malayan Union, in 1945. They conceived that it was necessary to get the Sultans to conclude new treaties that would enable them to apply the Foreign Jurisdiction Act and issue an Order-in-Council under it.[85] It was this process that provoked the Malay opposition that led to the creation of UMNO, the United Malays National Organisation.

The setting-up of the FMS suggested a model for Borneo. There the exercise of British power had been improvised in diverse ways, though they also testified to the restraints the Government sought to place on it. Under the treaty of 1824 arguably all Borneo was to be left to the Dutch, though it would be provocative to say so. But they had never established a connexion with Brunei – then including what was later to become the states of Sarawak and North Borneo [Sabah] – any more than they had with Aceh. Earlier of interest to the EIC when at odds with the Dutch, it was brought back into commercial connexion with the British by the establishment of Singapore, and into a political connexion by the endeavours of the adventurer James Brooke.

Given the attitude that despite the treaty of 1824 the Dutch were adopting towards British trade in the archipelago, he argued in 1838, Britain should take up the policy Raffles had advocated, and develop relations with princes of the archipelago who were still independent of them. He himself planned to set the change in motion by assuming the administration of Sarawak under the Sultan. Palmerston's Foreign Office not only considered that the Dutch were not abiding by the commercial clauses of the treaty, but also, after the opening of China, took an interest in the availability of coal in Borneo for the steamers that were coming into use. A public agitation, partly orchestrated by Brooke's agent in London, urged support for his venture, which was also associated with the accepted cause of suppressing piracy and the slave trade. Without Brooke, it seems clear, there would have been no 'British Borneo'. It is equally clear that the British government did not wish to reverse its basic policy, that politically the Dutch should prevail in the archipelago.

Yet it was just that which Brooke hoped to bring about. He was appointed Britain's Agent with the Sultan of Brunei in 1844. His intervention provoked a coup in Brunei against what he called the anti-piracy faction and a naval attack on Brunei followed. It was not, however, taken over. Instead in 1847 Britain made a treaty with the sultan, providing for extra-territorial jurisdiction, and binding him, under article 10, not to make cessions to other powers without the approval of the British government. Offshore Labuan, already offered to the British, became a colony. With such steps Britain went back on the treaty of 1824 but only in a limited way. Its emphasis was on bringing the Dutch to terms, not on establishing a rival empire. At home, too, a public campaign now developed against Brooke, provoked in part by the bloody conflict with the Iban 'pirates' at Beting Marau in 1849, but also concerned with the apparent incompatibility of the roles he had assumed, Raja of Sarawak, Governor of Labuan, and Commissioner and Consul-General to the Sultan and Independent Chiefs of Borneo. When a new British government appointed a commission of enquiry in 1853, the expansive policy of the 1840s, such as it was, was dropped.

The Labuan colony was not, however, abandoned, though it did not thrive. Nor was the treaty of 1847 undone. The raj of Sarawak was not withdrawn: public opinion would not have permitted the government to attempt to do so. Increasingly, on the other hand, Raja James now argued that Sarawak was an independent state. Accepting that, however, would set an undesirable precedent. The transformation of British subjects into sovereigns would be an unwelcome anomaly in a world of sovereign states and empires. Instead of the clear obligations of a colony, there would be the unclear responsibility of a pseudo-colony. The position of Sarawak under the treaty of 1847 would also be unclear.

Reporting in 1855, the commissioners differed. H.T. Prinsep compared Brooke's position as a British subject with 'the ordinary and frequent case of British subjects engaging in the service of a foreign Power from which they may legally be recalled by their native Sovereign, on pain of outlawry'. At Sarawak he was a vassal of the Sultan, and that the British government could not overlook in the light of the treaty of 1847, so long as Britain and Brunei remained on terms of amity.[86] The other commissioner, H. B. Devereux, could arrive at no clear conclusion. If the treaty applied, Brooke could not alienate Sarawak without British approval, and British subjects would come under the jurisdiction of the Consul at Brunei, not Sarawak's. If it did not apply, a British subject would be in the position of passing sentence on other British subjects, or of assuming inconsistent obligations to foreign powers. In the meantime foreign states acknowledging the independence of Sarawak might be guilty of aggression against Brunei.[87]

The government dropped the Commissionership but, as a gesture to Sir James, appointed his associate Spenser St John Consul-General. That was not enough. The raja insisted that St John could not operate in Sarawak without an exequatur from Sarawak. The government compromised on a basis suggested by Lord Wodehouse, the later Lord Kimberley: it would not recognize Brooke's sovereignty, but it would be ready to leave British subjects to be dealt with by his courts.[88] That new anomaly was accepted by the raja. He rejoiced in 'Our split with England'.[89]

The Chinese 'rebellion' of 1857, however, prompted him to seek more formal support. He wanted the British government to offer a protectorate. That it was unwilling to offer. He began to look to other powers, major and minor, France, the Netherlands itself, even Leopold, the future king of the Belgians. The Raja told the British government that their relations were terminated, a 'manifesto (qy. and declaration of war)' Wodehouse described as 'simply ridiculous'. At Lord Russell's instance, the Raja was told 'that the people of Sarawak are welcome to any independence they can achieve and maintain, but that a British subject cannot throw off his allegiance at pleasure. Practically things will remain as before and a ship of war will go from time to time to Sarawak.'[90] The Raja, however, chose to see this 'a great Victory … the treaty of Brunei does not now impede our negociations'.[91] It did, however. What would Britain say? Bentinck, the Dutch ambassador, asked.[92] Napoleon III gave no answer: Walewski had declared that the British would oppose the scheme by referring to the treaty of 1847.[93]

Belgium the Raja himself ruled out after meeting the future ruler of the Congo: 'he has no idea of native rights'.[94]

Brooke's friends had been largely against his foreign proposals, as had, for somewhat different reasons, his elder nephew and heir. One, the millionairess Baroness Burdett Coutts, offered financial support. Others worked on the Foreign Office. The outcome was that Governor Cavenagh was sent to Kuching to report. He suggested that Sarawak stood in the way of the Dutch, 'always inimical to British commerce in the Archipelago, and thus retains to us the whole of the trade of the north of Borneo'. He also made a strategic case. If the French retained their new settlement in Cochin-China, and there were a war, British vessels would have to go China by the Palawan passage, and Sarawak could be a harbour of refuge and a position where men-of-war could refit. If it were in foreign hands, however, 'Labuan could only be maintained by the presence of a large Force, and the safety of our trade with China might be seriously endangered'.[95]

The Governor-General suggested some recognition and protection. Making Sarawak a colony might 'give umbrage in certain quarters, and furnish a precedent which may be abused if not a ground for protest'. Extending 'such recognition and protection' as would enable Sarawak 'to maintain in tolerable safety its present status of independence' would be 'the safer and wiser arrangement, if care be taken to define properly before hand the extent which is to be given to this protection. It wd. never do to offer to the Govt. of Sarawak an absolute pledge of support.'[96] The Government had already more or less decided to appoint a consul at Sarawak and the report clinched it. Doing that implied Sarawak's independence, though the terms in which it was done sought still to avoid recognizing a subject's sovereignty. '[A]bstaining from all unnecessary interference … ', the consul was told to 'afford that moral support to the Ruling authorities which it is the desire of Her Majesty's Government to give to them'.[97]

Extending Sarawak was another matter. Was it not extending an anomaly? And if Sarawak was independent, would extension not risk breaching the treaty of 1847? Indeed in 1868 the Government opposed the attempt of Raja Charles, his uncle's successor, to extend up to the Baram. But the advance that Sarawak had already made contributed to the weakness of Brunei, and other adventurers sought concessions north of the capital from Brunei and also from Sulu. With the backing of a British merchant, Edward Dent, the Austrian Baron Overbeck told the acting Consul-General W.H. Treacher that the object was 'to form a British Company somewhat, tho on a smaller scale, after the manner of the late East India Company, the main desire being to develop the agricultural resources of the northern portion of Borneo'.[98] 'We should be saddled with a responsibility without any control', Meade commented. It might be better to establish a colony at once.[99]

The Foreign Office, with which the main decision rested, took a different line, advocated in particular by Julian Pauncefote. The concept of a charter could be reutilized so as to limit the British Government's responsibility, and yet impose some control on the operation of the Company. At the same time annexation would be avoided. Likely to be opposed in Britain, let alone Sarawak, it might also alienate other powers, such as the Germans who had displayed interest in the Sulu archipelago, and the Spaniards who claimed control of the Sulu sultanate. Salisbury was supportive: 'if this opportunity is allowed to pass by', he told his colleagues, 'it seems very probable that some other nation would interpose claims which would prevent it from being renewed.'[100] But his government fell before a decision was made.

Pauncefote renewed the proposal under the new Gladstone government. It was, the Colonial and Foreign Offices agreed, not desirable to establish a protectorate, but it was important that no foreign power should establish itself. The only option was to charter a British Company. So long as annexation were not involved, there need be no difficulty with any foreign power, unless its treaty rights were infringed. That could be covered by binding it to obey the Secretary of State's instructions as regards relations with foreign states. Was there any valid objection in international law, the Law Officers were asked, to an association 'as the governing power over those territories under the grants from the Sultans'? And was there any objection to a charter? The Law Officers saw none. But they suggested modifying the clause binding it to follow the Secretary of State's instructions, for that would mean Britain could 'hardly avoid responsibility to foreign Powers for acts of the agents of the Association'. Instead the charter should provide, more negatively, for its ability to object to any of the Company's dealings with foreign states.[101] The CO raised the question of sovereignty: had British subjects, or the Queen, become sovereign? The answer was that the Sultans of Brunei and Sulu remained suzerain.[102] The Charter was granted in August 1881.

Dent opposed the idea of capitalizing the lease payments the Company made to the Sultan of Sulu, 'as we should by that means be buying the Sultan out entirely and constituting ourselves the sovereigns of the country; in which case it seems very doubtful whether the British Government would recognize us and give us the support which it now does as an English Company holding the land under a lease from the Sultan of Sulu'.[103] The lease payments indeed continued and the 'State of North Borneo' did not formally become British North Borneo, though ruled by the British North Borneo Company. But though the re-invention of the chartered company was a useful precedent in Africa,[104] the status of North Borneo was changed.

If the Bruneians had hoped to play off Raj and Company, their policy proved a failure. Indeed it seemed that the two might divide the remnant of the Sultanate between them. That, Herbert argued, would be desirable: 'the insertion of any foreign power at Brunei would cause serious complications'.[105] 'Remember the new Principals [sic] Bismarck has introduced into Colonial Politics', Salisbury wrote. 'He might likely as not seize the Balance.'[106] The immediate obstacle was the new Sultan, Hashim: under the so-called amanat of S. Abdul Mumin. the Bruneis had decided to lease or cede no more territory.

In the circumstances the British Government decided to extend a protectorate over all three territories. '[B]y virtue of Treaties, Charters, Declarations', they were 'virtually under British control, but not sufficiently to exclude the pretensions of other Foreign Powers seeking some footing in these important regions.'[107] The Governor of the Straits Settlements should be appointed High Commissioner, his 'high position' adding 'great weight to his authority in the settlement of any difficulties which might arise in the Protectorate.' Sarawak, Brunei, and North Borneo would become independent protected states.[108] Britain retained the power to appoint consuls, so as 'to establish more clearly that the states remain independent of us as regards their internal Government', as Pauncefote put it.[109] The agreements were signed in 1888.

Officials in the Colonial Office in the 1890s believed that Britain should go further. Lucas thought that a Resident should be installed in Brunei, which, with the colony of Labuan, would become the nucleus of a kind of BMS, paralleling the new FMS. 'I look in future to an administration of North Borneo & Sarawak on much the same principles as the native states of the Malay peninsula, with a resident general at Labuan and residents on the mainland, the whole under the High Commissioner at Singapore: but that is some way on.'[110] Following the persuasive report of Stewart McArthur, a Resident was established in Brunei in 1906, the aged Hashim signing a FMS-style treaty, in which he undertook to receive a British Resident whose advice was taken and acted upon in all questions except those affecting the Mohammedan religion. Sooner or later, Lucas thought, all 'British Borneo' must come directly under the British Crown.[111] But it never did.

Colonies, protected states, protectorates, contracts, treaties, declarations long and short, suzerainty, chartered company, consuls, residents, resident-generals, and high commissioners were all among the improvisations that marked the extension of European power over Southeast Asia in the nineteenth century. Though their more precise legal status might turn out to be politically important when the world of empires was displaced, loosely speaking they might all be placed in the category of 'colonial states', and it may be possible to characterize them by common features that they possessed and others that they lacked.

Most obviously, they were political entities that were given frontiers in the style to which Europe had become accustomed, but those were settled out of European convenience, and frontiers like that between the British and the Dutch empires had no support in history or geography or ethnicity. Their maintenance and defence continued to be the responsibility of the colonial powers. Their diplomatic relations were conducted in Europe where Westphalia practices held sway. Nor were they in general expected to defend themselves. The stability of the whole region depended upon the predominance of the British – particularly of their naval power and their Indian soldiery – under whose hegemony the entities had grown up. The military forces at the disposal of each regime were largely constabularies, often recruited from alien or provincially differentiated sources.

Though often acquired for political or strategic reasons, the 'colonial states' were subjected to what was seen as 'development'. Capitalism was less often behind their acquisition than it turned out to be necessary to procure a tax base for the new forms of government that were introduced, and investment, often at least at first reluctant, was encouraged by the creation of infrastructure, by changes in land ownership, even by the advancing of government credit.

The states, like European states, claimed the allegiance of all those within their frontiers – and those beyond if they were 'protected persons' – despite the arbitrary way in which those frontiers had been established. But to back it up they could utilize neither the old methods nor the new. Their governors could not employ religious sanctions or ancient imagery nor adopt familial or patron-client relationships. Nor on the other hand were the peoples they ruled to be seen as citizens of an independent state. Governments thus relied to a large extent on collaborating elites, sometimes recruited during initial 'pacifications'. That was the more readily done because their purposes after all were limited and the range of government activity small.

Despite the risk of Whiggishness, it is hard not to conclude that the colonial state was not simply a facsimile, but also that, as some British commentators believed, a transitional form. It was, in Partha Chatterjee's terms, '*not just* the agency that brought the modular forms of the modern state to the colonies; it was *also* an agency that was destined never to fulfil the normalizing mission of the modern state because the premise of its power was a rule of colonial difference, namely, the preservation of the alienness of the ruling group.'[112] There were other obstacles, too. Though its range was limited, both the colonial and the capitalism it fostered brought social as well as economic change. Improved communication brought in different concepts of the state that involved the idea of the nation. Education had 'capricious outcomes'. And nationalists could reasonably argue that the colonial state could not realize even the prospects of development that it held out. Could a colonial state even risk dropping its connexions with the old elite and coming to terms with the new? Would the new elite challenge its control of the future?

Example was to play a role, but it was not provided by the one state in Southeast Asia itself that had indeed avoided formally becoming a 'colonial state', Siam/Thailand. It had sustained its independence by coming to terms with Britain and then with other powers on the basis of the extra-territorial system that had been forced on China but that, with the Bowring treaty of 1855, it readily accepted. Rama IV [Mongkut] readily achieved what Mindon failed to achieve, direct relationship with the British government. He wrote to Queen Victoria herself. The British Government appointed a diplomatic representative in Bangkok, whose presence indeed helped to constrain the ambitions of the Governors in the Straits. The Thai protest against the bombardment of Trengganu was strikingly effective.

Mongkut's successor, Rama V [Chulalongkorn], maintained the independence of his kingdom not only by expedient territorial concessions – some of them of territory in Laos and Cambodia only recently secured, and indeed partly secured with the possibility of concessions in mind – but also by 'modernizing'. His vision, David Wyatt argued, was to turn his kingdom into 'a miniature European colony' without the Europeans.[113] British and Dutch methods were adopted, Kasian says, to make Siam an 'authoritarian and centralized modernizing auto-colonial state'. '[T]he absence of western colonial rulers', he adds, ' … sterilized Siam of a nationalist mass movement and its possible radicalisation.'[114]

Siam also changed its relationship with China. Mongkut despatched a mission on his accession in 1851, but it was turned back owing to the death of the Tao-kuang emperor. Another mission, sent with a trading purpose, was sent the following year, and better received, though it was attacked on its way back by Taiping rebels. John Bowring, the Governor of Hong Kong, suggested that Siam should use that as a pretext for discontinuing the tributary pattern, 'since Siam was supposedly an equal sovereign state'. Mongkut sent no more missions. On Chulalongkorn's accession, Siam indicated that it wished to send an embassy, provided that it would be treated 'somewhat in the same manner as those which have been sent by Western nations'. The Manchu court rejected the idea. When it demanded tribute in the late 1870s, Siam was evasive. In 1882 it renounced all its tributary obligations and declared that it recognized only the Western system of international relations.[115]

Its own tributary pattern was brought to an end partly by foreign pressure. The vassalage of the northern Malay states had been weakened in the nineteenth century by the interposition of the British.[116] In the new century Chulalongkorn replaced the tribute pattern by a new Siamese adviser system in Kelantan, Kedah and Perlis.[117] That was soon followed by a deal with the British in 1909, under which Siam transferred its rights to Britain. The validity of the move was contestable. The rulers, moreover, were anxious to preserve an autonomy that they believed their peers in the FMS had lost. 'British Malaya' thus comprised the Straits Settlements, the Federated Malay States and the Unfederated Malay States. Yet entrenched interest made it difficult to set up a more unified structure.

Perhaps the Philippines offered a more relevant example for aspiring Southeast Asian elites than Siam. Britain had occupied Manila back in the Seven Years War, but in the interests of a larger strategy had relinquished it in 1764. In the nineteenth century it adopted towards the Spanish regime the kind of policy it adopted towards the Dutch regime, though without the equivalent of the treaty of 1824. Strategically the Philippines were best left in the hands of a minor power, such as Spain had now become. That would be commercially advantageous, too, if it abandoned its mercantilist policy. That indeed it did sufficiently to allow British capital a major role in the development of the Visayas. The only real difference arose over Sulu and the Muslim regions, which Spain had not effectively incorporated in its empire. Britain dropped any attempt to uphold the independence of Sulu when it concluded the Spain-Germany-Britain convention of 1885, under which Spain dropped its support of Sulu claims in North Borneo.

The Spanish government based itself on the 'friars' whom Palgrave admired and on a collaborating elite. It notably failed to come to terms with the new elite created by economic development, educational access, and foreign contacts, despite the lessons of Latin America and the advice the Catalan liitérateur and traveller Sinibaldo de Mas offered in 1842: not to preserve the colony but 'to decide on its emancipation and prepare it for freedom', leaving behind a constitutional form of government, perhaps under an Infante.[118] The elite sought collaboration, then resorted to confrontation, and finally took to revolution in 1896. Spain was also facing a revolt in Cuba, and its struggle with the Filipinos reached a deadlock in 1897, marked by the pact of Biaknabato. The outcome was to be decided by foreign intervention, but it did not favour the revolutionaries, as at first they had hoped.

Engaged in a war with Spain over Cuba, the US intervened in the Philippines. The revolutionaries renewed their insurgency and, after Dewey's destruction of the Spanish fleet in Manila, proclaimed independence in June 1898. But what the Americans had begun as a war strategy became an imperial strategy. An American military expedition had taken Guam late in May, and, after a token resistance, the Spanish forces in Manila surrendered in August. What policy should the US adopt towards the Philippines? Retain them, retain part of them, retain a naval base in them? They could hardly be returned to Spain. Were the Filipinos ready for self-government? Such were the questions President McKinley's cabinet debated. After a pre-election tour, he came down in favour of annexation. In the final treaty with Spain, signed in Paris in November 1898, the transfer of the whole of the Philippines was sweetened by the payment of US$20 million.

Selling a colonial territory was not a new concept, and it had a kind of finality about it: the US had bought Louisiana from Napoleon I and Alaska from Alexander II. But no nationalist movement had then been in question. Now there was, but it was left out of the transactions. The Filipino leader, Emilio Aguinaldo, was not invited to participate in the capitulation of

Manila. There was no Filipino representative at Paris. Six weeks after the Paris treaty, the Malolos convention proclaimed a constitution for the new Republic. A Nebraska volunteer fired on an 'insurgent' patrol in a disputed area outside Manila. That initiated a bitter conflict in the islands.

There was also a bitter debate in the US. Expansion across the continent was one thing; expansion across the Pacific was another. Was the acquisition of overseas territory not at odds with the founding principles of the American Revolution? The Anti-Imperialist League led a campaign against the ratification of the treaty. Ruling an overseas people without their consent was condemned as unconstitutional and undemocratic. An 'empire' would lead to foreign entanglements, to economic ruin, to the build-up of military forces. The expansionists won the day, talking both of duty and access to the China market. But the paradox remained. No Colonial Office was set up: the Philippines remained under the War Department even after pacification was at last achieved. The Americans adopted, more explicitly than other colonial powers, even the British, the argument that the Filipinos should have independence when they were ready for it. But both the criteria for readiness, and the timetable, became the focus of the argument, more or less resolved in the 1930s by the invention of the 'Commonwealth', a word used for Massachusetts and Puerto Rico, but in the Philippines meaning a state with no foreign policy powers, but due for independence in ten years' time.

The American decisions affected others besides the Filipinos. The decision to become a colonial power in a sense recruited the US to the maintenance of the Britain-dominated status quo in colonial Southeast Asia. The acquisitions of Germany after the war – it had already bought the Marshall islands – were limited to the Caroline and Mariana islands, excepting Guam, a deal involving paying Spain US$4.2 million. British fears that Germany would renew its interest in the Sulu region were ruled out when the still semi-independent Sultan reluctantly made a treaty with John C. Bates in August 1899, which in the event preceded a long campaign to 'pacify' the Moros. What other colonial powers came to fear – and to some extent the peoples they ruled to hope – was that the advance of the Filipinos towards independence would set an example and a precedent. The departure of the Americans might also make the colonial system that their acquisition of the Philippines had strengthened more insecure. Could an independent Republic survive? Would its weakness threaten the stability of the region?

Those were questions that were to be seen in the context of the 'rise' of Japan. 'We have in Holland great dread that your country may bestow autonomy on the Philippines', Dutch Foreign Minister Van Karnebeek was to tell US envoy Richard M. Tobin in 1925. 'I think it would be a dreadful misfortune if the United States were to disappear as an Asiatic power.' The Flipinos were incapable of self-government. 'If left to themselves they would fall into hopeless disorder and would undoubtedly become a prey to Japan.

It would be for us the beginning of the end, as undoubtedly we should be the next victim of the Japanese policy of imperialistic conquest.'[119]

Japan indeed stood at the borders of the region after its acquisition of Taiwan in 1895. In China the reformed regime had enjoyed some success, despite its reverses in mainland Southeast Asia. What were seen as the inner satellites had been retained, control over Korea, Tibet and Sinkiang intensified; and China had been successful in dealing with Russia in the Ili crisis. Some Chinese leaders indeed saw Russia as the main threat, rather than the maritime powers. But it was Japan, itself apprehensive of Russia, that delivered the main blow in the 1890s, going to war over Korea, defeating China decisively, and in the treaty of Shimonoseki securing the independence of Korea and acquiring Taiwan. In face of the Western advance in East Asia, it had westernized more effectively than its neighbour. How far would its ambitions extend? What form would they take? And what would their success prompt the Chinese to do? Those questions were, of course, to affect Southeast Asia. They were put in a new international context that helped to frame the questions. The result was the overthrow of the whole colonial framework in Southeast Asia, but it was first delayed and then violent.

Few historians include the Andamans and Nicobars in Southeast Asia, though geography suggests they should. The Andamans had attracted the attention of the British authorities in the 1790s – when Port Blair had been occupied as a naval base – and again in the 1850s when it became the site of a post-Mutiny convict settlement. Governed with the Nicobars under the Scheduled Districts Act of 1874, they were brought together as a Chief Commissioner's Province under the Indian Government Acts of 1919 and 1924.[120] It was in these remote islands that the Japanese handed over to Azad Hind Fauz as the 'Swaraj islands'. Its flag was unfurled at the Cellular Jail on 31 December 1943.[121]

5 The Co-Prosperity Sphere

Some saw World War I as an imperialist war; others have seen it as a war that occurred because the opportunities for settling disputes among European powers by imperial deals had been exhausted. Its origins are much better explained in terms of what A.J.P. Taylor called, in Nietzchean phrase, the struggle for mastery in Europe; better still perhaps by the failure to accommodate a shift in the distribution of power prompted by the industrial revolution. The 'rise' of Germany alarmed other powers, while it felt threatened by the precautions they not unreasonably took. To some extent, the war was begun because it was thought it would be short. In fact its length testified not only to the increased possibilities of defence as against the advantages of attack. It testified, too, to the enormous growth in the capacity of the state to organize its resources and mobilize its people, and to the national spirit that now identified itself with the state.

A war within Europe was bound to have its effects on the relationships between Europe and the colonial world. But the effects were rather long-term and indirect than direct and immediate. Certainly troops from the colonial world, Southeast Asia included, were drawn into the conflict, even into battle. But more significant – even for them – was the involvement of the US and the revolution in Russia, where the Romanov dynasty was overthrown and a Bolshevik regime set up.

The involvement of the US helped to bring about the defeat of Germany. But it also introduced new principles into international relations. President Woodrow Wilson distrusted the old diplomacy, its secret treaties, its concept of the balance of power, and, like others, tended to blame the war on them. He endorsed a different approach, represented by the creation of a League of Nations, though he failed to get endorsement from the Senate of his own country. The 14 points he had announced in his speech of 8 January 1918 also endorsed self-determination. The Westphalia state system was modified by the creation of the League and a number of associated international organizations. 'In combination with the League, self-determination was to take precedence over the integrity of the sovereign state, the foundation of international relations since the Treaty of Westphalia', Niall Ferguson writes.[1] It might be better argued that they came uneasily together: for the most part self-determining nations aspired to be sovereign states, and sovereign states aspired to be, or considered themselves to be, nation states. The Westphalia state became in a sense a Westphalia-Versailles state. State and nation were indeed identified in naming what was a league of states a League of Nations.

Such ideas were advanced the more strongly because they were intended to compete with an alternative world-view put forward by the Bolsheviks. The 14 Points were to a considerable degree a response to 'the voice of the Russian people ... a voice calling for these definitions of principle and purpose which is ... more thrilling and compelling than any of the moving voices with which the troubled air of the world is filled.'[2] Lenin had maintained that the first task of 'victorious socialism' was to bring democracy to its completion, and so it would have to realize 'the right of oppressed nations to self-government'.[3] The revolution took the Utopian stance that Marx ultimately endorsed: the state would wither away. But in practice Lenin and his colleagues compromised with nationalism: they had no choice. At home they invented what Terry Martin has not altogether aptly described as 'an affirmative action empire': 'a strategy aimed at disarming nationalism by granting what were called the "forms of nationhood"'.[4] They endorsed and promoted a cultural nationalism that they hoped would stop short of political expression. At the same time, however, they still looked for world revolution by encouraging communist movements in colonial and under-developed countries, though their treatment of them was complicated by their concerns for the security of their own new state.

'The announcement of the American President's 14 Articles caught the imagination of the whole world', Liang Ch'i-ch'ao declared. 'All the nations which had injustice done to them wanted to make an appeal to the president.'[5] The empires in the East were not, however, dislodged. The British Empire underwent some changes that affected the self-governing Dominions, whose contribution to the imperial war effort seemed, somewhat paradoxically, to justify their independent status. Britain and the Dominions, the Imperial Conference of 1926 was to declare, were 'autonomous Communities within the British Empire, equal in status, in no way subordinate one to another in any aspect of their internal or external affairs, though united by a common allegiance to the Crown, and freely associated as members of the British Commonwealth of Nations.'[6] India – its troops and its war effort also important to victory – won a reaffirmation that it was on its way to responsible self-government within the empire.[7] But Koreans and Vietnamese went unheard at Versailles.

The only change in the formal relationship between Europe and the colonial world was in the application of the new concept of the 'mandate', a way of breaking up the Ottoman Empire and of disposing of the former German colonies by emphasizing the trusteeship element that had been developing within the concept of the protectorate, and attempting to avoid what might otherwise appear as an unfashionable imperialist deal.

It applied on the periphery of Southeast Asia: the Micronesian islands went to Japan, New Guinea to Australia, which already had Papua as a colony. The colonies and protectorates of the victorious colonial powers did not change their status, though the requirements of some of the League agencies and international agreements on questions like the suppression of the opium traffic were to enhance the responsibility of 'protecting powers' and make the concept of the non-colonial protectorate, keeping internal and external apart, increasingly difficult to sustain.

When the US joined in the war in 1917, so, too, did China and Siam, both hoping to improve their international status. Siam was anxious to speed the end of extraterritoriality.[8] China, too, wanted to end the 'unequal treaties'. It entered the Family of Nations, as Zhang Yongjin puts it, by 'a revolt against the regime Europe introduced to regulate its relations with the outside world'.[9] The Chinese revolutionaries had seen the treaties, along with the 'loss' of Vietnam, Korea and Taiwan, as a humiliation brought on them by the Manchu dynasty. It was overthrown in 1911, but power fell into the hands of warlords, rather than an effective national government such as Sun Yat Sen and the Guomindang (KMT) envisaged. Though the revolution had aimed to strengthen China, it failed to do so. The peace treaty turned out to be only a further humiliation, for under it the German concessions in Shandong were made over to Japan rather than returned to China.

Throughout its history, Japan had always been concerned with China, with its changes of fortune and changes of policy towards its neighbours. The Japanese attitudes varied from an unspoken humility to an outspoken aggression. The combative policies of Hideyoshi in the late sixteenth century and the sakoku or closed country policies the Tokugawa shoguns followed in the seventeenth and eighteenth centuries were both policies towards China as well as towards its neighbours and dependencies. One was an aggressive policy that provoked China's military intervention in Korea. The other was a more realistic policy that accepted China's dominant position in East Asia without undergoing the formulae of tribute.

The nineteenth century marked a difference. Britain's success in the first Anglo-China war of 1840–42 prompted Japan to abandon the policy of sakoku. In 1854 the 'black ships' of the US Commodore Perry led the shogunate to make the first of Japan's unequal treaties. It was followed by further treaties, including one with Great Britain in 1858. The treaties not only revolutionized the conduct of Japan's foreign policy: they also contributed to the overthrow of the Tokugawa in 1868 and to the creation, in the name of the Meiji emperor, of a new regime, dominated by an oligarchy drawn from the western clans, Satsuma and Choshu, but dedicated to modernization. The object was to undo the treaties so that Japan should take its place as an equal with other nations. That was the aim, as the Meiji emperor told President Grant: 'We expect and intend to reform … so as to stand upon a similar footing with the most enlightened nations and to attain the full development of public right and interest. … It is our purpose to select from the various institutions prevailing among enlightened nations such as are best suited to our present condition and adopt them, in gradual reforms and improvements of our policy and customs, so as to be upon an equality with them.'[10]

What role should China have in this new policy? Was Japan to support it against the West? Or would it be better to anticipate the West and take advantage of its weakness? After the first Anglo-China war, the Satsuma daimyo argued that even a defensive policy required Japan to have bases in China, in Fujien and Taiwan, for example.[11] The other possibility was to ally with China against the West. That was the basis of the 'pan-Asian' (ajia shugi) approach. Japan's answer was ambivalent, but initially leant to the former. '[W]e have no leisure', Fukuzawa Yukichi wrote, to await the 'awakening' of China and Korea, 'and together revive Asia.' [We] must abandon Asia (datsu-A ron) and treat it 'just as Westerners do'.[12]

Even in the early 1870s the new regime incorporated the Liuchiu islands as Okinawa. Twenty years later, better prepared and facing a critical Diet, the government went to war with China over Korea. As a result of Japan's success, China recognized the independence of Korea by the treaty of Shimonoseki and also ceded the Liaotung peninsula in southern Manchuria. To the latter, however, France, Russia and Germany objected, and in face of this Triple Intervention, Japan backed down. But less than a decade later Japan defeated Russia, acquired southern Manchuria, and established its dominance in Korea, which it annexed in 1910.

Under the treaty of Shimonoseki Japan also acquired Formosa and the Pescadores. Two short-lived and often forgotten republics were proclaimed in opposition to the transfer, and guerrilla opposition continued after the Japanese flag was hoisted. Though Japan made a joint declaration with Spain on their respective spheres of interest,[13] moving further south was not entirely ruled out. The question arose because of the revolt against Spanish rule in the Philippines that began in 1896. The Filipino nationalists were aware of Japan's victory over China. Jose A. Ramos and Doroteo Cortes went to Japan to solicit its help before the uprising, and contacted the nationalist Oi Kentaro. The revolutionary Katipunan apparently delivered an appeal to the captain of a Japanese training vessel, the *Kongo,* in May 1896, looking for the aid of Japan, as France had once aided the American revolutionaries.[14] While, however, some super-patriots (shishi) wanted to go further, and while, indeed, some Europeans expected Japanese intervention, the ruling oligarchs, bearing the Triple Intervention in mind, were cautious. Japan, Floro C. Quibuyen suggests, 'did not want any power to interfere with her ambitions over Korea'.[15]

The intervention of the Americans only redoubled that caution. When the shishi, Sakamoto Shiro, suggested occupying Manila while Admiral Dewey was blockading it, the General Staff in Tokyo replied: 'The control of the South Sea is an idea [to be achieved] in Japan's national policy, but today is an inopportune time. You must positively not meddle in the war.'[16] For a while, however, it seemed uncertain that the US, when it defeated Spain, would retain the islands. Okuma Shigenobu, then Foreign Minister, told the Japanese representative in Washington that the extension of US sovereignty, or a protectorate, would be acceptable. If, however, the Americans did not wish to undertake either, Japan would be willing to join the US, singly or with another power, 'to form, subject to proper conditions, suitable government for the territory in question under the … protection of the guaranteeing powers'.[17] In the event, the US assumed sovereignty under the treaty of Paris of 1898.

The First World War – 'the grace of Heaven' for Japan[18] – helped Japan to become a creditor nation. While the Europeans were at war, there were other opportunities. Should Japan now take up the pan-Asian cause or continue to take advantage of China's weakness? The latter course remained the more tempting. On the outbreak of the world war, Japan absorbed the German concession in Shandong, and later in the year it acquired the islands in the Pacific that the Germans had picked up on the dissolution of the Spanish empire. In 1915 it turned back to China, and presented the 21 Demands. 'When there is a fire in the jeweller's shop', the Japanese minister in China explained, 'the neighbours cannot be expected to refrain from helping themselves.'[19] The demands – which required China's assent to any subsequent arrangement over Shandong, involved strengthening Japan's position in Manchuria, made Fujien a Japanese sphere of influence, and prohibited the cession of any port or island to another power – were later described by Chiang Kai-shek, the KMT leader, as 'the grand culmination of all the unequal treaties'.[20] Some Japanese argued that China was 'not a nation'.[21] But *realpolitik* had its critics, who evoked the concepts of 'co-prosperity and co-existence'.

China's failure to regain Shandong showed the weakness in Wilson's idealism, as had Japan's own failure to secure a declaration in favour of racial equality in the peace negotiations at Versailles. Yet there was a change – Heaven was not entirely gracious – and the Japanese recognized it. 'Today it is a worldwide trend to honor pacifism and reject oppression. Everywhere in the world the so-called Americanism is advanced', declared Makino Shinken, the plenipotentiary at the peace conference, 'and conditions have definitely altered since the days of the old diplomacy.'[22] 'China friendship' was Shidehara Kijuro's watchword. His vision of Japan was a democratic nation, with a developed commerce and industry, seeking and relying upon overseas markets, but not through territorial expansion, which would destroy international cooperation and provoke trade boycotts.

In face of a Chinese nationalism impatient to undo the unequal treaties – whether it was represented in an alliance with communism, as with the KMT cooperation before 1927, or whether it was at odds with it, as from 1927–28 – that policy was difficult to sustain. Nor was domestic support for Shidehara's approach unequivocal. The approach of the Northern

March of the Chinese nationalists to Manchuria produced a sense of crisis. It had yet to realize Japan's hopes of settling its population surplus or supplying its industries with raw materials. Yet Japan's position there rested on treaty rights, acquired by the expenditure of blood and treasure. 'Manchuria and Mongolia are Japan's lifeline', an official of the Japanese-owned South Manchuria Railway claimed in 1931. ' … Every nation has a lifeline that holds the key to its existence.'[23]

The economic depression after 1929 added decisively to the crisis. With some backing from the military at home, the local Kwantung army seized control in September 1931, fanning out from the railway zone. The cabinet at home was unable to check the army. Inukai Ki wanted to negotiate a settlement with the Chinese government that would preserve at least a fiction of Chinese sovereignty in Manchuria, while protecting Japan's interests. But he failed. In March 1932 his cabinet authorized the creation of a separate Manchurian government. His successor, Admiral Saito Makoto, recognized the new state of Manchukuo in August, the foreign minister, Uchida Yasuya, telling the Diet that it was his 'fervent hope that the day is not far distant when Japan, Manchukuo, and China, as three independent Powers closely linked by a bond of cultural and racial affinities, will come to cooperate hand in hand for the maintenance and advancement of the peace and prosperity of the Far East'.[24] These moves were a break with China, with the Western powers, with the League, with the Shidehara policy, and indeed with Japan's own colonial policy.

Taiwan was administered as a colony – the solidity and style of the buildings still to be seen in Taipei make it clear the Japanese meant to stay – its administration paralleling that of the homeland, with adaptations to meet local conditions. The bureaucracy, as in European colonies, 'relied greatly on native leadership and local initiatives for control and mobilization'. 'As Japan's first colony, Taiwan was also a laboratory of Japanese empire-building, so to speak,'[25] and its experience was transferred to Korea after 1910. After the war Taiwan received its first civilian government. The Korean independence movement of 1919 was met with a change of style rather than of substance: Governor-General Saito Makoto's administration 'strove to remove the more obnoxious trappings of colonialism while at the same time further entrenching Japanese rule'.[26] But Manchuria was to be treated in quite a different way. In a sense the Japanese – like the Bolsheviks – were taking account of and reinterpreting the ideology that was part of the novelty Makino had found in the conduct of international affairs during and after Versailles: that was the concept of self-determination. It formed part of the thinking of Ishiwara Kanji.

Japanese military thinkers had drawn from the First World War the lesson of a 'total defence state'. There would be a war, Ishiwara believed, between the US and Japan, out of which a new world order would emerge. In the meantime China and East Asia must be a supply base.[27] Japan should start by seizing Manchuria and Mongolia, setting an example there that would be heeded by the Chinese. But to legitimize that, Ishiwara argued that Manchuria and Mongolia were 'not inherently Chinese domain'. They 'do not belong to the territory of the han people, but rather are closely linked to our country. Those who speak of ethnic self-determination must recognize that … the Manchurian and Mongolian peoples are closer to the Yamato people than they are to the Han Chinese'.[28]

The argument did not convince even the army leaders. Instead the plan had to 'retreat' on the idea of an independent country under Japanese guidance, with the ideal objectives of 'ethnic harmony' and 'paradise of the kingly way'. Ishiwara accepted the change when 'influential Manchurians' proved ready to collaborate.[29] On 1 March 1932 the government of Manchukuo issued a state-founding proclamation. Changchun became the capital [as Xinjing] and as its foreign minister, Xie Jieshi, sought recognition from 17 countries.

Without legitimacy, it would be hard to refute criticism that Manchuria was a 'puppet' or 'bogus' state. In other words, it was now thought not only that it was not a matter of annexation, but that the state-founding act would need a form of legitimacy. That was sought in a mixture of 'traditional' Japanese jargon and modern popular self-determination. The PR desk at the General Affairs Department of the State Council of Manchuria suggested that the new venture would relieve the people of the warlordism and the despotism of the Guomindang. 'Our Manzhouguo is a newly arisen state rooted in the collective will of its thirty million people and born to implement a government of the Kingly way based on the great principle of following the way of heaven and bringing peace to the people, to embody ethnic harmony, and to advance in perpetuity the welfare of humanity. … The emergence of Manzhouguo is a phenomenon which introduces a new model of morality, the freshest of political forms in the world, and the world's political scientists will have to develop a new political theory for Manzhouguo.'[30]

At Gen. Tategawa's suggestion, the former Manchu Emperor Puyi became head of state ['chief executive']. He was a distinguished figure among the Manchus, and choosing him might avert international opposition. He was not at first made Emperor: that would have countered the argument that the new state was based on popular self-government. In fact the government was an autocracy controlled by the Guandong army under secret agreements with Pu Yi.[31] As Lord Lytton pointed out in his report to the League of Nations: 'although the titular heads of the Departments are Chinese residents in Manchuria, the main political and administrative power rests in the hands of Japanese officials and advisers'.[32]

The Diet in Tokyo recognized the independence of the state in September 1932: 'The Japanese nation recognizes the facts that Manzhouguo was created freely on the basis of the will of its inhabitants and that it is an independent state.'[33] This was done before the Lytton report was made public. That said that 'the present regime cannot be considered to have been called into existence by a genuine and spontaneous independence movement'.[34] The League adopted the report, Siam abstaining. The Japanese representative, Matsuoka Yosuke, walked out, and Japan withdrew from the League on 27 March 1933. Some Central and South American countries recognized Manchuria 'at a rather early stage'. It was a means of opposing the US, whose policy in Panama was seen as no different.[35]

Royama Masamichi argued that northeast China was colonial in nature, and that its people had low political consciousness. Political organization therefore had to take the form of 'some sort of oligarchic autocracy in which one ethnic group leads the other ethnic groups'. Over subsequent years the terms used to describe the Japan-Manchuria relationship became more hierarchical. The protocol of 1932 spoke of good neighbourly relations; the imperial rescript on the 10th anniversary referred to 'our senior [parental] country'. The Minister in Tokyo was to describe Manchukuo as 'the first child of the Greater East Asia Co-Prosperity Sphere'.[36]

That suggested another kind of hierarchy, a privileged position among the states of the sphere. Certainly, if Taiwan had been the model for Japan's earlier colonial venture, Manchuria was the model for its extension into Southeast Asia. In 1936 Taiwan became a 'stepping stone' for Japan's southward advance. Governor-General Kobayashi Seizo adopted the slogan: Marching South, Industrialization, Making Imperial Subjects.[37] The aim there was, however, to integrate Taiwan, and that was the purpose of 'mobilization'. The Manchuria approach was rather different, although the one-party mobilization there attempted – through the Concordia association Ishiwara had advocated – was to be adopted in the homeland as the Imperial Rule Assistance Association, as well as in the southern parts of the Sphere.

The model was unlikely to work. It had the intrinsic drawback of 'puppet' regimes. That had been encountered by protecting powers in the old colonial system. It was similar to a problem colonial regimes had found with their 'collaborators': they had to have enough influence to be useful; but they must not appear to be so closely controlled as to lose that influence. It was more of a problem with regimes dedicated to 'mobilizing' – by contrast to the limited aims of colonial regimes – amidst a popular rhetoric of independence or liberation.

Nor was it easy indeed to frame the rhetoric, and it could only become more difficult as the empire expanded. An obvious problem was with China itself. Already humiliated, it now lost Manchuria, too. How was it possible to evoke the old pan-Asian notions of co-prosperity and co-existence? The extension of the conflict in northern China following the Marco Polo Bridge 'Incident' of July 1937 led Prime Minister Konoe to declare early in 1938 that his government would not negotiate with the KMT government. In his speech of 3 November 1938 he spoke of a New Order and of a partnership between the two countries. His adviser, Ozaki Hotsumi, said the New Order had great potential in recognizing the vitality of Chinese nationalism; it would get the Chinese to collaborate.[38] In fact it was a step towards setting up a 'puppet' regime in China itself.

Based in Nanjing, that was headed by the ex-KMT politician Wang Ching-wei. It had great difficulty with the practice of Japanese power in wartime China, but it also had difficulty with the exclusivity of Japanese ideology. Against the emperor cult, Shinto, bloodline pan-Asianism or 'Greater East Asia' 'could never prevail', even if it might be argued that the Emperor was extending his beneficence. 'Nanjing sponsored public bodies such as the Greater East Asia League and the Sino-Japanese Cultural Association, but they proved incapable of formulating details of the new East Asian order. In view of the fundamental cultural exclusivism of Japan and the oppressive Japanese presence in China, such a task was futile.'[39]

Moreover the very attempt to deploy a rhetoric based on some kind of commonality between Chinese and Japanese tradition, vain as it was, could make it more difficult to find a rhetoric applicable to the rest of the Sphere when it extended outside the 'Confucian' limits. The Japanese, Royama declared, 'must be prepared to accommodate the nationalist desires of Asian peoples, and to weave them into a world policy which is readily distinguishable from Western imperialism'.[40] The New Order rhetoric adopted by Premier Konoe in 1938 was, as Kimitada Miwa says, presented in traditional terms so as 'to have a readier appeal to the sentiments of the Japanese public. It was also hoped that it would have a similar effect on the Chinese.'[41] But what could it mean elsewhere? It restructured the region hierarchically, but now with Japan, not China at the apex.[42] Could that be useful in Southeast Asia? There the Allies' wartime rhetoric, moreover, competed with that of the Japanese.

The colonial structure had remained in being until the opening of the Pacific war in December 1941, and the nationalist elites had enjoyed only limited success. The Philippines and Burma were constitutionally the most 'advanced'. In the former the quest for independence had dominated the politics that elections had introduced, even though the politicians were nervous about the future security of an independent state. The Wilson Administration was devoted to early independence for the islands, but the Jones law of 1916 spoke of independence when a stable government had been set up. The President's advocacy of self-determination prompted a Filipino mission to the US in 1919, seeking a fixed date, but it was in vain. The Democrats' interest in independence revived in the Depression, partly with a view to restricting the imports of sugar. The outcome was the Tydings-McDuffie Act, under which the Philippines would be granted independence after a ten-year period as a 'Commonwealth' with limited powers under an elected President and an uncertainty about its security.

In Burma political advance had been affected by the emergence of a nationalist movement, but also by the relationship with India, which both provided an example of constitutional change and aroused a fear of permanent inclusion in an Indian federation. In 1935 Burma was separated from India, and given a constitution of its own, with a cabinet responsible to an elected House of Representatives, and a wider suffrage than that in the Philippines. The parliamentary government did not, however, extend to the Shan states, nor did its powers extend to defence and foreign affairs or monetary policy. They thus stopped short of the powers of a 'Dominion'. U Saw, the premier, was seeking a promise of 'Dominion status' when the war began.

In 'British Malaya' and 'British Borneo', by contrast, constitutional change was largely avoided. The former continued to consist of a multiplicity of governments, Straits Settlements, FMS (Federated Malay States), UMS (Unfederated Malay States). Attempts made to alter this ramshackle system, limited as they were, met opposition which the British Government was not prepared to over-ride. The same applied in Borneo. Sir Cecil Clementi proposed federation in vain. The Brookes resisted the appointment of a Resident, though in 1941 they accepted a British Representative, shortly after, however, having proclaimed a constitution for their state. The British North Borneo Company wanted to sell out in the depression, but the Government would not buy.

In Netherlands India the early nationalist movements shifted away from the associationist path that liberal Dutch officials [Ethici] favoured, but Tjokroaminoto, the leader of the main mass movement, Sarekat Islam, favoured 'self-administration' rather than demanding independence. The Governor-General in the first world war, Van Limburg Stirum, was not unsympathetic, and believed he should indicate that the role of the new Volksraad was 'responsible government'.[43] But the mass support that SI secured, and the Communist penetration of it, alarmed both the Dutch and the *priyayi* elite, and the repressive policies of the 1920s were only intensified by the Depression. Cooperating nationalists were allowed only a limited role. The Sutardjo petition of 1937 – calling for a ten-year transition to autonomy – was rejected. Only in January 1942 did Governor-General Tjarda agree to a conference with the political parties (GAPI).

The French did not go even so far. Their concept of empire could not admit of a commonwealth in the British style, and they made no concessions to the nationalist movement that developed in the protectorate, and very few in the colony of Cochin China. As a result nationalism tended to fall under a Communist leadership. Their consciousness of the weakness of their hold on their remote empire encouraged the French to come to terms with the Japanese in 1940–41. Once broken off, their rule might never be restored. 'The position is unhappily very simple', wrote Paul Baudouin, the Vichy Foreign Minister; 'if we refuse Japan, she will attack Indo-China which is incapable of being defended. Indo-China will be a hundred per cent lost. If we negotiate with Japan, … we preserve the chances that the future may perhaps bring us.' Japan might respect French sovereignty and withdraw when its war with the KMT regime had ended.[44]

Japan's move on Indo-China followed the change in the European situation after the phony war. It had hoped that, over time, the colonial regimes in Southeast Asia would give way and allow it to dominate. It had watched the debate in the Philippines as had the Dutch. The consul-general, Kimura Atsuchi [1931–34], had said that Japan would be ready to guarantee the neutralization of the islands in cooperation with the US.[45] Time now seemed to be running out. But it was not till the US imposed its embargoes in 1941 – following the penetration of southern Indo-China – that Japan went to war, and undertook the dramatic and ruthless campaign that – more successful than the campaign in China – overthrew the colonial structure of Southeast Asia. The military planning, however, had been more thorough than the political, and the ideological was confused.

Konoe's 'New Order' had not been concerned with Southeast Asia. '[I]ts definitional extension to include Southeast Asia was the result of a sudden turn in international events and of Japan's opportunism in seizing upon this turn, rather than the consequence of a long-considered or widely held interest in the co-prosperity of the Southeast Asian peoples.'[46] Foreign Minister Arita began to evoke the rhetoric in April 1940, when urging the maintenance of the status quo in the Indies after Germany attacked the Netherlands. He referred to the 'intimate relationship of mutuality' binding Japan and Southeast Asia, and especially the Indies. Extending the war to Southeast Asia would interfere with maintaining and furthering 'economic interdependence' and 'co-existence and co-prosperity'.[47] On 29 June he went further. 'The countries of East Asia stand in close relationship to the regions of the South Seas in terms of geography, history, race, and economy. They are destined to enjoy prosperous coexistence by mutual help and accommodation and, by so doing, to promote the peace and prosperity of the world. It is a matter of course, therefore, to unite these regions into a single sphere on the basis of common existence so that the stability of that sphere be ensured.'[48]

The Konoe government, and its foreign minister, Matsuoka, put forward the vision of the Greater East Asia Co-Prosperity Sphere (GEAPS). Its rhetoric could not emphasize a common Sinitic heritage. It tended therefore to emphasize 'liberation'. 'To put it from the international point of view', Matsuoka declared on 1 August, 'the way of the Tenno is nothing but to allow every nation and every people to enjoy what is due to them.'[49] Four days after the Pacific war began in December 1941 the government announced that the Anglo-American war would be called a Great East Asia War 'because it is a war for the construction of a new order in East Asia'. It entailed the 'liberation of East Asian peoples from the aggression of American and Britain', which was to lead to 'the establishment of a genuine world peace and the creation of a new world culture'.[50]

The task force on ideology at the navy ministry in June 1941 had voiced its dismay over the contradictions within the concepts hakko ichiu (eight corners of the world under one roof, universal peace) and imperial 'benevolence' as the guiding principles of the Greater East Asia Co-Prosperity Sphere. The terms seemed limited to a Japanese audience. 'Don't we have any "slogan" comparable with the universality of America's "democracy"?' asked a naval officer. One adviser suggested redefining hakko ichiu as 'universal brotherhood', but soon all agreed that 'although we say "universal brotherhood", it probably means that we are equal to the Caucasians but, to the peoples of Asia, we act as their leader'. An academic adviser declared in October: 'The Greater Asia Co-Prosperity Sphere is not a reality, nor is it capable of becoming so. We are deceiving the world.'[51]

Royama admitted that working out the rationale of the Sphere was 'definitely not the simple task hoped for by politicians and the general public but an extremely difficult project full of impediments and obstacles'.[52] The task was not made easier by the words of the Atlantic Charter concluded between Roosevelt and Churchill in August 1941, and declaring that they respected 'the right of all peoples to choose the form of government under which they will live' and wished 'to see Sovereign rights and self-government restored to those who have been forcibly deprived of them'.[53] How could the traditionalism of the New Order rhetoric be combined with the Versailles spirit of the Charter?

The Total War Institute, an officially sanctioned think tank, struggled with the task early in 1942. One answer, already implicit even in Matsuoka's words, was an emphasis on hierarchy, displacing the equal sovereignty of Westphalia-Versailles, and echoing the 'parental' relationship that had appeared in Manzhouguo rhetoric. 'The Japanese empire is a manifestation of morality and its special characteristic is the propagation of the Imperial Way. It strives but for the achievement of *Hakko Ichiu,* the spirit of its founding. … It is necessary to foster the increased power of the empire, to cause East Asia to return to its original form of independence and co-operation by shaking off the yoke of Europe and America, and to let its countries and peoples develop their respective abilities in peaceful cooperation and secure livelihood.' The desire for independence of peoples in the Co-Prosperity Sphere was to be respected, 'but proper and suitable forms of government shall be decided for them in consideration of military and economic requirements and of the historical, political and cultural elements peculiar to each area'. Independence was to be based on the construction of the New Order, differing from 'an independence based on the idea of liberalism and self-determination. … The peoples of the sphere shall obtain their proper positions, the unity of the people's minds shall be effected and the unification of the sphere shall be realized with the empire as its center.'[54] Explaining the aim of the triumphing invaders to the House of Peers on 20 January, Premier Tojo Hideki echoed the rhetoric of the War Institute. Japan wanted to enable each country and people in the Sphere 'to have its proper place and demonstrate its real character, thereby securing an order of co-existence and co-prosperity based on ethical principles with Japan serving as its nucleus'.[55]

An advisory Council for the Construction of Greater East Asia was set up in February 1942. The haphazard nature of the policies of the occupying forces were an argument for a central planning agency, put forward by civilians on the Planning Board and in the Colonial Ministry. There was opposition. Some of it originated in bureaucratic rivalry, but by no means all. Former financial leaders, like Fukai Eigo, thought it a mistake to separate Asian countries from others. They thought, too, that the agency would symbolize compulsion, and alienate those whom it was intended to win over. After the defeat at Midway in mid-1942 the proposal was also criticized by the Foreign Minister, Togo Shigenori. 'Like the privy councilors, he thought an East Asian ministry would represent a point of no return in Japan's determination to separate the region from the rest of the world. It would be particularism in the extreme, making it more difficult than ever to come to terms with the Western powers.'[56] Though now flushed with victory and inflamed by hatred, the Japanese should be making plans to end the war. That task would be more difficult if policy towards Asia was left to a new ministry. It would, he told the prime minister, make it 'impossible to conduct a unified and consistent diplomacy' and 'affront' the pride of East Asiatic countries.[57] He argued in vain and resigned. The new ministry was established on 1 November 1942.

On 14 January 1943 the Liaison Conference decided to determine the future status of occupied areas according to two principles that Tojo had earlier enunciated. Areas of strategic importance and sparsely populated areas and regions lacking the capacity for independence were to be incorporated into the Empire. 'Independence shall be bestowed upon such areas as qualify for it in the light of their past political development, if this is deemed advantageous to the prosecution of the Greater East Asia war and the establishment of Greater East Asia.'[58] Togo's successor, Shigemitsu Mamoru, argued for the independence of Burma and the Philippines. The Liaison Conference of 10 March agreed that Burma's independence should be coupled with complete military collaboration and a treaty of alliance. The Philippines were to have independence 'when they have made substantial efforts to render hearty collaboration', it had been agreed in January.[59] The Liaison Conference of 26 June agreed on a deal like Burma's.

As Japan's position deteriorated, the war was increasingly presented in terms of liberation. The Allies were fighting to regain their colonies. Japan's aims were quite different, Shigemitsu told the Diet in October 1943. 'To East Asia and its peoples, this is a war of racial awakening – a war for the renascence of East Asia. No wonder that all the peoples of East Asia have risen *en masse* to join this supreme and stupendous enterprise. … The war of greater East Asia is a war for justice to combat aggression. It is a war of liberation.'[60] For the foreign minister, the rhetoric was a means of persuading the Japanese that they had won, as well as a means of stirring fellow Asians to greater efforts. It was something else as well. 'We must be prepared to make peace so soon as our aims have been attained. The emphasis on our war aims and the limits we assign to them will provide the groundwork for the restoration of peace.'[61]

A Greater East Asia Conference met in Tokyo in November, attended by leaders from Free India, Burma, the Philippines, though not by Pibun, the Thai leader, who failed to come, nor by the Indonesians, who were not asked. Tojo's welcoming speech again used the rhetoric he had used in 1942. In Greater East Asia, each nation was to have 'its proper place', 'enjoy the blessings of common prosperity', and 'practise mutual help'. Such was the 'spiritual essence of the culture of Greater East Asia'.[62] The declaration of principles adopted on 7 November was rather different. The countries of great East Asia were to 'cooperate together in order to secure the stability of East Asia and establish an order based on the principle of coexistence and coprosperity'. They were to 'respect their mutual autonomy and independence, extend aid and friendship to each other, and establish an intimate relationship throughout East Asia', and to 'respect their respective traditions, promote each people's creativity, and enhance the culture of the whole East Asia'. The countries were to cooperate closely 'according to the principle of mutuality, plan their economic development, and promote the prosperity of East Asia'. They would also 'maintain friendly relations with all nations, abolish systems of racial discrimination, undertake extensive cultural exchanges, voluntarily open up their resources, and thus contribute to the progress of the entire world'.[63]

The declaration had been drafted in the Foreign Ministry. Kase Shun'ichi had the Churchill-Roosevelt Atlantic Charter by his side when he drafted it, and it was, as many Japanese newspapers observed, a kind of answer to it. Indeed, while retaining key concepts like co-existence and co-prosperity, it was more universalistic in tone than pan-Asianist. Its invocation of universal principles, designed to stimulate the war effort, could also be a means of working towards peace. If they were accepted in Tokyo, they would give the Japanese a sense of achievement and avoid humiliation. At the same time they might also be accepted in Washington and, less readily, in London, and also perhaps in Moscow. 'Shigemitsu and others were preparing themselves and the nation for accepting defeat by calling it a victory for certain universalistic principles.'[64] 'It is clear', Iriye writes, 'that they were hoping to salvage the war from a complete disaster by devising a formula for a symbolic "victory"'.[65] It would, of course, be far more than symbolic. For any such plan, while bringing an end to the exclusivity of the Sphere, would also bring an end to the treaty system in China and to the colonial system in Southeast Asia.

That is evident, for example, in memorandum on the independence of Java produced by the Ministry of Foreign Affairs early in 1944. Granting independence would, it argued, 'naturally contribute to winning the hearts of the natives', and 'demonstrate the consistency of the Empire's moralistic Greater East Asian policies and contribute in no small way to the unity of Greater East Asia'. The 'tide' of the war was, however, 'running disadvantageously', and it might reach the Indies. Granting independence in such circumstances might restrict 'the Empire's pressing military and economic measures and obstruct military operations in no small degree'. If there were a stalemate, it might become a subject of negotiation: 'a hasty "commitment" of our diplomacy concerning Indonesia at this time may be harmful'.

'Nevertheless', the memorandum continued, 'the Greater East Asia war is fundamentally a struggle against the Anglo-American world order – in essence, a war between two world outlooks. Even if America and Great Britain, with their utilitarian outlook, do not comprehend the significance of the present war, regardless of whether or not the war is viewed as a clash in terms of the old concepts of national interests, and no matter whether circumstances are even now enabling complete restoration of the old order, the ideological foundation developed through the war of liberation in Greater East Asia by the Empire is, regardless of the course of the war, an eventuality which even the enemy must follow and accept; there should be a deep-seated conviction in this development.' Even if the independence of Indonesia were not finally 'upheld by diplomatic negotiations after the termination of the war' and were 'temporarily left in abeyance as a future problem', not even the enemy would be able to 'deny the fundamental truth that independence inevitably follows the formative development of a people; if so, and if independence is granted by us, then half the victory can be acknowledged as ours.'

Independence, moreover, could be modified to meet the Empire's requirements, 'should circumstances resolve in our favor; but should the war end completely disadvantageously, with the Empire also unable to honor its other international commitments, the granting of independence, if viewed on a long-term basis, would leave an invincible foundation which could be used in the future resurrection of Japan'. Clarifying Japan's position at this stage would 'make the Empire's war objectives more coherent and provide a constructive legacy for the future; moreover, it should not necessarily prove obstructive after the termination of the war'.[66]

Togo convened a second Greater East Asia conference in Tokyo on 23 April 1945, attended only by ambassadors, rather than heads of state, because of the physical conditions. One aim was to demonstrate Asian solidarity at the time of the UN conference in San Francisco. It 'set forth' the independence of the Indo-China states, where Japan had finally displaced the Vichy French, and looked towards that of the Indies. Its declaration stressed, not Japan's leadership, but cooperation, political equality, economic reciprocity, non-aggression.[67] Iriye's adjective is 'Wilsonian'. It was a response to the nations of Greater East Asia. It was also, perhaps, a signal to enemy nations, a means of conveying peace terms. 'More important', peace would not be a disgrace: 'it would simply mean an agreement with the enemy about an acceptable framework for Japanese foreign affairs.'[68]

Occupation policies varied, not only according to the shifting fortunes of war and the changes in the central government they precipitated, but also according to the current status of the territories the Japanese conquered and the attitudes of the population and its leaders. Japan's victory over Russia in 1905 had had a positive response among some of those under Western rule in Southeast Asia. It was 'hailed even by some of the new generation of Filipinos learning English in the American schools'.[69] Their treatment of China did not deny them a welcome in 1941–42, and they succeeded in securing collaborators, as had the colonial and protecting powers whom they had overthrown. They brought their own experience to bear, and, perhaps even more, that of Manchuria. The tonarigumi or neighbourhood associations, which became a feature of the occupation, had been made compulsory in the homeland in September 1940.[70] Konoe's Imperial Rule Assistance Association, itself based on Manchukuo's Concordia Association, was in turn the model for Putera in the Indies and the Kalibapi in the Philippines.[71] The emphasis was on control, but also on leadership, consensus, solidarity and harmony.

Burma and the Philippines were the Southeast Asian countries in which the Japanese saw fit to offer the greatest measure of constitutional advance. The last to be conquered, Burma was the first of the Southeast Asian countries to secure independence within the Sphere. The Liaison Conference of 10 March 1943 adopted 'Guiding Principles for the Independence of Burma'. The objective was 'to create, under the guidance of the Japanese government, a new Burma as one of the members of the Greater East Asia Co-Prosperity Sphere. Japan must promptly set to the task of guiding the new Burma to prepare herself both physically and spiritually so that she will be able to cooperate closely with Japan for the successful prosecution of the Greater East Asia War.' The military commander was to guide the Burmese in forming a preparatory committee, headed by a pre-war lawyer-politician Ba Maw, to plan the new Burma. It was to be proclaimed on 1 August, and to declare war on the US and the UK immediately after. 'The Burmese Government shall maintain an army and navy for the essential defense of Burma. But Japan shall in reality direct their decisions as to the size and manner of organizing Burmese forces.'[72]

Ba Maw, Thakin Mya, Thein Maung and Aung San arrived in Tokyo on 18 March for ten days' discussion. 'It is the firm belief of Nippon', Tojo told them, '… that the new Burma will be established upon the basis of ethical principles as a member of the Greater East Asian Sphere of Co-Prosperity in order to contribute to the creation of a new world order.'[73] The delegation was also granted an imperial audience on 23 March.[74] Back in Burma a Burmese Independence Preparatory Committee was set up. The constitution it produced provided that Burma would be ruled by a Head of State with 'full sovereign status and powers'.[75] Within a year, if conditions permitted, but in any case within a year of the end of the war, a constituent body would draw up the definitive constitution. Its members would be appointed by the Head of State, the Nainggandaw Adipadi.

On 1 August Ba Maw, designated Head of State by the Japanese, read the declaration of independence. In this he denounced the British and expressed Burma's gratitude to the Japanese. Established on the principle of one blood, one voice, one leader, Burma, 'now not only Burmese but East Asiatic as well', entered the 'free and equal partnership' of the Sphere. It pledged itself to the creation of a new Asiatic order, to be established as part of a new world order. It regarded the Great Asiatic War as its war.[76] The same day, Ba Maw, as Head of State, declared war on the US and the UK.[77]

Ba Maw and the newly-appointed Japanese ambassador, Sawada Renzo, also signed a treaty of alliance. The Japanese military wanted to refer to co-prosperity and co-existence; Shigemitsu wanted reciprocity. By compromise it referred to co-existence only.[78] Other states, besides Japan, recognized the new Burma, Germany and its satellites, Croatia, Slovakia, Bulgaria, and others in the Sphere, Thailand, Manchukuo and the Nanjing regime.

Yet, while it was the first Southeast Asian state to gain independence, its puppet nature was apparent. Nu records his humiliating position as Minister of Foreign Affairs: 'we received the Japanese Ambassador on his first arrival and he came to call on us once afterwards. That was all we saw of him at the Foreign Office. If I wanted to discuss anything I had to go to his office.' If he wanted to discuss anything, he went direct to the Adipadi.[79] 'This independence we now have is only a name. It is only the Japanese version of home rule', Aung San, the Defence Minister, told Ba Maw a little after the Normandy landings of June 1944.[80]

When Japanese forces had entered Manila, General Homma's chief of staff, Maeda Masami, sounded out Filipino leaders on the possibilities of cooperation and the formation of an administration. A group of Filipinos met at the home of the Speaker, Jose Yulo. Quintin Paredes and Benigno Aquino suggested working with the Japanese if they offered a republic; Jorge Bocobo and Rafael Alunan rejected a puppet regime, gobierno muneco. It was agreed to ask the Japanese to recognize the Commonwealth, with a provisional government.[81] Maeda would have nothing to do with the Commonwealth. A republic might be discussed in future. For now the alternatives were un gobierno de hierzo respalando por la forza militar, a government of iron backed by military force, or a gobierno muneco.[82] The group moved toward the puppet solution, minimizing alteration in the status quo.

The politicians' collective letter to Homma had declared that 'in compliance with your advice, and having in mind the great ideals, the freedom, the happiness of our country, we are ready to obey to the best of our ability and within the means at our disposal, the orders issued by the Imperial Japanese Forces for the maintenance of peace and order under the Japanese Military Administration', and were constituting a provisional council of state.[83] The draft had – at Benigno Aquino's suggestion – referred to the 'independence' of the country, and also, rather contradictorily, to a 'Commonwealth Council of State'. The words were all removed by Maeda.[84] Jorge Vargas, made chairman of an executive commission, welcomed Tojo's conditional promise of the 'honour of independence'. It 'personally … confirms my confidence and trust in the true and benevolent intentions of the Japanese Imperial Forces and I am glad I have been given the opportunity to co-operate and work with them'.[85]

Evacuated to head a government-in-exile, the Commonwealth President, Manuel Quezon, decided to ask Roosevelt's permission to issue a manifesto requesting immediate independence, demobilization, evacuation and neutralization, echoing in a sense long-standing aims of the Philippine nationalists. He feared that if Japan established an independent government, 'the masses of the people who knew very little of the history of Japan in Manchuria would fall into the trap and our leaders would be powerless in the face of such a situation'. If, on the other hand, Japan rejected the proposal, Tojo's perfidy would be apparent.[86] The request was, of course, rejected. Roosevelt pledged the US to drive the invaders from the Philippines and to fulfil its promise of independence. The promises Tojo made were valueless. 'I have only to refer you to the present condition of Korea, Manchukuo, North China, Indo-China, and … other countries … to point out the hollow duplicity of such an announcement.'[87] Leaving for Australia, MacArthur asked Quezon to join him there. The President finally left the Philippines on 18 March.

The military administration celebrated the first anniversary of the opening of the war with the creation of the Kalibapi, Kapisanan sa Paglilingkod sa Bagong Pilipinas (Association for Service to the New Philippines), a service organization on the lines of Concordia. On 4 December Vargas duly announced the dissolution of all existing political parties, and on the 6th, in his executive order establishing the Kalibapi, he declared that it was 'dedicated to the unification of the Filipinos in order to extend positive cooperation with the Japanese Military Administration and to secure a greater coordination and intensification of all efforts aimed at the rapid reconstruction and progress of the country, the rehabilitation of its people and the establishment of a sound and stable foundation for the New Philippines. One of its immediate objectives is to assist the Filipino in fully comprehending the significance of, and in strengthening his adherence to, the Co-Prosperity Sphere of Greater East Asia by subordinating himself and his interests to those of the Philippines.'[88]

On 19 June 1943 a special convention of the Kalibapi recommended those who should form the preparatory commission for independence. '[R]atified' by acclamation at a Luneta rally,[89] the names were approved by General

Kuroda on 20 June. Laurel, though recently wounded by guerrillas, was to be president of the committee, and it was openly expected that he would be president of the republic. So it turned out. The indignant Vargas, obsequious speeches unrewarded, was made ambassador to Japan.

During the preparation of the constitution Tojo visited Manila, and Colonel Utsunomiya Naonori, the assistant chief of staff, participated. Like the constitutions of the 1890s, Laurel indicated on 20 August, it was to be that of a republic: 'no other forms, such as a monarchy, could be established here'. A republic, he explained, was 'a commonwealth where the powers of the state are vested in the representatives who are directly or indirectly elected by the people.'[90] The constitution in fact removed the popular suffrage of the Commonwealth period. The president was elected by the national assembly. That was composed of the provincial governors and city mayors and delegates elected every three years, one from each province and city. Within a year after the end of the war, however, a constitutional convention, elected by popular suffrage, would create a new constitution. Taken to meet Tojo, though 'ill', Manuel Roxas, a released prisoner-of-war, joined a constitutional sub-committee. His aim was to secure a revision of the draft so that it did not commit the Philippines to the Sphere. A bill of rights was also inserted. The constitution was promptly ratified by a convention of the Kalibapi on 6 September, and that was followed by a mass rally. The Kalibapi also quickly produced the elected delegates. In his acceptance speech Laurel declared that he believed 'that every living Filipino, including those from the mountains [the guerrillas] who still entertain some doubts', would 'come down to help us'.[91]

On 29 September Laurel, Vargas and Aquino, elected Speaker, went to Tokyo. On his return Laurel announced that independence would be proclaimed on 14 October. That day Aguinaldo and Ricarte, revolutionaries of the first Republic, hoisted the new flag. The Filipino people proclaimed 'that they are, as of right they ought to be, a free and independent nation; that they no longer owe allegiance to any foreign nation; that henceforth they shall exercise all the powers and enjoy all the privileges to which they are entitled as a free and independent state; and that for the defense of their territorial integrity and the preservation of their independent existence, they pledge their fortunes, their lives, and their sacred honor.'[92]

A pact of alliance was concluded, but no declaration of war ensued, as in Burma. To that the activities of the guerrillas contributed, the Hukbalahap, the left-wing Chinese Hua Zhi,[93] and above all those affiliated to USAFFE (United States Army Forces in the Far East). 'Even Japanese military observers conceded that pro-American sentiment persisted in the Islands. … Involvement in the war might further divide opinion and might even bring about a civil war if there were a military draft.' The Japanese took the matter up again in September 1944, when the Allied invasion of the Philippines was imminent. Laurel planned to stick by his refusal and prepared to escape from Manila. Roxas advised compromise, since resistance was impossible: if the Japanese military administration demanded a declaration of war, the Republic should consent, but refuse to raise an army. The Council of State agreed: 'we will thus save our people from great and heavy sacrifices and the destruction of property', said Rafael Corpus. 'Would the sufferings of the people be greater if the Americans or [if] the Japanese considered us hostile?' Ramon Fernandez wondered. 'I prefer that the Japanese do not consider us hostile', Laurel replied.[94] He did, however, adopt a suggestion Recto made, and declared that 'a state of war exists'. He also avoided conscription.[95]

In Washington in January 1943 Quezon had considered asking Roosevelt for immediate independence, so that the US would not appear to be 'plagiarising the magnificent gesture of the Japanese'.[96] In a radio address the following month, he declared that the prospect was a 'Manchukuo': you could not rely on Japan's promise after 'the tragic end of Korea's independence'.[97] Later, however, Ambassador Elizalde approached Senator Tydings, who prepared a bill. Secretary Stimson was opposed: it would seem like recognizing the puppet republic now clearly under preparation.[98] In the event Tydings introduced resolutions pledging the US to drive the Japanese out as soon as possible, restore the democratic process, and then establish independence, and permitting the US president to declare that independence earlier than 4 July 1946. On 9 December the Senate passed a resolution approving advancement of the independence date.[99]

If the Atlantic Charter worked on the Japanese, it worked on the UK as well. Though drafted with an eye to Europe, it had, as had the 14 Points, an impact outside Europe. The Colonial Office recognized the need to advance from the 'trusteeship' approach and began to talk in terms of a 'partnership' in the advance towards self-government. '[W]e are pledged to guide Colonial peoples along the road to self-government within the framework of the British Empire', the Colonial Secretary told the House of Commons in July 1943.[100] News of the Japanese and American moves in respect of the Philippines also affected British discussions of the future of Burma. The Japanese, wrote Sir David Monteath, had made 'a high bid in the auction for Burmese cooperation which will not be easy to outcall'.[101]

None of the other colonial states in Southeast Asia, however, assumed puppet status under the Japanese. Thailand had entered an alliance with Japan and made some territorial gains at the expense of its neighbours. Pibun seemed to think the four northern Malay states and two Shan states 'a tasty but poisonous gift', Sato Kenryo observed.[102] Malaya was indeed treated in a cavalier fashion. Initially, the Japanese had envisaged the removal of the rulers, who were – like the daimyo after the Meiji restoration – to be 'induced to surrender voluntarily their political privileges', though that policy was abandoned in July 1943.[103] Singapore was a territory the Japanese intended to keep. The Vichy regime in Indo-China was retained until March 1945, though the Japanese then encouraged declarations of independence.

The attitude to Netherlands India was ambiguous. Steps were taken to mobilize support for the war effort, partly through mass movements. Nationalists sought to use them and gained prominence if not affection. 'Sukarno's face, not just his name, penetrated the Archipelago. I have the Japanese to thank for that.'[104] But it was only as the war drew to an end that the Japanese began to consider setting up an independent regime. In September 1944 the new Koiso government announced its plans for Indonesia. Officials had prepared draft statements for the premier to use when announcing them in the Diet. Those alluded to the goals of Greater East Asia, invoking 'stability', 'independence of national states', 'fraternal cooperation', 'co-existence and co-prosperity', and quoted the examples of Burma and the Philippines. The natives, said Koiso, had 'thoroughly comprehended the Empire's true intentions and consistently continued their tremendous efforts toward the successful climax of the Greater East Asia war; moreover, their cooperation with local military government has been truly something to behold. In response to these circumstances and in order to ensure the permanent welfare of the East Indies, the Empire here states that their independence will be sanctioned in the future.'[105] Only in 1945, however, did the military authorities set up preparatory bodies that involved Sukarno and other collaborating nationalists. And only after the surrender did they manage, rather discreetly, to declare independence on 17 August.

The concepts behind the GEAPS were a combination – not to say a muddle – of the traditional and the modern, inflected both by specifically Japanese ideas and by the hold that self-determination had already secured within the colonial states. That was underlined by the fact that the Japanese were competing with the Allies, who felt that it was necessary to offer what they implied was a more genuine liberation. Hierarchy was always part of the ideology the Japanese proffered: each nation should have its proper place. Dealing with one country at a time, they sought to bind by alliance, commitment, and mobilization. Not only, of course, were they trying to adapt and use an ideology. They were fighting a war and then seeking a peace and that put a premium on their pragmatism. It is impossible to work out what kind of Southeast Asia might have existed if they had succeeded. What would have been the status of the post-colonial states? How would they have been offered security?

In the event the legacy of the Japanese was more negative. They overthrew the colonial states and the British and American dominance that had provided security for them within the region. '[N]othing can ever obliterate the role Japan has played in bringing liberation to countless colonial peoples', Ba Maw wrote. Its victories 'really marked the beginning of the end of all imperialism and colonialism.'[106] Even so, it cannot be said that the Southeast Asian states owe their independence to the Japanese. Breaking the colonial continuity meant, as the French had seen, that it would be difficult to return. Securing independence out of the international situation at the end of the war was, however, very much the work of the Southeast Asian elites themselves. Some of their methods reflected their experience under the Japanese, in particular of the mobilization that reversed the practice of the colonial state. But their objectives were those that had forced their way into Japan's own ideologies since Manchuria: independent state and nationhood. If the elite utilized a non-national past – 'Why not recover the glories of our past?' Hatta asked[107] – that had after all been the practice in the West, and Western scholarship had uncovered some of those glories. What else was included in the legacy of the protectors who had failed to protect? Were the 'colonial states' to be 'successor states', their nationalism filling the frontiers the previous framework had created? What role would be played by those who had collaborated with colonial rulers or Japanese forces? What views had they imbibed? And how would they fare in the post-war world?

Initially the elites now faced the victorious Allies, the colonial powers in somewhat equivocal relationship with the triumphant US. They had developed plans for the future of their former states more or less comprehensive or forward-looking. All, even the French, recognized that their return, even if successful, could not be on the old basis, and their regimes would more clearly than ever be of a transitional nature and a shorter duration. None, not even the British, realized how intractable their task would be, how strong the nationalist feeling that the elites were able to evoke, how inadequate force would prove, how much their plans would have to change. Aside from the Timorese, not to mention the Andamanese, only the Vietnamese – caught up in a new war, cold for others, hot for them – were unable to secure independence for their countries within little more than a decade.

The struggles in Southeast Asia took place in a new international context. That, of course, affected their course, and their experience illustrates its nature. One feature of it was the decline in the power of Great Britain, under whose aegis the colonial system had been built up. In the war it was on the victorious side, rather than victorious, its power greatly depleted. Two 'super-powers' had emerged, the US and the SU (Soviet Union). Their antagonism developed into what was called a Cold War, and it was to shape and complicate the end of the European empires, the nature of the new states that emerged, the extent of their independence, and the means by which they sought security. KMT China had been treated as a great power in the war – the Allies abandoned extraterritoriality in 1943, at the same time as Japan made a similar concession to Wang Ching-wei, and also of course, as Chiang Kai-shek pointed out, the 'inglorious anniversary' of its inauguration at the end of the first Anglo-China war[108] – but by October 1949 its Communist rivals were able to proclaim a People's Republic. In 1950 it concluded an alliance with the SU, and the US believed that they constituted a Communist 'Bloc'. The regime was denied the China seat in the Security Council of the UN, the League of Nations' successor, strict adherent of Westphalia. In face of the Communist threat, the US encouraged the revival of Japan and its focus on Southeast Asia.

A striking feature of the new Southeast Asia was the extent to which its states retained the frontiers that the colonial period had established. The colonial elites had, of course, worked within them, challenging the particular imperial power to which they were subject. The Japanese had tampered with the framework and the Indonesians, in their preparatory committees, had contemplated a Greater Indonesia. The very fact that such changes were associated with the Japanese was an argument, however, for their post-war undoing. It was with particular colonial powers that the elites had once more to contend. In the Cold War phase, frontiers were nominally respected, if only because they were in practice undermined.

The imperial powers had been unable to 'protect' the colonial states against the invader. In turn Japan, despite its rhetoric, had been unable to provide security for the region or its territories. Its occupation was brief and contested. Moreover its concepts were confused. The war itself put a priority on resources and control, while its propaganda requirements pulled more than one way, as a result of the need to appeal both to a domestic constituency and to the nationalist aspirations in the territories they overran.

6 Independence

The Second World War had made it clearer than ever – especially in Southeast Asia – that a world of empires was to be followed by a world of nation states. The UN and its Charter envisaged that, clearly enunciating the 'Westphalia' principles, coupled with the Versailles ideals. But the process was complicated by the Cold War between the two super-powers, the US and the SU, that promptly ensued, and it was intensified by the outbreak of the Korean War in 1950. That both promoted the change and qualified it. The two super-powers, as at the end of the First World War, were in agreement that the old empires should come to an end. In some sense, they were, therefore, in accord: they accepted the nation state. Indeed they seldom openly challenged the frontiers of the states that emerged from the colonial states, questionable though they might be. But they did try to influence them, and there they competed. Sometimes they sought the allegiance of the new leadership, offering aid and advice, civil and military. Sometimes they sought to befriend it, sometimes to undermine it, to change its composition or manipulate it, often meeting the kind of difficulties the Japanese had met with their puppets. Sometimes they sought to draw the states into alliances or offer them protection at the risk of also making them targets. In such ways their independence might be modified, even though their sovereignty was nominally respected.

The Cold War entered a second phase in the 1960s. The PRC concluded an alliance with the SU in 1950. After the Korean War both followed a co-existence policy, but by the late 1950s the PRC was adopting a line that increasingly diverged from that of its partner. Mao believed that Khrushchev's Soviet Union was too ready to compromise with the West. The 'Communist Bloc' fragmented in the 1960s, though never quite disintegrating, and when the US came to terms with the PRC, the Cold War entered a new phase that lasted till the collapse of the SU in 1991.

China's rhetoric was generally one of struggle. But after the Korean War the super-powers did not come into open or direct conflict. Instead they took part in the conflicts of others, to some extent making them their own, though rarely holding sole responsibility for them. It is a mistake to regard them merely as proxy wars as was often done at the time.

Frontiers and sovereignty were acknowledged. But the emphasis was often on the nominal. Subversive movements were urged on by agents, money, and propaganda. Minorities were encouraged to oppose the majorities that now dominated the new nation states. And on the other hand the newly independent governments, seeking aid, sometimes paid the price of what opponents and critics at least called 'satellization' or, alternatively, victims of 'neo-colonialism'.

'Puppets' was another term of abuse that the super-powers employed to describe the allies of their opponents. Some rulers could rightly be termed puppets, though, like earlier puppets, they were not always easy to control. They differed from those that the Japanese set up, however, inasmuch as the states which they appeared to rule were in general widely recognized by other states as independent, were not within a Sphere, and were usually members of the United Nations. But they faced something of the same paradox. If their independence did not seem real, their usefulness would be less. But they might act too independently, like Pinocchio. The SU had limited control over Castro, and the US found 'counter-insurgency' in Guatemala 'running wild'.[1] Their patron would try to control them, wondering if aid were better or worse 'with strings attached'. Failing to do so, it might try to dispense with them. Replacing them was, however, even more difficult than replacing a collaborative elite in a colonial state or protectorate. It would signal a lack of independence and make the role of new puppets, if found, even less credible.

Independent states and their rulers indeed reacted in various ways. Some accepted aid and support, whether or not there were 'strings attached'. Some believed it possible to play off one super-power against another. Others adopted 'non-alignment', an Indian phrase, or 'neutrality'. A few went further and were or declared themselves ready to be neutralized, thus in fact formally sacrificing some of the rights and capacities of an independent state. Southeast Asia offers examples of all those reactions. Other territories seemed too small to survive in the dangerous world that had followed the overthrow of the colonial pattern and the security it had seemed to offer. Surely – as Leibnitz had argued in the late seventeenth century – some states were simply too small to be independent?[2] Should they become independent states or be joined with larger entities through incorporation or federation? Of those approaches Southeast Asia also offered examples. Though states finally succeeded empires throughout the region, the process was a prolonged one, and differentiated by style and timing. It also took place in changing international circumstances.

Those included not only the changes in the nature of the Cold War. They included the decline of British power both in Southeast Asia and the world at large, the emergence of an independent India, the decolonization of Africa, and the expansion of the UN, both in terms of membership and range of activities. Less obvious, and more difficult to define, was the emergence of the further elements that were necessary to a world 'system', the kind of practices and presumptions that makes a system operate or affects the extent to which it may operate. That involved not only the 'traditional' diplomacy of the Westphalian pattern and the new diplomacy of the UN and of 'summitry'. It also involved – to a greater extent than before – the play of 'opinion'.

In the imperial world colonial rulers had ultimately been responsible in some measure to metropolitan governments, and – for good or ill – to their expanding democracies. The Cold War contenders were not answerable to a metropolitan government: they constituted that government. They were responsible to their domestic constituencies, democratic or otherwise. They were responsible to 'world opinion', a developing phenomenon, not only stimulated by inventive technology and growing literacy, but also stimulated, if confused, by the propaganda the rival powers put out at the UN and through all the media, new and old.

Only at the end of the twentieth century had all the colonial states of Southeast Asia become nation states. Timor Leste was the last, a remnant of the first European empire in the region. Decolonization had been a clear aim, but the means had been much less clear. Like wars colonies were easier to get into than out of. Improvisation played a major role in the creation of the system. There was a role for it in its conclusion. Politics, domestic and international, practicality, precedent, prejudice and prestige were all factors in the forms decolonization took and in its timing.

The Philippines was the first to secure independence. The US was keen to mark its victory by sticking to the timetable envisaged when the Commonwealth had been set up. Some observers thought it was too soon. Certainly it came at a price. The Philippines won the double-edged advantage of continued preferential trade and it secured a promise of funds for rehabilitation after the destruction it suffered. But it had to allow Americans parity in the exploitation of its resources, peg the peso to the dollar, and provide American forces with bases. The State Department itself thought that some provisions in the trade bill were inconsistent with 'genuine independence', while others gave Americans special privileges when the US was fighting discrimination elsewhere.[3]

Granting independence was, however, seen not only as the fulfilment of a pledge, but also as an example to other powers. But their handling of the situation they met in the former colonial states was also determined, not only by the political situation they faced in their own metropolis, but by the influence of the British. Britain, the guarantor of the colonial system, also took the lead in most of Southeast Asia in the reoccupation that the Allies envisaged. Now more than ever it recognized that empire must give way to states. The Europeans should be putting their relationship with Asian peoples on a new basis. 'The Europeanised "Far East" has gone', as H.G. Walsh, the British Consul-General in Batavia, had put it in 1942, 'and the organization of European activities there in the future will have to be rebuilt on entirely different foundations from those prevailing before 1939.'[4]

The 'most important and most difficult problem', the Civil Planning Unit suggested late in 1945, was political advancement. 'We have not only to decide the proper tempo for political advancement, but also to convince the peoples concerned and the world at large that we are not yielding step by step to pressure, but are sincerely following out an enlightened policy.' The other European powers were confronted by 'similar problems'. Britain had 'a strong moral obligation' to restore their sovereignty. But, if there were to be 'just and stable systems of Government', Britain would have to play 'a leading part in the settlement of difficulties between the native peoples and our Allies'.[5] Britain recognized, as Walsh had put it, that relations between Europe and Southeast Asia would have to be on a new footing, one that accepted 'political advancement'.

The Cold War that followed brought another factor into play. Two superpowers emerged, with capacity far beyond that Britain now possessed. Britain certainly did not want the SU to dominate the world, threatening Britain's own security as well as its interests elsewhere. But nor did it want the US completely to predominate, though it was, of course, a necessary ally. And it had to be steered away from outright conflict. A Third World War would finally destroy Britain's power, if not the British state itself.

The nationalism that inspired post-war independence movements the British quickly saw, however, was a possible counter to communism, and the creation of states that were democratic, well-administered and development-oriented would counter its appeal. At the same time the emergence of such states would be a factor that the US would have to reckon with. In particular, the British thought, the US would have to take account of the policies of India after it secured its independence in 1947. Its insistent anti-colonialism was at times to be too much for the British. But in general they recognized its value as a constraint upon the more extreme attitudes the US was tempted to adopt as the Cold War intensified.

Another fundamental difference emerged. The British did not see the policies they were developing in Southeast and South Asia as inconsistent with the recognition of the Communist regime when it assumed power in China late in 1949. They believed that, if Communist China were treated like a normal member of the family of nations, it was more likely to behave like one, rather than like an outlaw or a subordinate of the SU or part of a Bloc. By contrast the Americans, frustrated by the failure of their policies in China, did not recognize the regime. They became more interested in the security of Southeast Asia particularly after the Chinese intervened in the Korean War. But their ways of providing for it and their purpose in doing so were likely to differ from Britain's ways.

The first of the colonial states to secure independence after the Philippines was Burma. Though the British were to depict their policy there, like that towards India, as an example to others, they had in fact had to yield to what the nationalist leader, Aung San, described as 'the fourth Anglo-Burman war', the one the Burmese were going to win. The concept of returning to direct rule and promoting rehabilitation, to be followed by a renewed advance towards a constitutional system, was abandoned. Independence was proclaimed early in 1948. Nor was Burma now interested in the Dominion status that it had sought before the war, even though India had accepted it. Though it concluded a defence agreement with Britain, Burma became independent outside the Commonwealth. At the time, a Dominion still had to accept the British monarch as head of state. Republics, such as Burma declared itself to be, were not accepted members of the club.

The form of the state was described as a Union. That was no mere constitutional matter either. In developing 'parliamentary Burma' before the war, the British had kept aside the Scheduled Areas, inhabited by non-Burman 'minorities', preserving there more of the powers of the Governor. Taking over a successor state, the nationalists intended to inherit the whole territory. Aung San negotiated the Panglong agreement early in 1947. As a result the Union included a Shan State, with a provision for secession after ten years. The Karen people, more intermixed with the Burmans, accepted no such solution, and were to initiate a long-term rebellion against the Union Government.

Britain, the Civil Affairs Unit had observed, was 'confronted in an acute form with the problem of maintaining friendly cooperation with the Dutch without putting herself into antagonism with the general cause of nationalism in Asia'. The sudden surrender of Japan had given the Indonesian leaders the opportunity to set up a republic before the Allied forces could arrive. Severe military clashes followed. The British sought to secure an understanding between the Dutch and the Indonesians before they withdrew their forces late in 1946, and their Special Commissioner, Lord Killearn, helped to bring about the Linggadjati agreement in November. When it seemed that it would collapse, Michael Wright of the Commissioner's office urged on the Dutch ministers Beel and Jonkman, who visited Singapore in May, the need to carry it out. 'We looked forward to the close co-operation of the Dutch as well as others, but always on the basis of a European/Asiatic partnership.' As yet the SU was not active in Southeast Asia on a major scale. There was a short-term opportunity to make 'a reality of a partnership between Asiatic people concerned and Western countries'.[6]

The policy was a failure. The Dutch police action followed in July. 'The action', wrote John Street at the British FO (Foreign Office), was 'basically stupid'. Most of the Dutch had 'never really understood the change which had come over the situation since 1941'.[7] A Security Council resolution provided for a Good Offices Committee (GOC) and negotiations began on the USS *Renville*. Street's colleague, W.D. Allen, thought that they would break down, and the Dutch march of Yogyakarta, the Republic's capital. They would prevail in the short-term. 'In the long run … their role and influence in the Indies will be swept away to a greater degree than ours in India, where we knew how to make our peace with Asiatic nationalism in good time.'[8] The prognostication was an accurate one.

The Good Offices Committee made slow progress. 'The Dutch understand that the policies which we have pursued in India, Burma and elsewhere, combined with our interest in retaining the support of public opinion in these and other countries in South East Asia, led us to believe that the Dutch approach to the Indonesian problem was on the wrong lines.' But they doubted if Britain's experiments in India and Burma were 'wise', and in any case, 'temperamentally and constitutionally', could not adopt precisely the same policy.[9] The Committee went beyond 'good offices' to secure the Renville agreement, but the truce was not followed by successful negotiations. 'This is all playing into Russian hands', Foreign Secretary Ernest Bevin wrote in May 1948.[10] In December the Dutch resorted to a second 'police action' and to a march on Yogya. Initial military success was followed by guerrilla warfare in Indonesia and by international opposition. US pressure conduced to the conclusion of the Round Table Agreement (RTA) in 1949.

That set up a Republic of the United States of Indonesia (RUSI) and a Netherlands-Indonesia Union. The Dutch had taken up the idea of a federal Indonesia. That would give expression to its regional diversity, but also make the Republic the nationalists had proclaimed but one of several units. While the GOC negotiations had been going on, the Dutch had indeed begun to set up federal states on a provisional basis, securing one way or another the cooperation of elite elements with whom they thought they could work. The RTA adopted the federal structure, but it did not last. Federalists themselves could not hold out against the Republic's identification of the nation with a single government. Indeed the association of federalism with Dutch latter-day imperialism made it difficult to conceive of any form of government but that of a unitary nation state.

The transfer of power under the RTA was not complete. West New Guinea had been under the authority of the Netherlands Indies government, but its transfer to its successor was not immediate. The Hague agreement provided that its status should be determined by agreement between the Netherlands and the Republic of the United States of Indonesia. Retaining a foothold in Asia made it easier to secure States General approval of the transfer of the bulk of Dutch territories to the nationalists. The Catholic leader, whose support was needed, had, moreover, become interested in self-determination for the Papuans. The Indonesians, on the other hand, believed that West New Guinea was rightfully part of their successor state, and that there was no call for further acts of self-determination. No agreement was reached, and a long and increasingly bitter dispute ensued.

Other powers were involved. The US was unwilling to come down on one side or the other between a NATO ally and a newly independent country it wanted to avert turning to its Cold War opponent. The Australians, possessors of Papua and still holding the Trust Territory of East New Guinea, wanted good relations with Indonesia, but hoped to keep West New Guinea out of its hands for as long as possible. The British had an interest in good relations with Indonesia, too: they had substantial commercial interests there; and it wrapped round their colonial and protected territories in the region. But good relations with Australia, a major Commonwealth partner, had to be preserved. The only answer, it seemed, was to put the issue into cold storage. But Indonesia's interest did not die away. It became associated, indeed, with the fiery nationalism of its first President, Sukarno.

Among the possible answers the British FO contemplated in 1950 was 'independent self-government', but that, it quickly determined, was 'out of the question',[11] not merely because Indonesia would not accept it, but because it would create a non-viable small state. The Dutch reaffirmed their policy of self-determination in 1952 but the Australians did not support it. They were ready to commit themselves to administrative collaboration between the two sections of New Guinea but not political. The time-frame for development might be different. 'Papua is Australian territory and Australian public opinion and opinion in the territory itself might look askance at any Government statement that foreshadowed possibility of our territories passing out of our control', James Plimsoll told the Netherlands Embassy in Canberra in 1957.[12]

These reservations were, of course, also an obstacle to another proposition that the British considered, but in the end found no way to advance. In February 1960 Theodore Bot, State Secretary in the Dutch Ministry of the Interior, told the press in Canberra 'that the union of Australian and Dutch New Guinea as an independent Melanesian State would be the wisest course for the future'.[13] The idea of 'a united independent Papua or even Melanesia' was supported in the British Commissioner-General's office in Singapore. Fred Warner, the head of the South East Asia Department in the British Foreign Office, saw merit in it, too. Though the survival of 'such a Palaeolithic Republic' was doubtful, 'it could perhaps be preserved by a joint Australian/Indonesian trusteeship in the early stage. But there seems little chance of achieving this and the idea must be dismissed for the immediate future.'[14]

His junior colleague, Justin Staples, suggested that an independent West New Guinea would be open to Indonesian penetration and attack: 'an independent and unified Papua would be a much more worthwhile unit.'[15] If the Dutch and the Australians kept in step in respect of the political progress in East and West New Guinea, self-determination might lead to an independent Papua, 'which might even be expanded', a FO memorandum suggested in September 1960, 'to become a Melanesian Union, including the Bismarck Archipelago, the Solomons and the New Hebrides'.[16]

The Australians was still against close collaboration. If they committed themselves to a unified New Guinea, the Indonesians might be encouraged, once established in West New Guinea, to lay claims to East New Guinea, too.[17]

An inter-departmental meeting was held in London on 4 January. Warner reported on it. Indonesia might get West New Guinea, but if the Dutch succeeded in bringing the territory to self-determination in about ten years, one possibility was a Melanesian federation. 'The main argument … is that an independent West New Guinea, even with considerable Dutch support, would be a poor and weak State, wide open to Indonesian penetration or attack. It would therefore make for the stability of the area if West New Guinea could become independent as part of (or with a clear prospect of becoming part of) a larger and more viable whole. Such a solution also offers a sensible future to some of the other small fuzzy-wuzzy territories of the area.'[18]

At the meeting Warner had reported that the idea had appeared 'spontaneously' in West New Guinea, and was 'written into the programme of one of the embryonic political parties' (Parna). What would the UK's attitude be if the idea caught on? The CO representatives thought the Solomon Islanders should be allowed to make up their minds when internal self-government was reached in about ten years' time. They might feel 'submerged'. The Dutch, Staples said, had ten years in mind. The Australians were talking 'much more vaguely in terms of about twenty-five years'. In ten years' time, if the Dutch remained till independence, Australia would be faced with a vulnerable West New Guinea. If the Dutch and the Australians coordinated their policies so that both halves of New Guinea reached self-determination at the same time, there would be 'a reasonable chance of the whole island emerging into independence as a unified whole'. For political reasons the Australians did not wish to commit themselves publicly to a 'One New Guinea' policy, but the foundation should be laid. The meeting agreed that there should be tripartite consultation on Netherlands New Guinea, and an inter-departmental meeting on the future of the Pacific territories as a whole.[19] But was there time? And would Indonesia be prompted to foreclose what there was?

Another possibility the FO considered was the possibility of self-determination by secession after ten years offered to the Shan states in the constitution of the Union of Burma. Impractical though that was, the idea perhaps had some impact on the deal that was finally made in the US-mediated Bunker agreement. That provided for the early incorporation of West New Guinea in Indonesia, but paid lip-service to the principle of self-determination by providing for a so-called act of free choice in 1969. In the event the choice was far from free. Papua New Guinea, on the other hand, emerged as an independent state, colony and mandate having been amalgamated, though it received substantial Australian aid. Coming in 1974, earlier than the Australians had envisaged, independence was even so too late to have an impact on the fate of West New Guinea, as some had hoped.

The West New Guinea 'solution' offered a precedent that Indonesia sought to take up in respect of Portuguese Timor, though it had never been part of the Netherlands Indies. The Carnation Revolution in 1974 had led the Portuguese to accept that their African territories must promptly become independent. The idea that so small a territory as East Timor could survive on its own was rejected in Indonesia, which argued that it would be a source of insecurity. The Suharto regime clumsily attempted a take-over, first by covert and then by open intervention, but it never secured the measure of international sanction that it secured in respect of West New Guinea.

By this time indeed the assumption that small states could not survive was less readily accepted. A UNGA (UN General Assembly) resolution of 1960 urged the end of colonialism irrespective of viability. 'Many new states acquired "negative sovereignty" – the right to be free of external interference – when they clearly lacked "positive sovereignty" – the right to satisfy the basic needs of their populations.'[20] Writing about 'quasi-states' Robert Jackson asked whether there should be a more effective system of global trusteeship to prepare colonies for full membership.[21]

Others were less concerned. Viability, David Vital suggested in 1967, was 'a relative quality fluctuating with circumstances'.[22] By 1991 Ramesh Thakur could write of it as 'a problem in search of a root rather than a small state phenomenon'. Some states were 'too large. And the world has become interdependent in such a way that the security and survival of nations anywhere have become hostage to policies and practices everywhere.'[23]

Size and viability had, however, clearly played a part in earlier attempts at combining security and political advancement. Federation had been an answer to the problem of decolonizing smaller territories that the British had favoured elsewhere, though the remedy sometimes proved worse than the disease. At the same time as they were contemplating it as the answer to the future of New Guinea and the Pacific dependencies, for example, they were also implementing it in the Malay world. There, of course, it seemed to have a precedent in the FMS, though that federation was more like a unification.

Post-war the British attempted to realize a plan for a Malayan Union, including all the states and settlements except Singapore, the site of their major base in East and Southeast Asia. Seeking to acquire sufficient jurisdiction in the states to enable them to apply the Foreign Jurisdiction Act (FJA) and so legislate, they negotiated with the Sultans, but were then faced with a wider Malay opposition in UMNO (United Malays National Organisation). They retreated to a Federation of Malaya, which would at least establish a single central government. Then, faced in 1948 with the Communist-led insurgency they categorized as the Emergency, they realized that it could be defeated only by coupling counter-insurgency with political advance. An inter-racial Malay-led Alliance secured independence for the Federation in 1957, coupled, as in Burma's case, with a defence treaty. But what should be done with Singapore? – about the same size as the Isle of Wight, as a FO official put it in 1956.[24] It secured internal self-government in 1959, but its leaders, Lee Kuan Yew and the People's Action Party, did not themselves believe that it was viable as an independent state. It had to be reconnected with Malaya.

And what of the Borneo territories, Sarawak and North Borneo, made colonies in 1946, and the protectorate of Brunei? Though there were Brooke loyalists who believed in an independent Sarawak, few believed that such a state would be viable. The Borneo territories, it was thought, might, despite their diversity, be drawn closer together, and ultimately, in the Grand Design put forward by the British Commissioner-General, Malcolm MacDonald, be associated with Malaya and Singapore in a Dominion of Southeast Asia. But, anxious throughout the region to avoid new troubles and new commitments, the British hesitated to take the necessary steps, particularly in face of opposition from Brunei, now a wealthy oil-producer.

Indonesia's confrontation of the Dutch over West New Guinea again raised the question of the Borneo territories. Would it try to realize the Greater Indonesia discussed by Sukarno and his colleagues before the Japanese surrender? In June 1960 the Malayan Prime Minister, Tunku Abdul Rahman, told Lord Home, Secretary of State for Commonwealth Relations, that they must be ready for an Indonesian move against Sarawak and North Borneo.[25] The following week he raised the question of enlarging the Federation of Malaya to include Singapore, North Borneo, Sarawak and Brunei.[26]

At the Foreign Office Warner remarked that Malaya was 'the only refuge' for the Borneo territories. Promoting federation might arouse hostility from the Indonesians and Filipinos, however. He thought it 'very likely' that Indonesia had 'secret long-term designs' on the Borneo territories, but believed 'that anything which helps us to build up Malaya must be counted a good thing, so long as the latter continues in its present condition'. Britain, he thought, should be ready to include Singapore: 'we have never in any case expected the present situation in Singapore to last for ever'. But was the Tunku? 'There must be some doubt whether the Tunku can absorb Singapore into such a Federation in the near future without upsetting the stability of Malaya. Perhaps he does not really mean to do so and is in fact just aiming to mop up the Borneo territories while continuing to exclude Singapore.'[27]

The British saw the scheme as a means of unburdening themselves of the Borneo territories, which could not exist on their own. They also wished, perhaps even more clearly, to put Singapore on a different footing. There was a risk that, at the next election, an extreme left-wing movement, possibly communist, could take over, making the base useless. If Singapore were in the larger scheme, the risk would be reduced, and so would accusations of colonialism. Britain's defence burden would, moreover, be diminished, since internal security would become a matter for the new federation.[28]

The scheme was pushed forward with remarkable speed. Indonesia was no doubt in mind. By August 1961 the Foreign Secretary could declare that the Tunku was showing much interest in 'Greater Malaysia', his idea, it was said, being that he could 'absorb the Chinese population of Singapore by bringing in the Borneo Territories to redress the racial balance; at the same time this might forestall Indonesian ambitions in the area'.[29] Speed, however, failed to avoid an Indonesian challenge, taking the form of another 'confrontation' like that with the Dutch. No war ensued. But, despite such attempts at compromise as the Maphilindo concept and the UN assessment of opinion in the Borneo colonies, the region came nearer to it than the British hoped, absorbed more resources than they wished, and conduced along with the sterling crisis to the decision to withdraw from Singapore that they announced, after the end of Confrontation, in 1967.

By this time, Warner's prophecy had come true. Singapore had been extruded from Malaysia in 1965. 'An independent Singapore was not regarded as viable three years ago. Nothing in the current situation suggests it is more viable today', wrote the Australian journalist Denis Warner.[30] But its leadership made decisive efforts to survive as an independent republic, not by going left, but by creating conditions that would encourage multinational investment. It was able to take the British withdrawal, finally effected in 1971, in its stride, though a sense of insecurity endured.

The extrusion of Singapore had delighted Subandrio, the Indonesian foreign minister.[31] But Malaysia did not break up, and indeed its government became all the more determined to retain Sarawak and Sabah [North Borneo]. Brunei, on the other hand, had not joined Malaysia. Though Sultan Omar Ali Saifuddien III seemed at times ready to do so, essentially he was unwilling either to lose control of the vast revenues that oil and natural gas were now bringing, or to abandon his attempts to secure a fuller political control of the Sultanate over against both the British Residents and the democratizing tendencies they were bound to encourage. The revolt of December 1962 was coupled with the proclamation of a state of North Kalimantan, which, as Warner put it, would be 'a weak state' that Indonesia would take over.[32] It was put down by British forces. Somewhat paradoxically, that enabled the Sultan to evade both democracy and inclusion in Malaysia, while retaining British protection. Unable to exert much pressure, the British government approved a new protection agreement in 1971.

In Indo-China, by contrast, the French had dissolved the federation they had proclaimed in 1887/1897, though the idea remained as something of a hope in Vietnamese minds and something of a fear among Cambodians. Yet another pattern was put forward by the Fourth Republic as a means of retaining its influence in the region: Vietnam, Laos and Cambodia would become Associate States in the French Union. Neither long-standing tradition nor current metropolitan politics made for a flexible policy towards the states. Cambodia's King Sihanouk was, however, to conduct a 'crusade' for independence in 1953, and Laos secured its independence in a treaty that year. Vietnam was another matter. The communist-led Viet Minh had proclaimed an independent Republic in Hanoi in September 1945. After the Allied occupation – there in the hands of KMT forces – had ended, the French and the Vietnamese reached an accord in March 1946. By the end of the year, however, the two parties were in open conflict. As a counter the French brought back the Nguyen emperor Bao Dai as Head of State in 1948, though not allowing him any real opportunity to build nationalist support. Unable either to fight decisively or negotiate effectively, the French took the opportunity of the 1954 Geneva conference on Korea to end their military struggle.

That was only a limited triumph for the government of the Democratic Republic in Hanoi. Because the Vietnamese nationalist movement was also and became even more a communist movement, the US could not accept its success, and saw the anti-colonial struggle as part of a much wider Cold War conflict in which failure would have ramifications across the world. On the other hand the Chinese communists, in power nearby from 1949, could not accept the defeat of the DRVN (Democratic Republic of Vietnam), even though the long-term relationship of the two neighbours had been marked by equivocation. Nor could they allow the SU to take the sole credit for supporting a communist and anti-imperialist government. If the emergence of nation states from colonial states elsewhere in Southeast Asia was complicated by the Cold War, nowhere was that so much the case as in Vietnam. Or perhaps one should say: Indo-China. For the neighbouring states of Laos and Cambodia, despite their independence, became almost unavoidably involved in the Vietnamese conflict.

The Korean War provided Southeast Asia not only with fears and apprehensions: it also provided models. On the one hand, it offered the image of massive troop movements. On the other, it offered the image of effective resistance to Communist forces, not only by US/UN troops from outside, but also by effectively trained local troops, with a determined, if tiresome, leader in Syngman Rhee. That example was greatly to influence American policy in Vietnam, before Geneva as well as after. The Korean War indeed made it unlikely that the US would again wish to deploy its own troops on the Asian mainland. But it also made it even more determined not to 'lose' any more territory to the communists. The answer was to deploy Asian forces.

Succeeding Ridgway in April 1951, MacArthur's replacement in Korea, James A. Van Fleet, built up over a 22-month tour of duty a ROK (Republic of Korea) army of 600,000 'fanatical' soldiers: he was, said Syngman Rhee, the 'Father of the ROK army'.[33] When the British Foreign Secretary of State Anthony Eden met the American Secretary of State Dean Acheson in Paris in May 1952, the latter told him that the Americans had concluded that 'a good deal' could be done by imparting to the French techniques used in Korea for 'the training and morale-building of local troops'. That should 'restore the confidence of the French Government in themselves', and 'by increasing confidence on the part of the Vietnamese authorities contribute to the process of enabling the latter to take over the government of the country'.[34]

Early in 1954 the US reluctantly accepted that the Korea peace talks might cover Indo-China as well. It was not prepared, however, to accept the 'loss' of Vietnam to the Communists implied by the semi-partition the British had in mind. The call for 'united action' Dulles made on 29 March became, however, a source of controversy. The Administration was not 'thinking of anything "silly" such as committing American ground troops, but they thought that with wise political action in Indo-China combined with energetic attempts to train native troops the situation could be mastered'.[35]

The Eden-Dulles meetings in London did nothing to resolve the differences in viewpoint, rather the reverse. As the Franco-DRVN battle at Dien Bien Phu reached a climax, moreover, it seemed that the Administration contemplated some military action, and that alarmed the British. Dulles told Eden he was 'no partisan of an immediate air strike'. But 'there was no hope that the French would stay in the fight unless they could be given some hope within the next few weeks that a common defensive system could be drawn up which would cover at least parts of Indo-China'. The Vietnamese, 'with proper training and support' could match the Vietminh, he thought. 'If some experienced general, such as General Van Fleet, could be sent out to make terms with the French for the reorganization of operations and training, much might be achieved.'[36] The day before Dulles had told Richard Casey, the Australian minister for external affairs, that better training – under a Van Fleet – was essential, but it would take time. 'The difficulty of how to bridge the gap in time of the necessary few months was a great problem.'[37]

Livingston Merchant of the State Department spoke of steps to 'shore up the French will': the ad hoc coalition, he told Harold Caccia and Evelyn Shuckburgh of the Foreign Office, was intended as a 'deterrent'.[38] In the event it was to become, partly through Eden's initiative, the basis of the SEATO (Southeast Asia Treaty Organization) alliance, concluded soon after the Geneva agreements. The British had long sought an increased US commitment to the security of Southeast Asia, but characteristically they also desired to limit it, and avoid its being provocative. They also wanted other Asian states, if not to join, then not to oppose such an agreement. Success evaded them. Signatories included Pakistan, but not India, now its antagonist over Kashmir. It included only two Southeast Asian states, Thailand and the Philippines. A 'protocol' of the Manila agreement envisaged action in support of unilaterally designated states – Laos, Cambodia and 'free' Vietnam – in the event of aggression or armed attack. That was designed to avoid objections from the PRC. It had taken part at Geneva, and Zhou Enlai had accepted that Laos and Cambodia would be independent states. Making them allies would have been unacceptable. Unilateral designation sought to avoid it. But it conveyed the impression that the states were still less than independent, under some kind of protection.

What of Vietnam? Though recognized by the UK, the US and others, Bao Dai's regime had never secured a firm hold. The Americans, again persuaded by their experience in the Korean War, were convinced that they could nevertheless create a stable non-communist regime in the south, and it was on that they now concentrated. '[I]n the land of the blind, the one-eyed are kings', President Eisenhower told the National Security Council in October 1954. 'What we want to do is simply to authorize O'Daniel to use up to x millions of dollars to produce the maximum number of Vietnamese units which Prime Minister [Ngo Dinh] Diem can depend on to sustain himself in power.'[39] Much more was needed. A state had to be created as well as an army, and in face of nationalism, rather than, as in Korea, with the support of it. Could that be done?

The programme raised the issues that the Japanese had earlier faced in Manchukuo. Colonial regimes had needed collaborators to achieve even their limited purposes. Yet they were useless if they seemed too dependent, and even if useless were difficult to abandon without shaking the foundations of the regime itself. The advance of nationalism worsened the problem. Could a puppet regime win support? Would that not be even more doubtful if it was faced with an alternative nationalist-oriented regime? The regime would certainly need to demonstrate its independence. But was that compatible with the objectives of the puppeteer? And if not, could it be displaced, given its alleged independence in a world of states?

In his book *Weak States in the International System*, the Israeli scholar Michael I. Handel pointed out that so far there had been no systematic study of patron–client relationships among states. 'The reason is clear. The unequal nature of the patron-client relationship is contrary to the accepted norms of international conduct. Therefore both sides try to cover it up, and that makes it all the more difficult to study.'[40] Vietnam might have been a possible topic. It was far from covered up, yet the relationship is still worth studying from that point of view Handel outlines. The US intervened with Korea in mind. But the parallel was inexact. They introduced their own troops, the very reverse of what the Korean example was supposed to suggest. In so doing, moreover, they seemed to be fighting for a state they increasingly presented as South Vietnam. That appeared indeed to be parallel to 'South Korea'. But it could not stand against the urge to national unity that the DRVN was determined and able to evoke and capture.

A 'weak state', Handel tells us, can exert what is called in bargaining theory 'coercive deficiency', threatening to collapse. That, he says, can work only if the continued existence or support of a weak state is of outstanding importance to a great power ally.[41] That applied to the final collapse of the Republic of Vietnam in the 1970s: the US was not willing to continue its support. In the meantime it had sought to determine the terms of its support. That proved counter-productive. It was possible to get rid of Syngman Rhee in 1960 when the students rioted against vote-rigging in the elections. The ambassador (Walter McConaughy) presented an aide-memoire that has been indignantly described as not unlike that the Japanese presented to the Emperor Yi (Kojong) in 1905, 'more like a grand jury indictment of a criminal than the friendly suggestion of one sovereign nation to another'.[42] But the treatment of the recalcitrant 'puppet' in Vietnam was different: worse, one might say.

Late in 1954 Gen Paul Ely, the French commander, had collaborated with Gen Lawton Collins, the US ambassador, on a plan for overhauling the Vietnamese National Army. They did not bring Bao Dai's Prime Minister into their discussions, but wanted the agreed programme to 'come from Diem himself in [a] manner designed to enable him to get credit for enlisting French and U.S. aid in strengthening Vietnam Armed Forces'.[43] Ely thought Diem a 'losing game',[44] and Collins soon came to agree. He wanted Diem to bring Phan Huy Quat, a former defence minister, into his cabinet. The initiative, Secretary of State Dulles reminded him, had to come from the premier 'on internal matters such as specific ministers'.[45] Diem declined to appoint him. The Prime Minister was, Collins thought, authoritarian, arbitrary, unwilling to delegate: he would be unable to unify the factions, and Vietnam would be 'lost to communism'. There was no choice but to continue support for Diem, Dulles replied. 'There [is] no other suitable leader known to us.'[46]

Just as Collins had finally persuaded Dulles to change his line, Diem won his battle with his Binh Xuyen opponents in Saigon in April 1955. His triumph, Dulles observed, put the situation in a different perspective. 'For us at this time to participate in a scheme to remove Diem would not only be domestically impractical but highly detrimental to our prestige in Asia.'[47] His position had now been strengthened, Collins admitted, but 'this will not change Diem's basic incapacity to manage the affairs of Govt. His present success may even make it harder for us to persuade him to take competent men into [his] Govt., to decentralize authority to his ministers, and to establish sound procedures for the implementation of reform programs.' If Diem did not demonstrate improvement in his administrative skills, 'we should either withdraw our support from Vietnam, because our money will be wasted, or we should take such steps as can legitimately be taken to secure an effective new premier.'[48] Dulles again did not follow Collins' advice.

That was, Philip Catton suggests, a point of no return: it became increasingly difficult 'to contemplate a diplomatic withdrawal'. But the relationship was conceived in doubt. US support for Diem's leadership 'depended on his ability to satisfy Washington's concerns. Like a prisoner on probation, his future rested on his good conduct, as defined by his new superpower patron.' US officials 'appreciated that their need to work through an indigenous government placed limits on their influence in Vietnam. Yet how could they afford to adhere to traditional American principles – anticolonialism, self-determination, non-intervention – in the case of a client whose policies threatened to increase his vulnerability to a communist takeover?' The dilemma proved 'inescapable'.[49]

A rigged referendum deposed Bao Dai and made Diem President of a Republic. Washington approved. Indeed, while not openly encouraging a coup, Dulles had told a press conference that '[t]here is always the possibility of changing the status of a country. France no longer has a king.'[50] 'You will continue to give complete, loyal, and sincere support to the government of President Diem', Dulles told Frederick Reinhardt, Collins' successor, 'and you should deal with it as the independent and sovereign government which we believe it is and should be. The U.S. has no right and no desire to dictate the composition of the government of an independent and sovereign state.'[51]

'At first', Chester Bowles, a former Under-Secretary of State, declared in 1971, 'Diem demonstrated a heartening degree of courage and understanding.'[52] But by 1963 he had become an embarrassment, in particular because of his treatment of Buddhist protestors, and his regime was failing to deal with the Communist uprising, stimulated by the creation of the National Liberation Front in 1960. What was the US to do?

'If you order Vietnam around like a puppet on a string', Diem asked Margaret Higgins in August 1963, 'how will you be different – except in degree – from the French?'[53] It was not merely a matter of pride, but of asserting nationalist credentials. He was not a puppet, Seth Jacobs argues. 'Rarely did the local viceroy's agenda mesh perfectly with that of his bankroller; indeed American journalists tagged Diem as a "puppet who pulled his own strings".' He knew he needed American support to stay in power, 'but he was also a Vietnamese patriot who did not like foreigners occupying his country. Moreover, he wanted to preserve the image of South Vietnam as a sovereign country. It galled him that the Viet Minh were able to point to his American advisers as evidence of neo-colonialism. No third-world leader found the label "puppet" as repugnant as Diem did, and none worked harder to prove his nationalist credentials.' One means, Jacobs suggests, was defying American instructions.[54]

On his mission as Vice-President in May 1961, Lyndon Johnson had described Diem as the Winston Churchill of Southeast Asia. When Stanley Karnow asked if such encomia were sincere, he replied: 'Shit, man, he's the only boy we got out there'.[55] His report to Kennedy said the same in more decorous, less Johnsonian, language: the 'existing government in Saigon is the only realistic alternative to Viet Minh control', though there was 'a significant level of disaffection', especially in the rural areas. He recommended increased aid. He had asked Diem if he wanted American combat troops.

Diem declined: 'it would give the communists a propaganda windfall'.[56] Putting troops in was 'a sensitive internal issue' for Diem.[57]

His possible replacement was discussed within the State Department even during 1961. While he exercised 'effective control' over the Government, the US should take no action, overt or covert. In a possible coup, the ambassador should support him until he decided 'that the time for change had arrived'. Then the US should be prepared 'quickly to support the non-Communist person or group who then appears most capable of establishing effective control over the GVN'. The support should be 'strong enough to achieve rapid results but not so blatant as to make such a person or group appear as a United States puppet'. Meanwhile reforms should be urged on him, perhaps through a Presidential letter, with the implication that if he did not carry them out, the US would have to reconsider its policy to Vietnam. 'Such a letter would require a prior decision that we would be prepared if necessary to run the risk of suddenly withdrawing our support from Diem and of almost simultaneously throwing our weight behind the most likely replacement. Such a move would require preparation, secrecy, surprise, and toughness.'[58]

Diem compared Maxwell Taylor's mission late in 1961 to Marshall's post-war mission to China: the attempt to impose reforms on Chiang Kai-shek had only helped the Communists. 'Vietnam does not want to be a protectorate.' The American demands threatened to give the communists a 'monopoly on nationalism'.[59] 'U.S. officials … had entered a diplomatic no-man's land in their attempt to fashion a relationship going beyond friendly advice but stopping short of colonial controls.'[60] If the US thought he was not in control, however, he felt the same about US advisers. 'They come without passports', he told the French ambassador [Roger Lalouette] early in 1963. 'I don't know how many there are nor how I can control them.' The US Defense Department said that they were 'creating a colonial impression among the people'.[61]

As the Buddhist crisis developed, Kennedy decided he needed someone in Saigon 'who could make Diem listen to American counsel'. He appointed a high-level Republican, Henry Cabot Lodge. 'They can send ten Lodges', Diem responded, 'but I will not permit myself or my country to be humiliated.'[62] Before Lodge arrived, he struck at the Buddhist pagodas. The State Department declared that his action violated his promise of 'a policy of reconciliation' and that the Administration deplored 'repressive acts of this nature'. 'Kennedy and his advisers began to talk about engineering a coup.'[63] Lodge later denied that he had been sent out to remove Diem. But at their first encounter, he insisted that there should be reform, otherwise aid would be cut, and then avoided contact with the palace. 'They have not done anything I asked. They know what I want. Why should I keep asking?'[64]

Nor, unlike his predecessor Frederick Nolting, did he cold-shoulder dissident generals. Indeed he thought the built-up ARVN (Army of the

Republic of Vietnam) was the only alternative, and Lucien Conein, a ex-CIA subordinate, was instructed to tell them that the US would not look unfavourably on a change of government. No coup leader emerged. Lodge hesitated: '[a]ction on our part in these circumstances would be a shot in the dark'. In the absence of more senior officials the response from Washington was drafted on 24 August 1963 by Roger Hilsman, assistant secretary of state for Far Eastern affairs (FE), with the collaboration of Averell Harriman, roving ambassador, and Michael Forrestal of NSC (National Security Council), opponents of the Diem experiment. 'Diem must be given [a] chance to rid himself of [his brother] Nhu. … If, in spite of all your efforts, Diem remains obdurate and refuses, then we must face [the] possibility that Diem himself cannot be preserved.' Lodge was instructed to tell key military leaders that the US would find it impossible to continue supporting the Vietnam Government if Buddhist grievances were not redressed and Nhu divested of power. He was instructed to 'examine all possible alternative leadership and make detailed plans as to how we might bring about Diem's replacement if this should become necessary'. Kennedy and Rusk cleared the cable 'hastily and over the phone'.[65]

Previously hesitant, Lodge now wanted to go further. He would not present Diem with another ultimatum, but go direct to the generals, and tell them that 'we [are] prepared [to] have Diem without [the] Nhus, but it is in effect up to them whether to keep him'. The State Department agreed. Paul Harkins, head of the Military Assistance Command (MACV), contended that there was no guarantee a new government would do better than Diem's, and argued that he should at least be given a chance to remove his brother. 'We are launched on a course from which there is no respectable turning back: the overthrow of the Diem government', Lodge responded. If the generals thought the US were hesitating, they would get cold feet.[66]

Kennedy, the fiasco of the Bay of Pigs enterprise in Cuba in mind, wanted to be able to change course if necessary. 'To be successful', Lodge replied, 'this operation must be an essentially Vietnamese affair with a momentum of its own. Should this happen, you might not be able to control it, i.e., the "go signal" may be given by the generals.' In fact they seemed reluctant. 'The days come and go and nothing happens. I am sure', Lodge told Rusk, 'that the best way to handle this matter is by a truly Vietnamese movement, even if it puts me rather in the position of pushing a piece of spaghetti.'[67]

In late September Defense Secretary McNamara and JCS Chairman Maxwell Taylor reported on a visit to South Vietnam. They advised sanctions designed to indicate disapproval of Diem's political programme, but declared that Washington should not 'encourage actively a change of government'. 'No initiative should now be taken to give any covert encouragement to a coup', Kennedy told Lodge on 2 October. But now Duong Van Minh told Conein that a coup was imminent. He did not want support: he asked only for assurances that the US would not thwart the plan and that aid would continue. An eighth Buddhist self-immolation followed the same day. Lodge recommended giving Minh the assurances he sought. 'While we do not wish to stimulate [a] coup, we also do not wish to leave [the] impression that [the] United States would thwart a change of government or deny economic or military assistance to a new regime', the President indicated.[68]

Lodge accepted that he would have limited advance knowledge of the coup: indeed he welcomed that. But again President Kennedy hesitated. The worst outcome would be failure, and the US wanted to consider the coup plans. Impossible, Lodge replied: the conspiracy would leak. Harkins, however, belittled the conspirators. There were 'no generals qualified to take over'. And the US had backed Diem for eight years. 'To me, it seems incongruous now to get him down, kick him around, and get rid of him.' The President disliked Lodge's advice that the coup could not be stopped. It was a reckless way to run foreign policy. He could not cancel the coup, Lodge declared, except by betraying the plotters to Diem, and that 'would make traitors of us'. America's word would never be trusted by Vietnamese again,[69] he curiously added.

The coup was quickly over and no civil war ensued. To that extent Kennedy's fears were unjustified. But the Gia Long palace had to be stormed – Nguyen Van Thieu, a colonel who commanded the Fifth Infantry, led the final charge – and then it was found that the brothers had fled to Cholon. They were murdered. Whatever Diem might have done, said Kennedy, 'it should not have ended like this'.[70] A series of revolving-door governments followed. 'I can scarcely believe the Americans would be so stupid', Ho Chi Minh remarked. 'Diem was one of the most competent lackeys of the U.S. imperialists.' The lackey administration could not now be stabilized. The coup would not be the last.[71]

'Neither Diem's regime nor any of the succeeding juntas and civilian cliques that Washington underwrote could take the mantle of Vietnamese leadership from Ho Chi Minh because they all owed their existence to a foreign power and were not expressions of indigenous nationalism.'[72] Washington could not win support for its Saigon client. A reverse was 'inevitable'. Diem's position was difficult, Pham Van Dong had noted. 'He is unpopular, and the more unpopular he is, the more American aid he will require to stay in power. And the more American aid he receives, the more he will look like a puppet of the Americans, and the less likely he is to win popular support.'[73] A former RVN (Republic of Vietnam) general made the same point. 'Since the dependence and subordination of the Vietnam government was so obviously demonstrated by the predominant presence and power of the Americans, the Vietnamese general public could not refrain from viewing their government as a puppet deprived of all national prestige, lacking in a national mandate and thus being untrustworthy.'[74]

The patron's position is problematic as well as the client's. If the latter is not meeting the former's expectations, what is to be done? In the colonial period a dependent could be displaced more readily, though even colonial governments were rightly wary of major changes. How could a head of state, necessarily alleged to be independent, be changed? The US Government clearly favoured a coup. The President was characteristically hesitant, but even he was more afraid of what would be said if it failed than apprehensive of what would happen if it succeeded. 'I still think that probably one of the most stupid, as well as the most shameful, instances in our policy was our cutting up of Diem a couple of years ago … without an alternative', John Hanes, an aide to Dulles, told a journalist (Richard Crowl) in 1966. 'I'm no great moralist, and I assume the Diem regime was many of the things that people said about it. So are a lot of regimes around the world. But to take a reasonably strong regime, to have no alternative, and to abandon it … is sheer stupidity.'[75]

Lodge's advice for the new President was hardly helpful. 'This unhappy country emerged from colonialism ten years ago and has been trying to get along since then with help from us that is, in all truth, advisory and not at all colonial', he wrote in May 1964. 'The question clearly arises as to whether this "advisory" phase is not about to be played out. … Whether it means that we will have a High Commissioner or a Commissioner-General, or a man who really gives the orders under the title of Ambassador, will have to be determined.'[76]

With the fall of the Quat government in 1965, there was no government in South Vietnam, said Ball. How could the war be won? 'You don't understand', Rusk replied, 'that at the time of Korea that we had to go out and dig Syngman Rhee out of the bush where he was hiding; there was no government in Korea either, and we were able to come through.'[77]

In neighbouring Laos, Dulles had pursued a different policy. The leading post-Geneva figure was Prince Suvanna Phuma. He believed that the future of the state could be preserved only by following a neutral foreign policy and indeed that his state had to have a neutralist government. Those views ran up against the policies of all three US agencies, CIA, State Department, and Pentagon. Their aim was to make the fragile newly independent kingdom into an anti-Communist bastion. That was, as the British ambassador John Addis put it in 1964, 'never physically or objectively possible. The main reasons for this were the nature and position of the country and the nature of the Laotian people. The more "success" the Americans had in setting up a pro-American and anti-Communist regime in Laos the more successfully (in the real sense) it was subverted by the [communist-led] Pathet Lao [PL] with support from North Vietnam. This was the inevitable process of cause and effect, which was demonstrated again and again right up to the settlement of 1962.'[78] Then Laos was neutralized. The negotiations in Geneva and elsewhere were exceedingly protracted.[79] One reason was the mutual attachment of the US and the army commander whom it patronized, Phumi Nosavan, and did not wish to abandon.

The US had created and sustained a large army in Laos. A United States Operations Mission (USOM) had been set up in Vientiane in January 1955, consisting of 200 men headed by Gen. John A. Heintges. The US Joint Chiefs of Staff considered that the army should be down-sized and focused on internal policing. '[T]aking into account the potential political influence of such an army and the stimulus to the economy that army salaries would provide', the diplomatic mission in Vientiane recommended an army of 23,600 men, and the Joint Chiefs acquiesced in view of the 'political considerations'. The Geneva agreements prohibited the establishment of a Military Assistance Advisory Group (MAAG).[80] In order to train this substantial force, however, the State Department set up 'an American military mission in disguise', the Programs Evaluation Office (PEO), attached to USOM.[81]

Perhaps with Korea again in mind, the State Department at times presented the Laos army in terms of the containment of China. It was, as Dommen stresses, not the kind of army that might have helped the RLG (Royal Lao Government) deal with the activities of the PL-backed Neo Lao Hak Sat and the mixture of suasion and coercion through which it extended its control in the countryside.[82] It was 'not a counterguerrilla force, but a conventional army'.[83] On the other hand the Royal Lao Army gave the US a political instrument, which it indeed never quite abandoned. But this 'cuckoo in the nest', as Stuart Simmonds called it,[84] was hard, if not counter-productive, to use. Would it not be seen as a tool of imperialism? Would it displace civilian politics and politicians? Was it amenable to control?

Distrusting Suvanna's neutralism, the US promoted, through the CIA, the 'Young Turks' of the CDIN (Comité de Défense des Intérêts Nationaux). Phuy Sananikone's government included some of them, excluded Suvanna, and added Phumi. When he reshuffled it at the end of 1959, Phumi attempted a coup. The US was unwilling to accept a purely military government. The new government, however, included him as Defence Minister, with control of 80 per cent of the budget. Konglae's neutralist coup followed in August 1960, and a new Suvanna Phuma government was set up. Phumi, supported by Prince Boun Oum and by Sarit of Thailand, and by the CIA, set up a Revolutionary Committee. Suvanna appealed to the SU, while the US aided the rebels. Phumi captured Vientiane after a 72-hour battle. But Konglae retreated on the Plain of Jars, and had the support of the Pathet Lao and also of the North Vietnamese. Apprehensive that the war might extend, the British sought to bring about a conference that would provide for the neutralization of Laos. The Kennedy Administration reluctantly agreed. It began to meet in Geneva in May 1961. Its main task was to establish effective and acceptable international controls. But, though it was not explicitly on the agenda, there was another task: to create a viable government.

The only possible head of it was Suvanna Phuma. The Americans, however, feared lest he would be too yielding so far as the Communists were concerned. After the Princes had met – along with Phumi in Zurich in June – the General was summoned to Washington. At the NSC meeting on 29 June, it was agreed 'that appropriate encouragement should be given to Phumi and that he should be given to understand that there are points at which the United States will intervene to prevent a Communist Laos this summer'. Those points, however, must be 'measured and decided' by the US, not by Phumi. Careful instructions were to go to Ambassador Brown in Vientiane and Phumi 'encouraged' to stay in close touch with him.[85]

In a most elaborate statement Rusk told Phumi that there were circumstances in which the US would find it necessary to send in its forces, but they could not be defined 'precisely and in advance'. The decision had to remain with the US. At the same he reiterated the advice the US had given not to make 'premature concessions' on the formation of a coalition government. 'The question arises how this advice can be followed, when it is accompanied by a feeling of uncertainty.' The only answer was to maintain 'daily contacts'.[86] The President took a similar line. Exotically, he adduced Talleyrand's achievement at the Congress of Vienna as a model.[87]

Phumi 'must have been rather confused', as Kaiser writes.[88] Though he surely realized that there was no prospect of an early US intervention, he was certainly encouraged not to be too yielding over the formation of a government. In Vientiane Ambassador Brown read part of his instructions to his British colleague. Addis feared that nothing had been said to Phumi 'to suggest that the Americans believe the possibility exists of reaching basis of an agreement between East and West on a peaceful settlement of the Laotian question'. Nor was he apparently told that, if American forces had to enter Laos, they would be 'limited to political objectives in support of negotiated settlement', rather than undertaking 'an unlimited military commitment'. A major purpose of the talks seemed to have been to boost Phumi's morale, overlooking the need to persuade him that it was necessary to work out 'a real compromise over possession and exercise of power in Laos'. The general effect, Addis feared, might be to encourage Phumi to 'go through the motions of reaching a negotiated settlement right to the last moment and then throw over the agreement in order to perpetuate the split and hold on to what he has got, in the confident belief that the Americans are bound to support him'.[89]

It was a percipient forecast. The Americans found it difficult to handle their 'puppets'. 'It is sometimes difficult, most great powers discover, to avoid becoming the satellite of one's "satellites"', as Hilsman later wrote.[90] But there was a special factor in this case. The Americans – even, perhaps, the President – retained a long-standing distrust of Suvanna. They were apprehensive that he could not, even if he would, sustain what they would consider a really neutral government. They argued that it was necessary to ensure that the right-wing was duly represented in a coalition, and that Phumi should not accept an unacceptable version. Indeed they were not willing to abandon reliance on the army they had built up until at least they were far more reassured about Suvanna's coalition, if ever. Phumi was to take advantage of their reluctance. Together these factors were to delay the formation of the coalition. Yet once more delays did not work to the advantage of the policies the Americans were basically pursuing. As time went by, Suvanna's independence of the communists diminished, and with it the prospect of a truly neutral government.

Though the negotiations in Geneva advanced, no Laotian government had emerged by October. Boun Oum and Phumi, said Harriman, were 'dragging their feet', and some Americans were not anxious that they should hurry.[91] Phumi was, he found, 'most difficult to handle'.[92] In a telegram for Rusk and Kennedy on 6 November, he argued that Ambassador Brown must now adopt a 'tough line' towards Phumi. He doubted that the general was acting or would act in good faith. '[E]ither from inertia or by adroit, deliberate action', he was leading the US into a war in Laos, in which, Harriman believed, China would join. 'It is fantastic that General Phumi, who is entirely US creation, should be permitted to continue to dictate American policy. Time is running out fast.'[93]

On 12 November the State Department gave Brown further guidance in the expectation that a three-prince meeting would take place on the Plain of Jars. If Suvanna kept the Defence and Interior ministries, Phumi could be a Deputy Premier, along with a PL Deputy Premier. He could then have a 'comprehensive view activities various ministries', and he, the King and other non-Communist elements could be assured that the US attitude to the Suvanna government would be 'strongly influenced by their assessment as to whether genuine neutrality is present or whether PL takeover is in process'. Suvanna must be reassured that the US wished to support him if he formed a government 'so composed as to provide maximum possibility of maintaining country's neutral status'.[94]

Yielding over the ministry of defence, and advising Phumi to do so, were risky, Brown responded. He would have to be forced into it, and he, and others in Laos and neighbouring countries, would question the 'reliability of US support', and conservative leaders, army officers and officials might be tempted 'to come to terms with what would appear to them to be the winning side'. Phumi might withdraw into exile 'or take the gamble of unsupported withdrawal to the south' or even persuade the King to reject Suvanna's slate. If the US did not support Phumi as minister of defence, 'or some alternative arrangement which Phoumi himself considers provides equal safeguards for conservative beachhead in Suvanna government', MAAG and the agencies believed that the Army would be demoralized and disintegrate, and Laos would become communist, which would have 'dangerous consequences for US prestige in the rest of Southeast Asia, probably all of Asia', and facilitate Viet Cong use of the south Laos corridor into South Vietnam.[95]

In the event Phumi sabotaged a further meeting of the princes. He saw the proposed coalition as diminishing his power and hampering his ambition,

Addis believed, and he therefore preferred to prolong the status quo in the hope that something better would turn up. The US was unwilling to impose sanctions: they were weapons that could be used only once, and would so weaken Phumi that he would be handicapped in negotiations and the balance in the coalition government would be impaired. But Suvanna Phuma's outline for a new government was, Addis believed, a necessary compromise that left little room for manoeuvre. The only option was to put pressure on Phumi. He might then resume fighting, resign, or do nothing. The most likely reaction was the last: 'he could exist for some time on his reserves'.[96]

In the State Department the desk officer told the Australians that it might ultimately be necessary to pull the rug out from under Phumi. 'Obviously United States did not want to do this since, however bad, Phumi was the West's principal asset in negotiations for coalition and in situation which would exist in Laos after establishment of coalition.'[97] The Americans, as Addis recognized from his conversations with Brown, tended still to think in terms of balance in a Suvanna-led government and also of control of the army. They thus tied themselves to a puppet who had his own agenda.

Ambassador Brown put his foot down, and a meeting was held on 26 December. The State Department now bought Suvanna's package for the structure of the coalition government. Phumi did not. He told his CIA adviser, Jack Hasey, that he was 'deeply shocked by defeatist policy of US'.[98] Brown, however, recommended the suspension of military deliveries, lest 'we fall deeper into Phumi's hands and remain at impasse in negotiations for formation of government'.[99] 'What we need now is action and action on Phumi where it hurts and where he still lingeringly hopes we will never desert him, namely in the military field.'[100] But the President had second thoughts about applying sanctions. American public opinion would not stand for it, Harriman said, even if the US government wished to impose them at that stage, and it did not.[101]

In the event, Phumi seemingly yielded. Brown had gone to see him on the morning of the 18 January. Phumi should allow Defence and Interior to go to neutrals and negotiate for a coalition government on that basis. Had he considered the consequences for the people of Laos if the US were unable to continue its support? 'Phumi said Brown should not threaten. … He realized that without US aid Laos was dead. If we wanted to stop aid, that was our privilege. We should just do it and not threaten it.' Brown appealed to Boun Oum, making a 'warm plea' for him to consider his responsibilities to the people and seize the chance to agree on a government. Phumi then said it was a 'very difficult decision', and he needed time to think. Harriman called in the afternoon, and, focusing on Boun Oum, urged him 'most earnestly' to get on with the negotiation. Phumi said he thought something would come of the meeting of the princes that had been arranged later that day. 'This was the first hint of any give in rigidity of position.' Harriman turned to him and said: 'you are a Lao for whom we have great respect. We hope that you, yourself, have a good future as well as your country.' He was 'obviously relieved and gratified'.[102] A communiqué was issued on 19 January. But the prospect of a settlement was put off by military incidents, in particular in the Nam Tha region late in January 1962.

The SD distinguished between Thailand as an 'ally' and South Vietnam as a 'client'.[103] Though Britain had thought that Thailand – which had allied with the Japanese and accepted territory from them – needed to 'work its passage' back into acceptance at the end of the war, the US had disregarded the Thai declaration of war and opposed what it considered a punitive policy. Under the wartime ruler Pibun again from 1948, Thailand sent troops to Korea, accepted US military aid, and joined SEATO. In the Laos crisis Prime Minister Sarit supported Phumi, and the US sought his support in handling their puppet. Before that was implemented, Nam Tha fell to neutralist/communist forces. Perhaps Phumi hoped that the reaction to that would enable him to wriggle out of a commitment to negotiate. Kennedy's answer, however, was not to back him, but to send troops to Thailand. That would show the US did not mean to give in to the Communists, but without assuring Phumi of further backing. American policy now had three objectives, Rusk told the British and French ambassadors on 14 May: to warn the Russians of the possible consequences of PL action; to reassure the Thais who were 'near to panic'; and to persuade Phumi that he could not 'suck them into Laos'. The move was not a formal SEATO action, but the US looked for a 'representational presence' in Thailand of forces from other SEATO countries. That would 'help domestically' and 'serve as an additional warning to the Communists and a further reassurance to Thailand (and South Vietnam)'.[104] Restraining a puppet led to propping up a client and an ally. But it is seldom noticed that, like Diem, Sarit was not keen on the presence of US troops.[105]

With this step the Laos crisis wound down. A coalition government was formed, and the conference concluded in July. But the neutralization of Laos did not mean that the US abandoned Phumi. Indeed the PL on the one hand and Phumi and the police and security apparatus on the other effectively destroyed the neutralists. Neither the DRV – which did not withdraw its forces – nor the US – which armed 15,000 Hmong guerrillas – honoured the Laos agreement.

Two forms of puppetry had been in use. One related the patron to a client ruler or state, the other related the patron to an important figure who was influential but not the ruler. In neither case was the puppet readily controlled. In the former case it was indeed clear that more control would reduce the value of the client: nationalist support would be lost, not won, if the puppet was clearly controlled by imperialists or neo-colonialists. In the second case that consideration did not apply. But the support the US afforded Phumi helped to prevent the neutralization of Laos and the creation of an effective government under Suvanna Phuma.

Puppetry was intrinsically problematic. But it is also true that in Vietnam and Laos it was deployed in difficult circumstances. Those related above all to the Vietnam War, in which the Communist-led struggle for unification was interlinked with the increasingly tripartite Cold War struggle. A war in South Vietnam was sure to involve its neighbours, Cambodia and Laos. The war also produced differences among the puppeteers. The Kennedy Administration, itself divided over Vietnam and Laos, was scarcely able to enforce the decisions it reached on the US officials in the region. The CIA was a state within a state like the Inquisition, Prime Minister Macmillan suggested.[106]

In some sense puppetry was a successor to and substitute for the collaboration colonialists had sought from rulers when they retained them or from elite elements when they sought to turn them to account. It echoed one of its problems. Could the US drop Phumi and give its full support to Suvanna Phuma? McGeorge Bundy wondered: 'the real problem would be how you can change horses in mid-stream without getting a complete deterioration of the situation.'[107] It differed, of course, in respect of the acknowledgment that independent states were involved and that they were part of world of states not a world of empires.

In practice 'puppetry' had another disadvantage. The Western powers, particularly the US, misunderstood the position of the DRV: it was assumed that it was a puppet or satellite of the 'Bloc' or of its increasingly antagonistic leaders. Moscow itself seemed to believe it, too: in the end North Vietnam would fall into line. 'In fact', as Ang Cheng Guan puts it, 'the Vietnamese Communists were remarkably in control of their own decision making.'[108] Even now, much less is known of the SU's decision-making, let alone the PRC's, than of that of the US or the UK. But it seems that their satellites followed an irregular orbit. Nor was it easy successfully to combine support for local Communist parties with support for national governments.

Though it was to fail, the neutralization of Laos attracted Prince Sihanouk, the Head of State of Cambodia. It would indeed be a high price to pay for the security it might offer, since neutralization – not the same as neutralism, a policy, or neutrality, a unilateral stance – involved abandoning some of a state's sovereignty. It 'seemed potentially attractive only to relatively minor states'.[109] But a small state might find it worthwhile to pay that price if it was preserved from greater powers. A neutralized Cambodia, as the British FO put it in 1963, would be 'much more limited in its freedom of action than Prince Sihanouk is today'.[110] Indeed Sihanouk did not see his neutralist policy as attractive in itself: it was not an ideology but a necessity.

His stance should be seen as another reaction to the problems emergent states faced in the region in the Cold War phase. Once an independent state – indeed one of exemplary power and influence – Cambodia had been much reduced by the nineteenth century, to the benefit of its now greater neighbours, Vietnam and Thailand, but it escaped a final disaster by turning to the French and accepting their protection in the 1860s. They made it part of French Indo-China, in which it preserved its autonomy, though subject to Vietnamese migration as well as French controls. French Indo-China could not be re-established when the French attempted to return after the Second World War. As King, Sihanouk captured nationalist support by his 'crusade' for independence, rewarded in 1953. But how could that independence be preserved in the face of ancient enemies like the Thais and the Vietnamese and in the context of a Cold War among the super-powers? Now there was no French protection. One of his neighbours was an 'ally' of the US, another a 'client'. Sihanouk's answer was 'neutrality'.

He would not become the puppet of one of the super-powers, avoiding 'satellization'. That would only attract the intervention of its opponent. But there was more to it than that. The position of those powers changed as time passed. The Americans became more deeply involved in Southeast Asia, but Sihanouk could not convince himself that they would stay there forever. The Chinese, themselves passing through the Great Leap Forward and the Cultural Revolution in the late 1950s and 1960s, sustained a rhetoric about the future. Ultimately they might be in a position of power, and they were more likely to be a permanent feature of the future of mainland Southeast Asia than the US.

Nor was the position of more immediate neighbours stable. Thailand and Vietnam Sihanouk saw as historical enemies and contemporary threats. Would the US restrain them or encourage them? Perhaps leaning towards China – without abandoning neutrality – would encourage the Americans to adopt the former course rather than the latter. Again it made sense not to alienate China, if not to become what James Cable at the British Foreign Office called 'a protected Satellite'.[111] In addition, it might be expected to restrain the ambitions of a Vietnam reunified under Communist leadership and prevent any attempt on its part to recreate a kind of Indo-China under its control.

Beneath a great deal of posturing – mixed with an extraordinary vanity – good sense, striking forethought and sound analysis were the foundation for Sihanouk's views. But – apart from those personal features, themselves to some degree intended as part of the policy, perhaps, but too exaggerated in fact to support it – their realization was inhibited by the expansion of the Vietnam war. Cambodia's territory was used by the DRV to back up the Liberation Front in South Vietnam, and the Americans and the South Vietnamese crossed the frontier to deal with them well before the fall of Sihanouk in 1970. The war made it impossible to secure a neutralization agreement. It also made it impossible to sustain neutrality, except by allowing both sides to fight it out on Cambodian territory, and that stimulated criticism within Cambodia. Opposition to Sihanouk could seize on the nationalism that he had done nothing to diminish. The Vietnamese were now in Cambodia after all.

His handling of the opposition was indeed his undoing. His was a right-wing regime at home, whatever its neutralism in foreign policy. Yet the right-wing was increasingly dissatisfied. Nor did he conceal his contempt for politicians, or his unwillingness to listen to the advice of others. He cannot have expected his overthrow in March 1970. But he rather expected that successors would pursue unwise policies, as indeed they did. Attacks on resident Vietnamese were followed by attempts to drive out the DRV/FLN from their sanctuaries and by open intervention by South Vietnamese and US forces. The war destroyed the new Cambodian Republic and brought the Khmer Rouge to power.

Aside from Brunei, only Timor now remained under a colonial power, and its fate was decided in the context of the debacle of US policies in Indo-China. In a talk with a member of the British High Commission, Rajaratnam of Singapore had tended to discount the idea that Malaysia might find Indonesia's intervention in Timor a precedent for its own handling of Brunei. But under the Tunku's successor Abdul Razak Malaysia was disposed to challenge the Sultanate's continued dependence on its British protectors. In 1975 it sponsored a Partai Rakyat Brunei delegation to the UN Committee on Decolonization.[112] Indonesia's action might be more than a question of precedent. 'The Malaysians are said to have taken the attitude that "what pinches Indonesia pinches Malaysia"', the British embassy in Jakarta reported in respect of a visit Ghazali paid in September 1975. 'It seems not to have been lost on the Indonesians that any assistance they seek from Malaysia over Portuguese Timor might involve some future quid pro quo over Brunei.'[113]

Suharto was resolved at that point still to focus on covert intervention in Timor. Rather ironically, he was anxious to avoid renewing the reputation his predecessor had gained for Indonesia in the latter stages of Confrontation. The Malaysians in fact thought he should act promptly. The Malaysian ambassador in Jakarta told his British counterpart, John Ford, that his government favoured the incorporation of Timor, and that elements in it, such as Ghazali, thought the Indonesians were 'being over-slow about the whole business'.[114] The Prime Minister shared his view. The Prime Minister's principal private secretary had told the British High Commissioner on 8 December that Razak's only criticism had been that the Indonesians 'had not acted firmly earlier'.[115]

In 1976 Malaysia sponsored a UN resolution in favour of elections in Brunei, the end of the ban on political parties, and the return of post-rebellion exiles; and in 1977 the resolution was adopted.[116] It was, as Leifer put it, seeking to destabilize the sultanate, 'ostensibly from a fear that it would become a contagious source of insecurity in northern Borneo in much the same way as Indonesia's military establishment had contemplated the deteriorating situation in East Timor'.[117] Such actions only made the sultanate more unwilling to relinquish Britain's protection.[118]

Razak's successor, Hussein Onn, took steps to improve relations, however, and, meeting in nearby Labuan in May 1978, he and Suharto expressed the hope that the sultanate would join the Association of South East Asian Nations (ASEAN) when it became independent.[119]

That line was supported by Singapore, 'which had come to regard membership [of ASEAN] as a political asset'.[120] Prime Minister Lee Kuan Yew had sustained a close relationship with the sultans and stood aside from the challenge Malaysia had mounted in the UN.[121] In March 1979 he became the first ASEAN leader to visit Brunei. Attending the 1982 ASEAN Ministerial Meeting as observer, Prince Md Bolkiah said Brunei was now 'more confident of the support and co-operation' of ASEAN countries, and stressed 'mutual respect for the sovereignty, independence and territorial integrity' as 'the basis for good relations'.[122] ASEAN thus helped Brunei towards 'full independence' in 1984, and itself moved a step towards regional inclusion on the basis of national sovereignty. Brunei retained a close connexion with Singapore: both were 'wary of their giant neighbours', as V. G. Kulkarni put it.[123] 'Timorization' remained a Singaporean concern, Indorf suggested in 1984.[124] In the event, however, Timor was to become independent, finally replicating the 'successor state' character of the post-colonial world.

A system of Westphalia-Versailles states emerged in the Southeast Asian region by a tangled and varied route. Their political format also turned out to be very diverse. They had, however, much in common. One feature was the inheritance of frontiers from the colonial states by states that by whatever means they were ruled regarded themselves as nation states. Another might be described by the novelty of independence. They differed not only in political system, but in wealth and power. Now they had to make foreign and defence policy for themselves, both in respect of their neighbours and of other powers in the region and beyond. Their stances differed, both according to their domestic circumstances and their international position. How could they sustain security among themselves and within the wider world? Would they have to modify their newly acquired sovereignty?

If the Andaman and Nicobar islands are part of Southeast Asia, their position was as ever exceptional. Site of the Azad Hind government, they were made over to India when it became independent and seen as strategically important to it. India speaks the language of a latter-day colonial power in the islands and recalls the ambiguities of the past amidst the ambitions of the present. What is the position of 'aborigines' under a settler regime? What is the objective of 'development'? How much self-government should the settlers enjoy? The Union Territory of the Andaman and Nicobar Islands has no elected assembly, but a Pradesh Council with the Administrator as ex-officio chairman. There are calls among the settlers for more democratization. But no one imagines that an independent state will be created, even if a 'state' emerged within India.

7 Regionalism

The emergence of independent states – and in some cases their failure to emerge – had taken place in a changing international context, without which it cannot indeed be fully understood. The conflict between the two super-powers, the US and the SU, continued throughout the 1970s and 1980s. Indeed it took on new dimensions, with the Soviet attempt to recreate a world-wide fleet and its invasion of Afghanistan and the US 'star wars' initiative. The disintegration of the Union in 1991 came as a surprise to almost every observer, though there was wisdom after the event. That seldom recognized the risks that Lenin and Stalin had built into the empire they had created. Their view that nationalism could be cultural, but not political, was mistaken.

China, of course, played a role in the dénouement. The second phase in the Cold War had begun in the latter days of the Cultural Revolution, well before the death of Mao. But after his death and the succession struggle that followed, China changed its domestic as well as its foreign policy. Under Deng Xiao-ping it resolved to utilize its resources and its people in a new way. China began, in the loose phrase of the day, to 'rise'. That had implications for the world at large, particularly after the collapse of the SU, and for Southeast Asia, too. China had at last clearly joined the 'Westphalia' world. But how would it use the rules? If the world now accommodated mini-states, how would it accommodate a maxi-state? – one, too, that rapidly industrialized in the context of a new economic globalization.

The shifts were promptly recognized in Southeast Asia. The indication in the late 1960s that the US would not keep its forces there forever, as Sihanouk put it, had been coupled with the withdrawal of the British from their base in Singapore. States in maritime Southeast Asia would need to reconsider their attitude to China. Perhaps victorious Vietnamese would follow a more traditional policy? In the event, provoked by the Khmer Rouge, they invaded Cambodia. That rescued it from a murderous regime, but also revived the apprehension that they were aiming to realize a new Indo-Chinese federation. China engaged in a rather ineffective punitive action. It also offered the Khmer Rouge political support. And in that it was joined by ASEAN. The diplomatic pressure, coupled with the exhaustion of

Vietnam and the implosion of the Soviet regime that backed it, led to the installation of a new regime in Cambodia under the auspices of the UN.

The combination might seem surprising, and at the time seemed discreditable, such was the evil reputation of the Khmer Rouge. But it had a logic. Several states in Southeast Asia – Indonesia, Malaysia, Thailand, the Philippines and Singapore – had drawn together at the end of Confrontation. The basis of their association in ASEAN was eminently Westphalian: sovereignty, non-interference, territorial integrity. Designed partly to accommodate Indonesia's claim to primacy without yielding to its control, such principles echoed those adopted in the previous decade by the Afro-Asian conference held at Bandung in 1955. Those in turn echoed the principles that Zhou had agreed with Nehru in 1954 during the co-existence phase in the PRC's foreign policy. Entering the UN at last in 1972, the PRC would, it could he hoped, endorse and support those principles.

The 1954 agreement followed Nehru's acceptance that Tibet was part of China. A preamble to the agreement, signed shortly before the opening of the Geneva conference, declared that the governing principles should be mutual respect for sovereignty and territorial integrity, non-aggression, non-interference in each other's internal affairs, equality and mutual benefit, and peaceful co-existence. In an exchange of letters on the occasion, Zhou suggested that those principles could be the basis of agreement on any outstanding questions, and Nehru made 'a suitable reply'.[1]

Those principles, as Coral Bell put it, were to become 'rather a theme song with the Chinese communists'. They were, she adds, 'unexceptionable sentiments'.[2] Chen Jian suggests that for the Chinese leaders the principles represented 'a series of new basic codes in conducting international affairs and politics that were fundamentally different from dominant codes and norms created by Western powers'. China's initiating them would 'further justify its claim to China's centrality in international relations'.[3] But they were no more and no less than core principles for a world of states, and as such an echo of those that underpinned the UN itself, and indeed of those that the US had seen as a basis for peace with Japan back in 1941. At no cost, indeed, China was demonstrating that, though not yet a member of the UN, it deserved to be treated as one.

The principles were employed at Geneva, which Zhou saw as an opportunity to raise China's international status. At Bandung the following year he was at his most conciliatory. China, it had been decided, should 'strive for expanding the united front for world peace, promoting national independence movements, and creating conditions for establishing and enhancing our country's ties and diplomatic relations with various Asian and African countries'. The delegation resolved to 'emphasize that China shared history, culture and the modern experience of suffering from imperialist and colonialist aggression with other asian and African countries, so as to ensure that the conference would be successful'.[4]

A number of more pro-Western countries led the conference to amplify and qualify the principles – five principles became, as the State Department saw it, ten commandments.[5] But generally it was the five principles that a reference to Bandung continued to evoke. Inter alia, they became a basis for ASEAN – scarcely what Zhou and its delegation had intended – and subsequently for its recent attempt to extend its approach, the 'ASEAN Way', to the relationships among all the nation states of East Asia. That approach, though based on Westphalia principles, might be regarded as another state system within Southeast Asia, if not within East Asia as a whole. It was Westphalia-Versailles modified.

'Sovereignty and independence are highly valued, not least because it is still within living memory for many that they were denied by Western and/or Asian imperialists.'[6] The 'ASEAN Way' accepts the sovereignty of individual states, which was indeed the founding principle of the Association. But it seeks to avoid conflict among them, resolving difficulties if it can, putting them off if it cannot. It does not modify the Westphalia principles as much as the EU. Far from it. But security is bought at some cost to the exercise of sovereign powers, however strongly the founding principles are stated.

The Association stopped short of a region-wide neutralization, such as Malaysia once advocated. That would have meant, as had been apparent when the neutralization of individual states was undertaken or contemplated, a substantial curtailment of the normal exercise of power, if not, as was at first suggested, the introduction of outside guarantors. But with the 'rise' of China, ASEAN sought to extend its 'Way' in to a wider region, again evoking the five principles that China had earlier endorsed. Its 'rise', along with the change in American policies and the collapse of the SU, would alter its relationship to the region, though it was not clear how. ASEAN hoped it would continue to see the five principles as some kind of 'moral interdiction', abide by codes of practice built upon them, and abstain from establishing the 'hegemony' it had foresworn, let alone reconstructing the older hierarchy in some form. Had it not promoted the independence of Cambodia? Or was that merely to be explained by its traditional distrust of Vietnam?

Regional organizations distinct from those headed by outside powers like SEATO began to emerge with the creation of an independent Malaya in August 1957. The reason its government took the lead was that it was anxious to avoid the dominance of the largest state in the archipelago, Indonesia, without remaining dependent on outside powers to counter it. It was an aspect of the decolonization of the region. The new states had to develop a foreign and defence policy, taking account of their neighbours and the stance of the great powers. New relationships had again to be improvised. Of all the relationships Malaya had to develop, the relationship with Indonesia was most crucial, even if it was not always wise to say so.

The relationship was novel: Malaya's policy was not now that of a major power nor Indonesia's that of a minor one. Indonesia, too, was not only wrapped around Malaysia, but had armed itself to deal with domestic revolts, and it was challenging the Netherlands for West Irian [Papua]. The most populous state in the region, proud of its record in winning independence, it was also conscious of a leadership entitlement in international affairs that Bandung had itself illustrated. By not joining the US-led SEATO Malaya avoided challenging Indonesia as well as China, and it did not want merely to rely on its defence agreement with the UK that had accompanied independence. A merely bilateral engagement with Indonesia that extended beyond a cultural agreement would, however, imply another kind of dependence. Malaya's regional initiatives sought an answer to the conundrum.

After visiting Colombo early in February 1958, the Prime Minister, Tunku Abdul Rahman, urged closer co-operation among the smaller Southeast Asian states. Southeast Asian countries were 'should not concern themselves unduly with the world and Afro-Asian politics when they had problems of their own nearer at hand. An effort should be made to build up their own unity and understanding. If they did not do this, they would have to look outside the area for protection and the full meaning of independence would be lost.'[7] The dig at Indonesia was not welcomed there. 'Indonesia is almost certainly unready to sacrifice what she considers to be her position of influence among the larger group of Bandung powers for any formal alliance, Pan-Malayan, Southeast Asian or otherwise', Canadian officials reported. '… Indeed the Indonesians may well resent the suggestion that they accept leadership from Malaya, a nation they regard as their junior in age, experience and influence.'[8] The *Times of Indonesia* thought it would be 'a charitable act' if the Indonesian Government 'nipped in the bud the puerile, vain and flamboyant hopes' of 'an economic and cultural union of Southeast Asia'.[9]

'The Tunku's plan is now passing through a period of consolidation and elaboration', Arthur Menzies of the Canadian High Commission in Kuala Lumpur (KL) reported in March 1959. The founding members of what was now to be called SEAFET were to be Malaya and the Philippines. They would like to bring Indonesia in, but Indonesia preferred to seek closer bilateral ties with Malaya and trying to sell it a more comprehensive treaty than the Federation wanted to accept. Beyond the 'inner circle', Thailand was the most likely candidate for membership.[10]

The Tunku had mentioned the idea to Foss Shanahan, the New Zealand representative in Singapore, during a break in the meetings of the working party on the UK-Malaya Defence Agreement. While he had 'a strong feeling of affinity' with the UK and welcomed the Defence Agreement, 'he is anxious to create another area of balance or strength within the region of South East Asia itself'. He told Shanahan that all the countries of Southeast Asia were small and 'would be noticed and effective only if they found some way of getting together'. In the Tunku's mind one of the values of a treaty and the cooperation it should promote was 'greater political understanding which may lead to some affirmation of a general position on the question of the regional security of its members'. The Indonesians might be reluctant to join, given reasons of prestige, 'and the feeling that they have a role to play not just regionally but essentially on the world's stage'.[11]

Felixberto Serrano, the Philippines Foreign Minister, visited Kuala Lumpur on his way to attend the SEATO conference in Wellington. On SEAFET he was 'hopeful but vague'. It would at first be bilateral, then Malaya and the Philippines would consider bringing others in.[12] Razak and Ismail, the Malayan leaders, found the Thai leaders enthusiastic when they visited Bangkok in June 1959, it was reported, and they had undertaken to put some comments on Malaya's draft proposals in writing.[13] Foreign Minister Thanat subsequently visited other mainland capitals. He concluded that it would be 'fatal to force the pace. … Cooperation had to come naturally in response to the genuine feelings of the countries concerned and if the proposals were quietly discussed he thought that progress would eventually be made. When asked whether in view of Indonesia's attitude he thought the scheme should be confined to the peninsular countries plus the Philippines, Thanat said that he believed that eventually Indonesia also might be interested.'[14]

By November Malayan tactics had changed. Ismail said that the Tunku had written to the Prime Ministers in Vietnam, Laos, Cambodia, Thailand, Burma, the Philippines and Indonesia.[15] There had been a danger, a diplomat at the British High Commission commented, that the agreement might look too restrictive. That was probably why the Federation had dropped the original idea of a bilateral agreement with the Philippines, to which others could accede, in favour of a simultaneous approach.[16] The following month, however, Sihanouk made it clear that Cambodia could not join, lest it forsook its neutrality. Thailand and the Philippines were both in SEATO, and only one part of Vietnam, the south, had been invited.[17] By March 1960 it was clear that the SEAFET proposal was, in the words of J.C. Crombie at the Commonwealth Relations Office in London, 'doing very poorly'.[18]

In the event the Tunku decided to go ahead with SEAFET on the basis of membership by Malaya, the Philippines, and Thailand alone. A start had to be made somewhere, he said: an organization in being might after all be more attractive than a mere plan.[19] The new association, he announced in July, would be called ASAS, Association of South East Asian States, not SEAFET.[20] At the end of July 1961 the three foreign ministers met in Bangkok, and their declaration, issued on 31 July, established the Association of Southeast Asian States (ASA). Its machinery was to include an annual meeting of foreign ministers, preceded by a meeting of the joint working party; a standing committee, chaired by the foreign minister of the host country, and including the diplomatic representatives in its capital;

ad hoc and permanent specialist committees; and a national secretariat in each country.[21]

The fledgling organization was thus set up at the very time the Tunku was pursuing the concept of Greater Malaysia. Could such an inter-state organization survive a member's challenge to the territorial integrity of another member? How would it cope? The answer was as yet unclear, since Malaysia was only in the process of formation. It was as a result of that process, however, that the Philippines determined to put in its claim to Sabah, based on that of the heirs of the Sultan of Sulu in respect of the 'leases' secured by the British North Borneo Company. That had lain relatively dormant since the establishment of the Philippines Republic in 1946, since it would have involved presenting a challenge to the UK. The prospect that North Borneo would be 'decolonized' to the advantage of an independent state made it necessary to put in the claim: if it were ever to be made, it would have to be made before that process was complete.

The next ministerial meeting was postponed till April 1963, as a result, as the New Zealand High Commission in KL put it, of the Philippines claim, and the need for what the Tunku termed 'a better atmosphere'. That the meeting was finally held was 'a tribute to the genuine concern of all three nations, and especially Malaya and Thailand, not to allow contentious issues to mar the future of the organisation'. Its achievements were modest, but it 'proved the will of the three countries to preserve ASA in the face of disruptive political issues, is there, even if the way has not been found'.[22] Here, perhaps, was a pointer towards the 'ASEAN Way'. But Indonesia was, however, not yet a member.

The revolt in Brunei in December 1962 indeed determined Indonesia to 'confront' the new Malaysia federation that was being set up. At the same time as he advanced the Sabah claim, President Macapagal had proposed a Malayan confederation, evoking an earlier Filipino concept as a means of raising Philippines prestige and alleviating conflict among the new sovereign states. Was that a 'mere tactic'?[23] Perhaps it was, or became, something more: a means of restraining Indonesia by bringing it into a confederation. Certainly, as Indonesia's 'confrontation' policy shaped up, Foreign Minister Pelaez wanted to use it as a framework for tripartite discussions on the future security of the region. Three-way officials meetings followed the ASA meeting, but not the summit that Pelaez wanted. Late in May 1963, however, Sukarno and the Tunku met in Tokyo, and recalled the friendship treaty they had made in 1959.[24] The foreign ministers, meeting in Manila on 7–11 June, decided that an 'impartial authority' would endeavour to ascertain whether the Borneo peoples wished to join Malaysia or not, and Macapagal won approval for his confederation in the form of MAlaysia-PHILippines-INDOnesia,[25] 'a grouping of states which would work "together in closest harmony but without surrendering any portion of their sovereignty"'.[26] The three countries, the report declared, shared 'a primary responsibility' for the security of the area.[27]

The summit took place on 31 July to 5 August 1963. The joint statement now made reference to such Indonesian concepts as musjawarah or consultation and the Afro-Asian spirit. It also declared that the foreign military bases in the region – those in Singapore and in the Philippines were in mind – were 'temporary in nature', and 'should not be allowed to be used directly or indirectly to subvert the national independence of any of the three countries'. In accordance with the principle in the ten-clause Bandung declaration of 1955 [6a], the three countries would 'abstain from the use of arrangements of collective defense to serve the particular interests of any of the three big powers'.[28] Indonesia no doubt had in mind the rebels' use of foreign bases in the civil strife of 1958, but the clause also staked a larger claim to leadership as part of the price for accepting Malaysia. The Tunku said he would postpone the founding date for a few days if necessary. A UN team began to assess Borneo opinion, but new arguments arose over the number of 'observers' each country might send. The Tunku announced on 14 September – one day after Thant conveyed the conclusion[29] – that Malaysia would come into being on 16 September. Indonesia and the Philippines announced that they could not at once recognize it.[30] Manila–KL relations were severed, and Confrontation deepened.

The subsequent development of confrontation left Macapagal and Pelaez's successor Lopez exposed to domestic criticism. In May 1964 Lopez was relieved from his post. Consular relations with KL were re-established. Eventually Macapagal declared that he deplored the dropping of Indonesian guerrillas on the Peninsula,[31] though the Sabah claim was not abandoned. A few weeks later Singapore was extruded from Malaysia in August 1965. But a few weeks after that the Indonesian coup of 30 September 1965 held out the prospect of an end to Confrontation, though the ruling triumvirate, Suharto, Adam Malik and the Sultan of Jogjakarta, did not abandon it at once.[32] What would happen to Maphilindo?

The Tunku's sights were set on reviving ASA, reported Michael Walker at the BHC (British High Commission). If it prospered, the Malaysians did not exclude the possibility that Indonesia might join, 'just as they were in favour of Indonesian participation when it was first set up in 1959'. Malaysia wanted to avoid an association based on 'purely racial affinities', 'understandable enough in a multi-racial country'. It also wanted to build up a viable relationship with Thailand and the Philippines through ASA, in order 'to produce a counterbalance to the far greater size and potential of Indonesia which will be needed when the time comes for trying to establish a sensible relationship with that country as well'.[33]

In more or less his last act as acting minister for foreign affairs, however, Tun Ismail took a different line. 'The stage is now set for full-scale resumption of ASA', he said. 'There is every reason to hope for an early participation of Indonesia in a wider grouping of South-east Asian states. … We, in Malaysia, … look forward to a regional association embracing Thailand, Burma, Indonesia, Singapore, Malaysia, Philippines, Cambodia,

Laos and Vietnam.' The nations and peoples of Southeast Asia had to 'pull together and create, with hand and brain, a new perspective and a new framework'. The ASA principles were a good starting point, but the name did not matter. Ismail envisaged 'an organization which would be, first and last, pro-South-east Asia, pro-development, pro-regional cooperation and pro-peace.'[34]

The formal ending of Confrontation was negotiated during these months. The Indonesian Foreign Minister, Adam Malik, told reporters after meeting Razak in Bangkok at the end of May that he, and the Malaysian, Thai and Filipino foreign ministers had all been thinking of an association of Southeast Asian nations 'which might be regarded as an expansion of Maphilindo under a different name'.[35] Indonesia could not join ASA. What was needed was another body involving elements of ASA and Maphilindo. Indonesia could not see itself 'simply stringing along with a group of South-East powers already in association', commented Horace Phillips at the British embassy. '[B]y virtue of its size and position', it regarded itself as 'the potential leader in the area and, as such, will insist on being a founder-member of some new regional grouping'.[36]

In KL Walter Ayathuray, head of the Malaysian ASA secretariat, gave the British High Commission a copy of the first draft of an agreement Thanat sent the Tunku in December. It was in the form of a joint declaration by foreign ministers. It began by reciting their belief that the countries of Southeast Asia shared 'the primary responsibility for ensuring the stability and maintaining the security of the area from subversion in any form or manifestation in order to preserve their respective national identity and to ensure peaceful and progressive national development in their respective countries and in their region in accordance with the ideals and aspirations of their peoples'. It also stated their agreement 'that foreign bases are temporary in nature and should not be allowed to be used directly or indirectly to subvert the national independence of their countries, and that arrangements of collective defence should not be used to serve the particular interest of any of the big powers'. Peace, freedom, social justice and economic well-being, they affirmed, could best be attained by 'fostering good understanding, good neighbourliness and active cooperation among their nations'. Their conviction was that 'mutual cooperation in the economic and technical fields and cultural relationship' would contribute to the welfare of their peoples and their mutual understanding.

Desiring to establish 'a firm foundation for common action to further regional cooperation in South East Asia', the foreign ministers declared the establishment of the South East Asian Association for Regional Cooperation [SEAARC]. It aimed to 'promote mutual understanding, harmonious relations and friendly cooperation among the nations of the region', 'strengthen regional peace and security', cooperate in promoting Southeast Asian studies, and generally 'consult and cooperate with one another so as to achieve the aims and purposes of the association, to contribute more effectively to the work of existing international aid agencies, as well as to resolve any problems that may arise between them'. It also aimed to establish an effective machinery for consultation, for 'active collaboration', and for 'mutual assistance in the economic, social, cultural, technical, scientific and administrative fields'; to provide training and research facilities in member countries for nationals and officials of other members; to provide machinery for collaboration in using resources, developing trade and industry, improving communications, and raising living standards; and to 'consult and cooperate … in the study of the problems of commodity trade'.

Under the draft the Foreign Ministers also declared 'that the association is in no way connected with any outside power or power blocs and is directed against no country, but represents the collective will of the nations of South East Asia to associate themselves for the mutual benefit of their respective peoples without surrendering any portion of their sovereignty, having as its objectives and through joint endeavour, the promotion of the well-being and the economic, social, technical and cultural progress of this region'. It would adopt ASA-type machinery.[37]

In mid-April Malik declared that plans were going ahead for a new organization. The Tunku declared, however, that Indonesia could join ASA. 'We already have our regional economic grouping.'[38] But at a meeting with Thanat on 20 May, according to MFA (Ministry of Foreign Affairs) officials, the Tunku 'surprised everybody' by changing his line. 'He apparently told Thanat that, though he was convinced the new association would be a failure, Malaysia could not afford to stand out from it and he was therefore prepared to see its formation announced as soon as Thanat thought fit.' ASA, he said, 'was in any case moribund because of the Philippines increasingly difficult attitude over Sabah.' Officials could not explain the Tunku's about-face, 'except possibly in terms of recent reports of increased Philippine interference in Sabah', including alleged attempts to encourage secessionism, a British diplomat [Bentley] reported. But it was 'equally possible' that the Tunku saw no point in maintaining ASA 'once an essentially parallel organization had been set up'.[39]

The five foreign ministers held informal discussions at Bangsaen, then drove to Bangkok, 'rewrote' the draft, and issued the ASEAN declaration on 8 August 1967. Press reports indicated that the preambular statement attracted most controversy during the discussions. The resulting declaration modified the 'Thanat' draft to read: 'foreign bases are temporary and remain only with the expressed concurrence of the countries concerned and are not intended to be used directly or indirectly to subvert the national independence and freedom of states in the area'. Malik remarked after the meeting that Indonesia left it to the countries concerned to determine how long bases would remain. 'The statement concerning collective defence arrangements that served the interests of big powers was conspicuous by its absence.'[40]

A Philippines draft included a provision from the Manila accords of 1963 that international relations in the area be conducted in conformity with international law. The Malaysians were 'naturally suspicious' that that was 'a backhanded attempt to introduce the contention that the Sabah claim should be considered at the International Court'. Eventually they secured a redraft included in the main declaration, indicating that the association would 'promote regional peace and stability through abiding respect for justice and the rules of law in the relationship among countries of the region and adherence to the principles of the United Nations Charter'. A Malaysian official thought that 'would sufficiently confuse the issue and remove any obligations over the Sabah claim'. Foreign Minister Ramos, it was felt, had to come back to Manila 'with a piece of paper demonstrating that the establishment of ASEAN had not prejudiced the Philippines' hopes in Sabah'. In fact there was renewed resentment of the Philippines in KL, a New Zealand diplomat reported, the Tunku being 'particularly bitter' at its 'irresponsible' pursuit of the claim.[41]

Even before the Bangkok meeting, officials in Canberra concluded, it was obvious that the Malaysians had 'changed their attitude towards the prospect of a new regional body. Earlier misgivings about Indonesia's intentions and capacity for harm seem to have been subordinated to the more urgent need of not foregoing the opportunity, through regional arrangements, of drawing Indonesia into harmonious and constructive relations with its neighbours.' Economically there were 'severe practical limits to what the five countries can do together'. The importance of ASEAN was more political than economic. In promoting a new organization, 'Indonesia was seeking to exert a leading role, thereby restoring some of her self-respect and what she regards as her rightful place of pre-eminence in the region. Such expansion is likely to take place in any case because of Indonesia's size, population and potential economic and military strength. However, ASEAN may prove useful in providing a framework for orderly and peaceful development in this direction.'[42] ASEAN, it was suggested in Wellington, provided 'a context within which Malaysia can achieve a satisfactory relationship with Indonesia. ... At the same time Indonesia's preponderant influence is moderated and contained by other members, especially Thailand.'[43]

By adopting mutually agreed policies of self-restraint, the states that joined the Association were providing themselves within additional security in respect of their potential antagonisms. Though not formally modifying their sovereignty, they were thus reinsuring their territorial integrity. They were also limiting the role of powers outside the region that they were defining. One of those powers was already known to be limiting its future role and another was unlikely to stay for ever, but others might expand their activities. Not all the states wanted to abandon outside connexions, but none wanted to see Southeast Asia the prey of extra-regional intervention as it been throughout history. In a sense the intended UK and probable US withdrawals were an opportunity as well as a threat. But not all were quite reassured over Indonesia's claim to primacy, given more recent history, nor were they prepared to rely on Indonesia to defend them against outside powers, which some of Indonesia's military leaders seemed to think was its task.

The Vietnam war was still on: indeed it was about to reach its turning point, Tet 1968. Even before that, however, Tun Ismail had presented the idea of neutralization, not of particular states, but of the whole region. In a debate on defence in the Dewan Rakyat back in January 1968, he argued that it would save money that could be spent on social services. 'The time is … ripe for the countries in the region to declare collectively the neutralization of South-East Asia. To be effective, the neutralization … must be guaranteed by the big powers, including Communist China … it is time that the countries in South-East Asia signed non-aggression treaties with each other. Now is also [the] time for the countries in South-East Asia to declare the policy of co-existence, in the sense that the countries in the region should not interfere in the internal affairs of each other and [should undertake] to accept whatever form of government a country chooses to elect or adopt'.[44] It was a plea to end the Vietnam war. It was also designed to allow the states in the region to live alongside one another in the future. But the outside guarantee seemed somewhat inconsistent. Perhaps it was a matter of interpretation.

Ismail, now Deputy PM, led the Malaysian delegation at the 4th ASEAN Foreign Ministers meeting (AMM) in Manila in March 1971. 'The tragedy of Vietnam', where, despite the Paris peace talks, no settlement was in sight and war continued to 'wreak havoc', was, he declared on 12 March, 'a telling testimony to the dangers of big power interference, involvement or intervention in the internal affairs of small countries'. The lesson of the war was clear: 'big powers should leave small countries to themselves, to evolve their own systems of government and to work out their own programmes for progress and prosperity'. With Vietnam in mind, 'together with the withdrawal of the American and British from Southeast Asia', Malaysia advocated '*a policy of neutralisation for Southeast Asia* to be guaranteed by the big powers, viz. the U.S., the U.S.S.R. and the People's Republic of China. The policy is meant to be a proclamation that this region of ours is no longer to be regarded as an area to be divided into spheres of influence of the big powers. It may be regarded as a project to end or prevent small countries in this region from being used as pawns in the conflict between the big powers.' It was a programme designed to ensure peace and stability and permit development.[45]

In October 1971 Ghazali published a defence of the proposal and outlined the steps Malaysia envisaged for implementing it.[46] At the first level, he argued, the individual countries of the region must 'respect each other's sovereignty and territorial integrity, and not participate in activities likely to directly or indirectly threaten the security of another. Non-interference and non-aggression are basic principles which Southeast Asian countries must unequivocally accept before any further steps can be taken.' All foreign powers were to be excluded from the region, which 'should not be allowed to be used as a theatre of conflict in the international power struggle'. The countries of the region should ensure peace among member states, and present 'a collective view before the major powers on vital issues of security' and 'promote regional cooperation'.

At the second level, the three major powers had to agree that Southeast Asia was 'an area of neutrality', and 'undertake to exclude countries in the region from the power struggle amongst themselves'. They should 'devise the supervisory means of guaranteeing Southeast Asia's neutrality in the international power struggle. Just as the Southeast Asian countries will be responsible, under the neutralization plan, for maintaining peace among themselves, so will the guaranteeing powers be responsible for preventing externally-inspired conflict in the region'.[47]

There were objections both practical and political. Some of the issues in respect of individual states had been evident in the negotiations about Laos and discussions about Cambodia. Those were part of a critique made by one of the states before the ASEAN FMs met in November 1971. 'A neutralized state must give up any aspirations to great or middle power status.'[48] Indeed it modified the very sovereignty of the states it was designed to protect.

There were precedents for neutralizing states, but not regions. That raised further questions, practical and political. How would differences among states within the region be dealt with? If outside powers were to intervene, foreign troops might have to be introduced.[49] What would the 'guarantee' of which the Malaysians spoke imply? The Indonesians, not surprisingly, did not care for it. 'Neutralisation that is the product of one-way benevolence on the part of the big powers', Malik said, 'at this stage, would perhaps prove as brittle and unstable as the interrelationship between the major powers themselves.' He believed that it was 'only through developing among ourselves an area of internal cohesion and stability, based on indigenous socio-political and economic strength, that we can ever hope to assist in the early stabilisation of a new equilibrium in the region that would not be the exclusive "diktat" of the major powers'. Southeast Asian nations should work towards the day when the security of the region was primarily their responsibility.[50]

A guarantee by outside powers not only undermined Indonesia's position: it was, as Malik said, impractical. The UK FO had long favoured the neutralization of Southeast Asia, though its ability to pursue it had been checked by its special relationship with the US. Now it thought that it would be able to take a positive attitude to a declaration of neutralization which the Chinese would find it difficult not to respect, but which would not inhibit regional cooperation or 'the freedom of South East Asian countries to maintain arrangements with friendly powers which they think necessary for their security'. But the suggestion that external powers – presumably US,

SU, PRC – should 'underwrite' it would be difficult to endorse publicly. 'There is a distinction between self-denying ordinances whereby the great powers would undertake not to interfere in the affairs of South East Asian countries and to respect their territorial integrity, sovereignty and existing systems of government and an international agreement (which in itself would give the outside signatories a droit de regard in the area) under which each great power would guarantee the neutrality of countries in the area. A positive agreement of this sort would involve reconciliation of differing interests of the powers concerned to an extent which is not practical politics at present. It could also involve weakening of existing Western position in the area. Furthermore, Malaysians would presumably want above all to obtain undertakings by China not to support Communist subversive movements in the area: we cannot expect the Chinese to give any undertakings of this sort in the foreseeable future.'[51]

How would the major powers check each other without the risk of intervening? Perhaps the Malaysians saw this difficulty. Their phrases often used words that implied a declaratory or proclamatory approach. They certainly proved ready to accept that line when it proved that such was as much as they could hope to secure: 'an expression of creative ambiguity', as Leifer called it.[52] Perhaps it was what they wanted all along: an agreement not to interfere rather than to guarantee.

The ASEAN foreign ministers met in KL on 26–27 November 1971 and signed a declaration announcing their agreement 'that the neutralisation of Southeast Asia was a desirable objective' and that they should 'explore ways and means of bringing it about'. The preamble alluded to UN principles, the Bandung conference of 1955, and the Bangkok declaration of 1967 that had founded ASEAN, and took cognizance of the move towards nuclear-free zones in Africa and Latin America. The declaration itself stated that Indonesia, Malaysia, the Philippines, Singapore and Thailand were 'determined to exert initially necessary efforts to secure the recognition of, and respect for, Southeast Asia as a Zone of Peace, Freedom and Neutrality, free from any form or manner of interference by outside Powers'.[53] A joint communiqué indicated that the ministers would encourage other countries in Southeast Asia to associate themselves with the declaration and would establish a committee of senior officials 'to study and consider what further steps should be taken'. Great powers and guarantees were not mentioned.

Many miss the point, the Canadian High Commission suggested, that the Malaysian government was not promoting neutralization for tomorrow 'but rather for an indeterminate date in the future when the USA's role in this part of the world has diminished, the five power defence arrangements [which had replaced the Anglo-Malayan defence agreement] are over and China, Japan and Indonesia are exerting the major influence in the region'. Razak, the Commission noted, had spoken in the past of guarantees, but the Declaration used the words 'recognize' and 'respect'. The Malaysian Foreign Ministry spokesman 'indicated that the use of "recognize" was calculated and meant to imply the recognition of Southeast Asia's neutrality in the same way that all recognized Switzerland's neutrality. To "guarantee" the area's neutrality could imply a role for the super powers to police the guarantee and presumably the countries of the region do not wish this.'[54]

Officials met in Jakarta in December 1972. They 'sought to establish the principles on which neutralisation should be set up and to consider the ways of promoting the conditions in which a zone of peace would prosper and survive', Albert Talalla of the Malaysian Foreign Ministry said. 'They ... succeeded in establishing a code of conduct for states both within and outside the region and they had made some progress on lines of action for the promotion of the zone.' The guidelines were to be referred to the Foreign Ministers, perhaps at their regular meeting in April. He admitted that there was a long way to go. 'In particular time had not permitted the completion of their study of guarantees or on the mechanism of conflict resolution (and this, of course, could be much more contentious).' But he was pleased with the cooperation received: even the Singaporeans were in a 'less argumentative frame of mind'.[55]

The AMM in Pattaya endorsed the guidelines on neutralization that the officials had worked out in Jakarta in December. The next officials meeting would address the question of great power guarantees. 'Are these needed, and if so in what form? Will they not give the great powers the excuse to meddle in the affairs of the region? And so on.'[56] The meeting was held at Baguio 19–21 June 1973. The statement issued referred to the steady progress that had been made towards realizing the objectives of the KL declaration. Instead of seeking guarantees from the outside powers, 'the conference was reported to have agreed ... on letting the big powers recognise and respect the zone'. To do that, one source said, 'we have to be ready with a specific blueprint which we could show these big powers so that it would be also to their own interest to insure the neutrality of the region. Of course we cannot impose on the big powers although we can initiate dialogues with them.'[57]

In the meantime the US and North Vietnam had signed a communiqué on Kissinger's visit to Hanoi in February 1973. That declared that the fulfilment of the Vietnam cease-fire agreement reached in Paris would make a positive contribution to peace in Southeast Asia 'on the basis of full respect for the independence of the countries of that region'.[58] The prospect of a regional neutralization seemed to improve.

Sir J. Johnston, the British High Commissioner in KL, suggested in October 1973 that regionalism was 'a present reality', and neutralization 'a convenient aspiration, of which we must take account not because of its realism, but because of its convenience to its proponents'. ASEAN was no longer, as in 1967, 'a talking shop', but a 'genuine vehicle for consultation and cooperation, with increasing political content, and ... on the way to being institutionalised'. It consulted on neutralization, the recognition of Bangladesh, relations with China, and in respect of the southern Philippines

ASEAN had priority over Islam. In the economic field members were working more closely together, trying to present a common front to the EEC (European Economic Community) and in international negotiations.

With enlargement to include the Indo-China states and Burma, the discussion moved from 'reality' to 'aspiration', and regionalism began to link up with neutralization. 'The aspiration is that at some time in the future the association will extend to include the other five SE Asian countries: and that together the Ten will form an area of "peace, freedom and stability", collectively persuading the super powers to remain at a political equidistance which none singly could hope to achieve.'

'Faced with prospect of an assortment of SE Asian States, appearing in the aftermath of one or another kind of colonialism, disunited, uncertain and obvious take-over targets – the classic "power vacuum" after British, French and partial US withdrawal – the Malaysians believe that the regional acceptance of the common policy goals they have described as neutralisation will give the region the appearance and possibly a genuine sense of direction and unity of purpose, and strengthen its position vis-a-vis the super powers.' They believed, perhaps rightly, 'that if these aims and objectives are sufficiently reiterated and successfully put across, they may possibly derive from their acceptance as objectives some of the benefits that in theory would flow from their eventual realisation'.[59]

The New Zealand High Commissioner in Singapore made reference to *Neutralization and World Politics* by Cyril E. Black, Richard A. Falk, Klaus Knorr and Oran Young, published by Princeton University Press in 1968, following on their report to the Senate Foreign Relations Committee of 10 October 1966. Envisaging a possible outcome in Vietnam, the book included documents on the neutralization of Laos in 1961–62 and also the 'draft outline of a model treaty of neutralization'. That was concerned with a single state, and it provided for guarantors.[60] But what if neutralized states differed? It seemed from the Princeton study, Assistant Secretary of State for Far Eastern Affairs Bundy commented for Rusk, that 'violations from one "neutralized" state against another "neutralized" state may have to be accepted as "tolerable" (i.e. from Vietnam to Laos or Cambodia). We find this argument difficult to accept.'[61] Even Lee Kuan Yew did not seem to see the problems in extending the concept of neutralization from state to region. 'The best way to maintain peace and security would be to leave South-East Asia as a neutral area in which no major power will use any of the smaller countries as an extension of its own might', he had told the Socialist International in Sweden in April 1966, 'and at the same time guarantee the integrity of each of the smaller powers against encroachments by the others'.[62] How could that be done?

Was a neutral Southeast Asia possible, J.L.S. Girling had asked in 1973. '[I]t provides no solution either for internal conflicts within Southeast Asian countries or for intra-regional disputes. In fact by "freezing" the status quo, it may make peaceful change more difficult to achieve and may even divert the forces of change into armed conflict'. But the alternative – interference by one or other rival power or 'dominance by one great power' – was worse.[63]

Malaysia had initially sought guarantors in the ZOPFAN (Zone of Peace, Freedom and Neutrality) discussions of a regional neutralization, and the British FO had pointed to the difficulty. In a sense ASEAN's regionalism was, however, a substitute for them. If neighbours did not fall out, there would be no need to call in outside help. The answer was 'the ASEAN Way'. ASEAN's was 'an essentially declaratory regionalism that originates not only from natural circumstances, but in the political will of Southeast Asian policy elites'.[64] Blaming outside powers for past interventions rather than inside appeals for help was part of a sustaining rhetoric, partial view of history though it involved.

At the time of the Laos negotiations Prince Sihanouk – in the event vainly – suggested a neutral belt in Southeast Asia, covering at least his country and neighbouring Laos. The British FO saw advantage in it: 'it enshrined the "Sacred Cow Principle"', as Warner put it. 'It was easy enough for powers to knock around a little ping-pong ball like Laos but once you had established a neutral belt this became a major feature of the world political scene and it would be considered a great sacrilege to tamper with it.'[65] Recognizing that 'constructivist' principle, the Malaysians were to be more ready to drop the difficult issue of guarantees, if indeed they had ever determined to insist on them.

The seventh ministerial meeting was held in Jakarta on 7–9 May 1974. Adenan of the Indonesian Ministry told the Australians that the Philippine proposal on the formal machinery for settling disputes had not been well received. '[T]he Indonesian way was to do this by informal bi-lateral or tri-lateral contacts whenever necessary.'[66] Malaysia was also concerned about the concept of 'machinery'. 'This could have been interpreted as implying the establishment of a rigid system of referral to a tribunal or court of arbitration and it caused the Malaysians some disquiet, particularly because of their long-standing difficulty with the Philippines over the problem of Muslim insurgency.' The Philippines agreed to change the term to 'procedures'.[67]

The eighth meeting – held in KL on 13–15 May 1975 – followed soon after the collapse of the regimes in Saigon and Phnom Penh. Razak expressed a 'fervent hope' that the countries of Indo-China would join in building 'a strong foundation of regional co-operation and regional peace'. The founders of ASEAN had envisaged that it would eventually include all the countries of Southeast Asia. 'Surely the moment has come for that community of Southeast Asia, which has been our dream, to be realised?'[68] Malik evoked Bandung. Adjustment to the new situation should not be inspired by fear, nor by perceived vacuums in power relationships. 'He proposed instead a framework of power relationships based on the Bandung principles of peaceful coexistence, noninterference, respect for sovereignty and territorial integrity, equality and justice.'[69]

In their final statement, the foreign ministers expressed their willingness to enter friendly relations with the Indo-Chinese countries – differences in social and political systems should not be 'an obstacle to the development of constructive and mutually beneficial relations'[70] – and to cooperate in 'the common task of national development', but made no mention of expansion.[71] The meeting agreed to accept for consideration by governments a draft treaty of amity and cooperation. 'This was hailed as an important step towards the realisation of the Zone of Peace, Freedom and Neutrality. It was moreover noted with satisfaction that progress was being made by Senior Officials in working out a "blueprint" for the Zone.'[72] The changes in Indo-China, coming more quickly than expected, put a new urgency behind the institutionalization of ASEAN. Whether it would be able to welcome Indo-China or not, it would need to set its house in order first. It was agreed to hold the first 'Summit', a meeting of the Heads of State.

At the Pattaya meeting of Foreign Ministers that preceded the Summit in Bali in February 1976, there were, the Australians in Singapore learned, 'problems' with the Treaty of Amity.[73] 'In essence, the Malaysians want it made crystal clear that the treaty does not impose on ASEAN members a binding obligation to submit bilateral disputes to the organization for settlement', New Zealand diplomats reported. Officials were dealing with the issue at their pre-Summit meeting in Jakarta. 'The Malaysians are apparently confident that they will get what they want. But if the Filipinos dig their toes in, it may well be that the treaty, at this stage, may simply take the form of a statement of principles.'[74]

The Treaty of Amity, as concluded at the Summit meeting on 23–25 February, covered the 'machinery'. The preamble alluded inter alia to the desire 'to enhance peace, friendship and mutual cooperation', consistent with the UN Charter, the ten principles of Bandung, the Bangkok declaration of 1967, and the KL declaration of 1971. Article 1 declared that the object was to promote peace, amity and cooperation, and Article 2 that the parties would be guided by the principles of 'a. Mutual respect for the independence, sovereignty, equality, territorial integrity and national identity of all nations; b. The right of every State to lead its national existence free from external interference, subversion or coercion; c. Non-interference in the internal affairs of one another; d. Settlement of differences or disputes by peaceful means; e. Renunciation of the threat or use of force; f. Effective cooperation among themselves.' The parties agreed to promote mutual understanding and cooperation, and to collaborate [Article 6] 'for the acceleration of the economic growth of the region in order to strengthen the foundation for a prosperous and peaceful community of nations in Southeast Asia'. The parties were 'to strengthen their respective national resilience in their political, economic, socio-cultural as well as security fields in conformity with their respective ideals and aspirations, free from external interference as well as internal subversive activities in order to preserve their respective national identities' [Article 11]. They were also to 'cooperate in all fields for the promotion of regional resilience, based on the principles of self-confidence, self-reliance, mutual respect, cooperation and solidarity' [Article 12].

Articles 13–17 covered the pacific settlement of disputes. Article 13 required the parties to have 'the determination and good faith to prevent disputes from arising'. If they did, they were to refrain from force or the threat of force, and to settle the disputes through friendly negotiations. 'To settle disputes through regional processes', Article 14 prescribed the setting up of a High Council, a continuing body comprising a representative of each of the parties to the treaty, 'to take cognizance of the existence of disputes or situations likely to disturb regional peace and harmony'. In the event that no solution was reached through direct negotiations, the High Council was, under Article 15, to recommend appropriate means of settlement, or offer its good offices, or, with agreement of the parties in dispute, 'constitute itself into a committee of mediation, inquiry or conciliation'. That provision was not to apply unless the parties to the dispute agreed, but, under Article 16, that would not prevent parties to the treaty not party to the dispute 'from offering all possible assistance to settle the said dispute', and parties to the dispute were to be 'well disposed' to such offers. Nothing, said Article 17, precluded recourse to the modes of peaceful settlement prescribed in the UN Charter, Article 33 (1). But parties to a dispute were 'encouraged to take initiatives to solve it by friendly negotiations before resorting to the other procedures provided for in the Charter of the United Nations'. The treaty, signed by Indonesia, Malaysia, the Philippines, Singapore and Thailand, was, Article 18 declared, 'open for accession by other States in Southeast Asia'.[75]

The treaty did not cover neutralization, but the idea of ZOPFAN was brought formally under ASEAN's auspices.[76] In a Declaration of ASEAN Concord, the leaders agreed, inter alia, to consider initial steps towards obtaining recognition of and respect for ZOPFAN, and to strengthen 'political solidarity by promoting the harmonization of views, coordinating positions and, where possible and desirable, taking common actions'. They also adopted a plan of action put up by the meeting of Economic Ministers, and covered, in very general terms, cooperation over social development, population programmes and narcotics control. The Declaration also stated – 'allaying fears about incipient militarism' – that there should be a 'continuation of cooperation on a non-ASEAN basis between member states in security matters in accordance with their mutual needs and interests'.[77]

The summit, Yusof of the MFA in KL told the Australians, decided not to act as a bloc vis-à-vis the Indo-China states, since that would be 'unnecessarily provocative', be 'counter-productive' in respect of ZOPFAN, and 'be ineffective because ASEAN did not possess sufficient strength'. Now, however, was not the time to encourage the Indo-China states to join ASEAN: some matters would be 'awkward' to discuss in their presence; and their approach to industrial projects would differ. 'It was thought better to let the states of Indo-China settle down further and get over some of their old "hang-ups" before participation in ASEAN.' But an Indo-China state could participate in one ASEAN activity and build up its involvement step by step.[78] In the event relations between ASEAN and Vietnam deteriorated, and, accompanied by many references to proxy wars and satellites,[79] the conflict over Cambodia interposed before it became possible for the Indo-China states to join. But that took place amidst further major changes in the world at large, including the 'rise' of China.

Indeed the rise of China, and its influence with the military regime in Burma was a reason for admitting Myanmar into ASEAN as well. The generals, who ignored the outcome of the 1990 elections, wanted to diminish the role of the opposition and secure legitimacy. For ASEAN, too, there were 'hidden interests'. Indonesia and Malaysia were 'mostly concerned with China's growing power in Burma. ... Already faced with diplomatic difficulties with Beijing in regard to territorial disputes in the South China Sea, ASEAN's attempt to prevent any Sino-Burmese links was seen as a move to counterbalance Chinese influence.'[80]

There were further responses. ASEAN, as Hiro Katsumata puts it, was constituted by 'norms at the global level', stipulated in the UN Charter. 'Yet the Southeast Asian countries have incrementally reconstructed these ideational elements in the Asian context, thereby developing the "ASEAN Way", through a process of interaction over the decades since the 1960s.'[81] One of its objectives was to extend this approach beyond Southeast Asia, while trying to retain ASEAN's centrality. The ASEAN Regional Forum (ARF), which first met in 1994, followed an 'Asean' approach, as Jose Almonte, adviser to President Fidel Ramos, put it in 1997–98: 'it accentuates the positive – focusing not on controversy, but on areas of common interest from which multilateral cooperation can be developed and expanded. Divisive issues are simply passed over for later resolution – or until they have been made either irrelevant or innocuous by time or events.'[82]

Another approach was more traditional. Stuart-Fox argues that in China there has been a 'carry-over' from the Confucian past into the Marxist-Leninist present in foreign as well as domestic affairs. China 'has always had difficulty seeing itself as just another nation-state'. In reality, it is, he suggests, the last great empire, and a civilization 'whose historical pretensions to superiority are deeply embedded in the national psyche'. Formally it treats other nations as equal just as the emperor treated vassal states impartially. But the world of nation states is in fact a hierarchy of powers, and for China 'a hierarchy of international status'. Chinese leaders have to regain international standing. And if it is to be a global great power, it has to be recognized as such within the region.[83]

The Westphalia system insists that states have equal sovereignty in principle, and does not formally recognize their differential power. That is a matter of judgment, spoken and unspoken, an informal matter, lesser states deciding how much they should accept the superiority of the larger if they are to retain the maximum security and larger states deciding what they might accept or demand. There is a hierarchy of power but the differences of status are not and cannot be expressed in the formal terms of vassalage. Instead there is an implicit deal. Recognizing China's status and its security interest is the price of security – non-intervention, political support for the regime, fair economic exchange – for the mainland states, Stuart-Fox argues. Would maritime Southeast Asia be more ready to oppose 'hegemony'? he wonders.[84]

The ASEAN 10, he suggests, have chosen the path of 'accommodation'. They will try not to provoke China, but try to make room for it. No new tributary system is about to evolve, but 'certain elements central to historical bilateral relations regimes are likely to carry over. These include Chinese respect for the independence and territorial integrity of Southeast Asian nations in return for tacit acceptance of de facto Chinese regional hegemony.' There would be no kowtow. But Southeast Asia leaders were 'adept at polite, some might say deferential, diplomacy'.[85] When it becomes the 'equal or dominant regional or local power', Wayne Bert wrote in 2003, China might end up 'accepting most of the norms of the present system'.[86] China endorsed the five principles when it was weak: it could still do so now it is strong.

Indeed what Stuart-Fox describes can be arranged within the Westphalia system. But the ASEAN Way is a gloss on Westphalia which the adept leaders wish to extend so that, while ASEAN yet remains central, it may be adopted elsewhere in the wider region. But can it apply to so different a region as Northeast Asia? The ASEAN leaders also try to develop more particular codes of behaviour, for example over the South China Sea, where the extension of the power of nation states provided for under the Law of the Sea agreements threatens relations both among Southeast Asian states and between them and the PRC.

Those issues might be regarded as part of a horizontal view of ASEAN's policies, those that relate its members to one another and relate it and its members to the outside world. There is a vertical one, too. 'What was more vital to make ASEAN permanent was the participation of its people in its activities', Hussein Onn had declared in 1976.[87] It was an elite organization, emerging partly because of the 'will' of the leaders. Could it be otherwise? The second Bali concord of 2003 implied a wider agenda. But if ASEAN became more popular in style, it might have to do more, and then, like a colonial government though in a different context, it might become less acceptable. Some leaders, such as Jusuf Wanandi, came to believe it should. Hiro Katsumata believed that it neither could nor should, since it was fundamentally based on the Westphalia principles. If it was to go beyond talk, it should act only by setting an example.

Epilogue

If it is presumptuous to think that such a work as this can contribute to the debate which seems to be frustrating the theorists of IR, it has to be admitted that it is unlikely to satisfy the writers of H. For the former it may tip too little towards the theoretical, for the latter too much. It may speak too little of systems for the one, too much for the other.

The historian indeed deals in personality and in specificity. Warned by Herbert Butterfield, the historian will be anxious to avoid what he called a 'Whig interpretation'. Yet it is hard not to see the long history through which this book has sought to cover the international relations of Southeast Asia as the story of the emergence of one system, 'Westphalia'.

If the historian were to hazard an account of the future – something that the profession would generally regard as risky, if not mistaken – it would surely question the possibility that the system was being displaced or indeed that it was likely to be. It faces many challenges and will undergo continuous modifications, but a substitution seems quite improbable.

The economic globalization set in motion in the 1970s has certainly involved compromises, but they have not all been on the side of the nation state. It has not disappeared, but, obstacle at times, saviour at others, it has endured, negotiating a vast variety of agreements on trade and IP, baulking at a global agreement. What its role will be in the search for mechanisms for regulating fiscal globalization that the crises of the early twenty-first century seem to call for remains to be seen.

Nor will it readily abandon its insistence on non-interference in other fields, such as 'human rights'. 'We must defend the principle of intervention by the international community, under U.N. auspices, to bring relief to the victims', the French Prime Minister urged in 1999. 'The U.N. mission is not limited to the settlement of conflict among states. … This mission extends to defending human dignity within each State where necessary – as the Charter permits – against States.'[1] But such a doctrine – often resisted – has not been easy to apply.

The new media are in themselves both a help and a hindrance. They have given non-state actors and non-governmental organizations (NGOs) and even individuals a new means of acting. But they have also given protest groups what Rosemary Righter has called 'a spurious homogeneity'.[2] And, of course, they have given governments a new instrument of control. If 'intelligence' has been important to all the systems this book has mentioned – from the mandala to the colonial state, from seventeenth-century Mataram to 'British Malaya' – there has been no precedent for the 'surveillance state' of our own time, in which a government's capacity to monitor its citizens is limited by its possession of too much information rather than too little.

Difficulties with the system aside – and they extend to other fields, including the vexed question of 'climate change' – no alternatives are on offer. Interpreting world politics in terms of a 'clash of civilizations' is far from persuasive. Too clearly it recalls George Kennan's warning in the Cold War, his fear 'that we could not adopt an adequate defense position without working our people into an emotional frenzy, and this emotional state, rather than cool and unemotional appraisal of national interest, would then have to be the determinant of our action'.[3] The 'war on terror' – another poorly defined concept – has in fact intensified the control of the state.

Whatever the concepts of the world Islam offers, the Islamic states in general act within the Westphalia system. The foreign policy of the Islamic Republic of Iran, according to Article 152 of its constitution, seems to echo the five principles: it is 'based on the negation of exercising or accepting any form of domination whatsoever, safeguarding all-embracing independence and territorial integrity, defence of the rights of all Muslims, non-alignment with domineering powers, and peaceful and reciprocal relations with non-belligerent states'.[4]

Islam is diverse. So, too, are the relationships between the ummah, the community of believers, and the nation state. In some states nationhood overshadows Islam; in others the reverse may be true; in yet others there is harmony.[5] The state that contains the largest population of Muslims is in Southeast Asia. But what is of significance to young Indonesian Muslim leaders is 'the implementation of Islamic values and *shari'a* principles at the societal level, rather than delving into the muddy debates on the symbolic terms and forms of the state'.[6] Only a small minority support the idea of a univeral khilafah. Mainstream Muslims are 'simply not interested'.[7]

In the past, new systems have emerged from changing circumstances as well as themselves changing circumstances. But systems have also adapted to changing circumstances as well as adapting them. It is impossible – at least for the historian – to see at present beyond the latter process.

Southeast Asian states share the problems and challenges other states face. Given their post-colonial insistence on 'Westphalia', it could hardly be otherwise. But they have added to it a distinctive kind of regionalism that this book has ventured, perhaps questionably, to consider a further 'system', inasmuch as it has involved the so-called 'ASEAN way'. Its main success has been in providing the region as a whole, and the states within it, with a measure of security, even at the cost of partly unspoken modifications of their status as fully independent states. That was indeed its main task. Whether it can deepen its approach is in question. Whether it can add to its security, or that of its members, by extending its approach remains to be seen.

Regionalism in itself is, after all, no guarantee against the assertion of hierarchy, with the limited security it provides even for states of subordinate status. But, if approached in the ASEAN manner, it may help to provide lesser states with a degree of security and independence over against greater states that supplements the guarantees offered by the world-wide acceptance of the Westphalia principles. Diplomacy will still, of course, be required, and a degree of make-believe, too: but that has been true of all systems.

Historians rarely include Southeast Asia in their more general surveys or analyses. Students of IR may find its experience too peculiar for their models. Yet, as this book has been able only to hint, it provides rich material for both. And so, too, for those who themselves practise international relations now and in the uncertain future.

Notes

1 Introduction

1 TLS, 21.4.2004, p. 27.
2 Robert M. Crawford, *Idealism and Realism in International Relations,* London, New York: Routledge, 2000, p. 34.
3 Torbjorn Knutsen, *A History of International Relations Theory*, Manchester: Manchester University Press, 1992, p. 193.
4 Scott Burchell et al., *Theories of International Relations*, Basingstoke, New York: Palgrave, 2001, p. 6.
5 E.H. Carr, *The Twenty Years' Crisis 1919–1939*, London: Macmillan, 1939/81, p. 8.
6 Knutsen, p. 193.
7 Gunhild Hoogensen, *International Relations, Security and Jeremy Bentham*, Abingdon: Routledge, 2005, pp. 1, 17n.
8 William Olson and Nicholas Onuf, 'The growth of a discipline: reviewed', in Steve Smith, ed., *International Relations: British and American Perspectives*, Oxford, New York: Blackwell, 1985, p. 12.
9 Christopher Hill, 'History and International Relations', in Steve Smith, ed., *International Relations: British and American Perspectives*, Oxford, New York: Blackwell, 1985, pp. 131–2.
10 Kenneth Waltz, *Theory of International Relations*, New York: McGraw-Hill, 1979, pp. 91–2.
11 Ibid., p. 96.
12 Crawford, pp. 78–9.
13 Thongchai Winichakul, *Siam Mapped*, Honolulu: University of Hawaii Press, 1994, p. 14.
14 M. Stuart-Fox, *The Lao Kingdom of Lan Xang*, Bangkok: White Lotus, 1998, p. 15.
15 David Reynolds, *Summits*, London: Penguin, 2008, p. 18.
16 Thongchai, p. 81.
17 C.H. Alexandrowicz, *An Introduction to the History of the Law of Nations in the East Indies*, Oxford: Clarendon Press, 1967, p. 156.
18 Introduction to *The Expansion of International Society*, Oxford: Clarendon Press, 1984, p. 1.
19 Quoted in Ian Hall, *The International Thought of Martin Wight*, Basingstoke, New York: Palgrave Macmillan, 2006, p. 100.
20 Jan Wisseman-Christie, *Theatre States and Oriental Despotism*, Hull: Centre for South-East Asian Studies, 1985, p. 10.
21 C. Geertz, *Negara. The Theatre State in Nineteenth-Century Bali*, Princeton, NJ: Princeton University Press, 1980, p. 13.

22 H. Schulte Noordholt, *Bali: Colonial Concepts and Political Change, 1700–1940*, Rotterdam: Erasmus University, 1986, p. 9.
23 M. Ricklefs, 'Unity and disunity in Javanese political and religious thought of the eighteenth century', *Modern Asian Studies*, 26, 2 (May 1992), p. 665.
24 Janet Lippman Abu-Lughod, 'The world system in the thirteenth century: dead end or precursor', in Michael Adas, ed., *Islamic and European Expansion*, Philadelphia, PA: Temple University Press, 1993, p. 95.
25 The phrase is Stephen Gould's. 'Evolution and the triumph of homology', *American Scientist*, 70 (1986), p. 64.
26 Gomara, quoted in J.H. Elliott, *The Old World and the New*, Cambridge: Cambridge University Press, 1970, p. 10.
27 Dona Torr, Introduction to *Marx on China*, London: Lawrence and Wishart, 1951, p. xvi.
28 Alexandrowicz, p. 213.
29 John E. Wills, *Embassies and Illusions*, Cambridge, MA: Harvard University Press, 1984, pp. 31–2, 154.
30 Quoted in F.H. Hinsley, *Sovereignty*, London: Watts, 1966, p. 194.
31 Quoted in James R. Fichter, *So Great a Proffit*, Cambridge, MA: Harvard University Press, 2010, p. 67.
32 E.H. Pritchard, *The Crucial Years of Anglo-Chinese Relations*, Pullman, WA: State University of Washington, 1936, pp. 256–7.
33 Quoted in David Scott, *China and the International System 1840–1949*, Albany, NY: SUNY Press, 2008, p. 16.
34 Quoted in Julia Lovell, *The Great Wall*, London: Atlantic, 2006, p. 280.
35 Quoted in Alfred P. Rubin, *The International Personality of the Malay Peninsula*, Kuala Lumpur: Penerbit Universiti Malaya, 1974, p. 198.
36 Ibid., p. 252.
37 Quoted in W.G. Beasley, *Great Britain and the Opening of Japan*, London: Luzac, 1951, p. 89.
38 Hinsley, p. 206.
39 Kobkua Suwannathat-Pian, *Thai-Malay Relations*, Singapore: OUP, 1988, pp. 1, 4, 44.
40 C.P. Fitzgerald, *The Chinese View of their Place in the World*, London: OUP, 1964, pp. 60–1.
41 Tony Day, *Fluid Iron*, Honolulu: University of Hawaii Press, 2002, pp. 91, 292.
42 Ibid., p. 297.

2 Traditional hierarchy

1 Hermann Kulke, 'The early and imperial kingdom in Southeast Asian history', in David G. Marr and A.C. Milner, *Southeast Asia in the 9th to 14th Centuries*, Singapore: ISEAS; and Canberra: RSPacS, Australian National University, 1986, p. 2.
2 *Les états hindouisés d'Indochine et d'Indonésie*, Paris: E. de Boccard, 1948.
3 Kulke, pp. 5–8.
4 Leong Sau Heng, 'Collecting centres, feeder points and entrepots in the Malay Peninsula, 1000 B.C. – A.D. 1400', in J. Kathirithamby-Wells and John Villiers, eds, *The Southeast Asian Port and Polity*, Singapore : Singapore University Press, 1990, p. 20.
5 Ibid., p. 21.
6 Ibid., p. 31.
7 Jan Wisseman Christie, 'Trade and state formation in the Malay Peninsula and Sumatra, 300 B.C. – A.D. 700', in Kathirithamby-Wells and Villiers, p. 42.
8 Ibid., p. 47.

9 Ibid., p. 46.
10 Ibid., p. 55.
11 Ibid., pp. 54–6.
12 Nik Hassan Shuhaimi bin Nik Abd. Rahman, 'The kingdom of Srivijaya as socio-political and cultural entity', in Kathirithamby-Wells and Villiers, pp. 65, 67.
13 Ibid., p. 64.
14 Christopher I. Beckwith, *Empires of the Silk Road*, Princeton, NJ: Princeton University Press, 2009, pp. 12, 14.
15 N. Davies, *God's Playground*, London: OUP, 2005, I, p. 56.
16 O. Wolters, 'Southeast Asia as a Southeast Asian field of study', in O. Wolters, ed. Craig J. Reynolds, *Early Southeast Asia Selected Essays*, Ithaca, NY: Cornell University SEAP, 2008, pp. 48–9.
17 O.W. Wolters, *History, Culture and Region in Southeast Asian Perspectives*, Singapore: ISEAS, 1982, pp. 16–19; revised edition, Ithaca, NY: SEAP; Singapore: ISEAS, 1999, pp. 27–9.
18 Nik, p. 78.
19 S.J. Tambiah, *World Conqueror and World Renouncer*, Cambridge: Cambridge University Press, 1976, p. 30.
20 Ibid., pp. 40–1, 46–7.
21 Ibid., p. 70.
22 Tambiah, pp. 102, 110, 112–13, 123.
23 V. Lieberman, *Strange Parallels*, Cambridge: Cambridge University Press, 2003, I, p. 33.
24 Davies, *God's Playground*, I, p. 30.
25 L.Y. Andaya, *Leaves of the Same Tree*, Honolulu: University of Hawaii Press, 2008, p. 66.
26 Wolters, ed. Reynolds, 'Restudying some Chinese writings on Sriwijaya', p. 127.
27 Wolters, *History, Culture and Region*, 1999, pp. 27–8.
28 Wolters, ed. Reynolds, 'Ayudhya and the rearward part of the world', pp. 157, 158, 162–3.
29 Jan Wisseman-Christie, *Theatre States and Oriental Despotism*, Hull: Centre for South-East Asian Studies, 1985, pp. 20, 21, 38.
30 John K. Whitmore, 'The last great king of classical Southeast Asia: Che Bong Nga and fourteenth-century Champa', in Tran Ky Phuong and Bruce M. Lockhart, eds, *The Cham of Vietnam*, Singapore: NUS Press, 2011, p. 169.
31 R. Hagesteijn, *Circles of Kings: Political Dynamics in Early Continental Southeast Asia*, Dordrecht: Foris, 1989, p. 139.
32 Ibid., p. 102.
33 Ian Mabbett, 'Kingship in Angkor', *Journal of the Siam Society*, 66, 2 (July 1978), p. 29.
34 Wolters, ed. Reynolds, 'Ayudhya', p. 158.
35 Michael D. Coe, *Angkor and the Khmer Civilization*, London: Thames and Hudson, 2003, p. 194.
36 Ian Harris, 'Rethinking Cambodian political discourse on territory', *Journal of Southeast Asian Studies*, 41, 2 (June 2010), p. 224.
37 M. Stuart-Fox, *The Lao Kingdom of Lan Xang*, Bangkok: White Lotus, 1998, pp. 45, 48.
38 Whitmore, pp. 169, 177, 178.
39 Soemarsaid Moertono, *State and Statecraft in Old Java*, Ithaca, NY: Cornell University Press, 1968, pp. 111–12.
40 W.F. Wertheim, 'The sociological approach', in Soedjatmoko et al., eds, *An Introduction to Indonesian Historiography*, Ithaca, NY: Cornell University Press, 1965, p. 349.

41 B. Schrieke, *Indonesian Sociological Studies II Ruler and Realm in Early Java*, The Hague: Bandung, 1957, pp. 221, 228.
42 E. Locher Scholten, *Sumatran Sultanate and Colonial State*, Ithaca, NY: Cornell SEAP, 2003, pp. 45–6.
43 Luis Felipe Ferreira Reis Thomaz, 'The Malay Sultanate of Melaka', in A. J. S. Reid, *Southeast Asia in the Early Modern Era*, Ithaca, NY: Cornell University Press, 1993, p. 77.
44 C.M. Reber, 'The Sulu world in the eighteenth and early nineteenth centuries', MA thesis, Cornell University, 1966, p. 64.
45 P. Wheatley, 'Desultory remarks on the ancient history of the Malay Peninsula', in J. Bastin and R. Roolvink, eds, *Malayan and Indonesian Studies,* Oxford: Clarendon Press, 1964, p. 58.
46 Brantly Womack, *China and Vietnam. The Politics of Assymetry*, New York: Cambridge University Press, 2006, p. 136.
47 J.K. Fairbank, 'A preliminary framework', in J.K. Fairbank, ed., *The Chinese World Order*, Cambridge, MA: Harvard University Press, 1968, p. 4.
48 Ibid., p. 249.
49 Womack, p. 113.
50 Truong Buu Lam, 'Comments and generalities on Sino-Vietnamese relations', in E. Wickberg, comp., *Historical Interaction of China and Vietnam,* Lawrence, KS: Center for East Asian Studies, University of Kansas, 1969, p. 47.
51 Ibid., p. 57.
52 Quoted in O. Wolters, *The Fall of Sri Vijaya in Malay History*, London: Lund Humphries, 1970, p. 50.
53 Wang Gungwu, 'Early Ming relations with Southeast Asia', in J.K. Fairbank, ed., *The Chinese World Order*, Cambridge, MA: Harvard University Press, 1968, p. 54.
54 M. Stuart-Fox, *A Short History of China and Southeast Asia*, Crows Nest, NSW: Allen and Unwin, 2003, p. 86. G. Wade in G. Wade and Sun Laichen, eds, *Southeast Asia in the Fifteenth Century*, Singapore: NUS Press, p. 28.
55 Stuart-Fox, *Short History*, p. 87.
56 Karl Hack and T. Rettig, *Colonial Armies in Southeast Asia*, London, New York: Routledge, 2006, p. 19.
57 Geoff Wade, 'Ming Chinese colonial armies in Southeast Asia', in ibid., p. 77.
58 Julia Lovell, *The Great Wall*, London: Atlantic, 2006, p. 184.
59 Wolters, *Fall*, p. 37.
60 O.W. Wolters, *Early Indonesian Commerce,* Ithaca, NY: Cornell University Press, 1967, p. 223.
61 Derek Heng, *Sino-Malay Trade and Diplomacy from the Tenth through the Fourteenth Century*, Athens, OH: Ohio University Press, 2009, p. 26.
62 Ibid., p. 53.
63 Ibid., p. 65.
64 Ibid., p. 211.
65 Stuart-Fox, *Short History*, p. 93.
66 Wolters, ed. Reynolds, 'China Irredenta: The South', p. 68.
67 Wolters, ed. Reynolds, 'Chinese writings', pp. 143, 145.
68 Wang Gungwu, 'China and South-east Asia 1402–24', in J. Ch'en and N. Tarling, eds, *Studies in the Social History of China and Southeast Asia,* Cambridge: Cambridge University Press, 1970, p. 397.
69 Wang Gungwu, 'The opening of relations between China and Malacca in 1401–5', in J. Bastin and R. Roolvink, eds, *Malayan and Indonesian Studies,* Oxford: Clarendon Press, 1964, p. 101.
70 Stuart-Fox, *Short History*, p. 92.
71 Wolters, *Fall*, p. 155.

72 Danny Wong Tze Ken, *The Nguyen and Champa during 17th and 18th Century*, Paris, San Jose: International Office of Champa, 2007, pp. 62, 64.
73 A. Woodside, *Vietnam and the Chinese Model,* Cambridge, MA: Harvard University Press, 1971, p. 259.

3 Conquests and contracts

1 Michael Donelan in Hedley Bull and Adam Watson, eds, *The Expansion of International Society*, Oxford: Clarendon Press, 1984, p. 81.
2 Ibid., p. 81.
3 Lewis Hanke, *The Spanish Struggle for Justice in the Conquest of America*, Philadelphia, PA: University of Pennsylvania Press, 1949/1959, p. 27.
4 Quoted in ibid., p. 125.
5 Quoted in Donelan, p. 83.
6 Quoted in Hanke, p. 154.
7 Donelan, p. 83.
8 Hanke, p. 151.
9 Martin C. Orten, 'Vitoria and the universalist concept of international relations', in Ian Clarke and Iver B. Neumann, eds, *Classical Theories of International Relations*, Basingstoke: Macmillan; New York: St Martin's, 1996, pp. 105–6.
10 Hanke, p. 151.
11 Donelan, p. 84.
12 Hedley Bull, 'The emergence of a universal international society', in Hedley Bull and Adam Watson, eds, *The Expansion of International Society*, Oxford: Clarendon Press, 1984, p. 120.
13 P. Brummett, *Ottoman Seapower and Levantine Diplomacy in the Age of Discovery*, Albany, NY: SUNY Press, 1994, p. 21–2.
14 Ibid., p. 22.
15 T. Naff, 'The Ottoman empire and the European states system', in Hedley Bull and Adam Watson, eds, *The Expansion of International Society*, Oxford: Clarendon Press, 1984, p. 144.
16 Alfred P. Rubin, *The International Personality of the Malay Peninsula*, Kuala Lumpur: Penerbit Universiti Malaya, 1974, p. 8.
17 Brummett, p. 22.
18 Naff, pp. 146–8.
19 C.H. Alexandrowicz, *Treaty and Diplomatic Relations between European and South Asian Powers in the Seventeenth and Eighteenth Centuries*, Leyden: Sijthoff, 1961, p. 251.
20 Bernard Lewis, *The Muslim Discovery of Europe*, New York, London: Norton, 1982/2001, p. 49.
21 Quoted in Brummett, p. 45.
22 James J. Boyajian, *Portuguese Trade in Asia under the Habsburgs, 1580–1640*, Baltimore, MD, and London: Johns Hopkins University Press, 1993, p. 1.
23 Ibid., p. 1.
24 Ibid., pp. 6–7.
25 A. Watson, 'European international society and its expansion', in Hedley Bull and Adam Watson, eds, *The Expansion of International Society*, Oxford: Clarendon Press, 1984, p. 19.
26 S. Subramanyam, *The Portuguese Empire in Asia, 1500–1700,* London, New York: Longman, 1993, p. 78.
27 Hedley Bull, 'The revolt against the West', in Hedley Bull and Adam Watson, eds, *The Expansion of International Society*, Oxford: Clarendon Press, 1984, p. 227.

28 Boyajian, pp. 72–3.
29 Ibid., p. 9.
30 Boyajian, p. 110.
31 Ibid., p. 114.
32 P. Borschberg, *Hugo Grotius, the Portuguese and Free Trade in the East Indies*, Singapore: NUS Press, 2011, p. 123.
33 M.J. van Ittersum, *Profit and Principle*, Leiden: Brill, 2006, pp. lvi, 29, 57.
34 Ibid., pp. 361–3, 387–8, 430.
35 Ibid., pp. xxvii, xxviii.
36 Ibid., pp. xxix, xxx.
37 James A. Nathan, *Soldiers, Statecraft and History*, Westport, CT, and London: Praeger, 2002, pp. 13, 16.
38 Paul W. Schroeder, 'Not even for the seventeenth and eighteenth centuries …', in Ernest R. May, Richard Rosecrance, and Z. Steiner, eds, *History and Neorealism*, Cambridge: Cambridge University Press, 2010, p. 82.
39 Hedley Bull, *The Anarchical Society*, Basingstoke: Palgrave, 3rd edition, 2002, pp. 12–13.
40 Quoted in Edward Keene, *Beyond the Anarchical Society*, Cambridge: Cambridge University Press, 2002, p. 20.
41 B.W. Andaya, *To Live as Brothers*, Honolulu: University of Hawaii Press, 1993, p. 61.
42 Ibid., p. 147.
43 Borschberg, *Hugo Grotius,* p. 154.
44 Ibid., p. 157.
45 L.Y. Andaya, 'Cultural state formation in eastern Indonesia', in A.J.S. Reid, ed., *Southeast Asia in the Early Modern Era*, Ithaca, NY: Cornell University Press, 1993, p. 35.
46 Leonard Y. Andaya, *The World of Maluku*, Honolulu: University of Hawaii Press, 1993, pp. 186, 190.
47 Quoted in B.W. Andaya, *The Abode of Grace*, Kuala Lumpur: OUP, 1979, p. 78.
48 Ibid., p. 93.
49 Ibid., pp. 79–80.
50 Quoted in ibid., p. 230.
51 Ibid., p. 239.
52 L.Y. Andaya, 'De VOC en de Maleise wereled in de 17de en 18de eeuw', in M.A.R. Meiliink-Roelofsz et al., *De VOC in Azië*, Bussum: Unieboek, 1976, pp. 120–1.
53 L.Y. Andaya, *The Kingdom of Johor 1641–1728*, Kuala Lumpur: OUP, 1975, pp. 57–8, 137.
54 P. Borschberg, *The Singapore and Melaka Straits*, Singapore: NUS Press, 2010, p. 200.
55 Reinhout Vos, 'The broken balance. The origins of the war between Riau and the VOC in 1783–84', in G.J. Schutte, ed., *State and Trade in the Indonesian Archipelago*, Leiden: KITLV Press, 1994, p. 116–17.
56 Quoted in ibid., p. 127.
57 Quoted in B.W. Andaya, *To Live as Brothers*, Honolulu: University of Hawaii Press, 1993, pp. 193–4.
58 Dianne Lewis, *Jan Compagnie in the Straits of Malacca 1641–1795*, Athens, OH: Ohio University, 1995, pp. 127–8, 132.
59 George Brian Souza, *The Survival of Empire*, Cambridge: Cambridge University Press, 1986, p. 2.
60 Ibid., p. 6.
61 Wolters, *Fall*, p. 178.

62 Souza, p. 16.
63 R. Ptak, 'Sino-Portuguese Relations circa 1513/14–1550s', in *China, the Portuguese, and the Nanyang*, Aldershot: Ashgate, 2004, Variorum ed., p. II 21.
64 Sarasin Viraphol, *Tribute and Profit Sino-Siamese Trade 1652–1853*, Cambridge, MA, and London: Harvard University Press, 1977, p. 30.
65 Ibid., pp. 2, 5–6.
66 Ian Hall, *The International Thought of Martin Wight*, Basingstoke, New York: Palgrave Macmillan, 2006, pp. 389–91.
67 Viraphol, pp. 145, 153, 158.
68 Dhiravat na Pombejra, 'Conflict and commerce in the Gulf of Siam, c.1629–42', in V. Grabowsky, ed., *Southeast Asian Historiography Unravelling the Myths*, Bangkok: River Books, 2011, p. 147. Kobkua Suwannathat-Pian, *Thai-Malay Relations*, Singapore: OUP, 1988, p. 57.
69 Hall, pp. 169–70.
70 Hall, p. 409; Truong Buu Lam, 'Intervention versus tribute in Sino-Vietnamese relations', in J.K. Fairbank, ed., *The Chinese World Order*, Cambridge, MA: Harvard University Press, 1968.
71 C.M. Reber, 'The Sulu world in the eighteenth and early nineteenth centuries', MA thesis, Cornell University, 1966, pp. 129, 148.
72 M. Stuart-Fox, *A Short History of China and Southeast Asia*, Crows Nest, NSW: Allen and Unwin, 2003, p. 88.
73 Quoted in Andrew Hurrell, 'Vattel: Pluralism and its limits', in Ian Clarke and Iver B. Neumann, eds, *Classical Theories of International Relations*, Basingstoke: Macmillan; New York: St Martin's, 1996, pp. 239, 243, 245.
74 Quoted in N. Ferguson, *The War of the World*, London: Penguin, 2007, p. 92.

4 European empires

1 S. Crowe, *The Berlin West Africa Conference*, New York: Longmans, 1942, p. 190.
2 Quoted in James A. Nathan, *Soldiers, Statecraft and History*, Westport, CT, and London: Praeger, 2002, p. 96.
3 N. Tarling, *The Burthen, the Risk and the Glory*, Kuala Lumpur: Oxford University Press, 1982, pp. 339–40.
4 Quoted in Yao Jen-to in Ping-hui Lao and David Der-wei Wang, eds, *Taiwan under Japanese Rule*, New York: Columbia University Press, 2006, p. 39.
5 L. Blussé et al., eds, *Pilgrims to the Past*, Leiden: Leiden University, 1996, p. 18.
6 W. Gifford Palgrave, *Ulysses or Scenes and Studies in Many Lands*, London, New York: Macmillan, 1887, p. 150.
7 Percival Spear, *India*, Ann Arbor, MI: University of Michigan Press, 1961, p. 243.
8 Quoted in N.A. Pelcovits, *Old China Hands and the Foreign Office*, New York: King's Crown, 1948, p. 125.
9 Palmerston to Brooke, 18.12.1849. FO 69/1, National Archives, Kew.
10 Quoted in Ella Laffey, 'The content of the Sino-Vietnamese tributary relationship in the late nineteenth century', in E. Wickberg, comp., *Historical Interaction of China and Vietnam*, Lawrence, KS: Center for East Asian Studies, University of Kansas, 1969, p. 26.
11 Quoted in Eugene K. Lawson, *The Sino-Vietnamese Conflict*, New York: Praeger, 1984, p. 17.
12 Churchill/Viceroy, 5.11.1885, quoted in Md Shamsher Ali, 'The beginnings of British rule in Upper Burma', PhD thesis, London University, 1976, p. 120.
13 Ibid., p. 121.

14 Sun Laichen in G. Wade and Sun Laichen, eds, *Southeast Asia in the Fifteenth Century*, Singapore: NUS Press, Hong Kong University Press, 2010, p. 60.
15 Michael Symes, *An Account of the Embassy to the Kingdom of Ava*, London: 1800, pp. 463–4.
16 Quoted in D.G.E. Hall, *Europe and Burma*, London: Oxford University Press, 1945, p. 96.
17 Quoted in G.P. Ramachandra, 'Anglo-Burmese relations, 1795–1826', PhD thesis, University of Hull, 1977, p. 391.
18 Ibid., p. 433.
19 Quoted in W.S. Desai, *History of the British Residency in Burma*, Rangoon: University of Rangoon Press, 1939, p. 71.
20 Quoted in ibid., p. 196.
21 Ibid., pp. 295–6.
22 Quoted in D.R. SarDesai, *British Trade and Expansion in Southeast Asia*, Columbia: South Asia Books, 1977, p. 115.
23 Quoted in Myo Myint, 'The politics of survival in Burma', PhD thesis, Cornell University, 1987, pp. 277, 287.
24 C.L. Keeton, *King Thibaw and the Ecological Rape of Burma*, Delhi: Manohar, 1974, pp. 127, 370–1.
25 P. Tuck, *The French Wolf and the Siamese Lamb*, Bangkok, Cheney: White Lotus, 1995, p. 76.
26 Quoted in Keeton, p. 243.
27 Grantham/Fitzherbert, 18.12.1783. FO 27/3.
28 Quoted in N. Tarling, *Anglo-Dutch Rivalry in the Malay World 1780–1824*, Cambridge: Cambridge University Press; St Lucia: University of Queensland Press, 1962, p. 9.
29 For an account of their struggle, see S. Schama, *Patriots and Liberators*, London: Harper Perennial, 2nd edition, 1992, ch. 3.
30 Leeds/Auckland, 1.2.1791. FO 37/33.
31 Quoted in Holden Furber, *Henry Dundas*, London: Oxford University Press, 1931, pp. 103–4.
32 Raffles/Minto, 10.6.1811, in Sophia Raffles, *Memoir of the Life and Public Services of Sir Thomas Stamford Raffles*, London: Murray, 1830, pp. 69–82.
33 Memorandum on Mr Raffles' letter and Minute to the Governor-General dated 11 February 1814. Java Factory Records 64, British Library.
34 Quoted in John Bastin, 'Raffles and British policy in the Indian Archipelago, 1811–16', *Journal of the Malayan Branch of the Royal Asiatic Society*, 27,1 (May 1954), pp. 108–9.
35 Quoted in Tarling, *Anglo-Dutch Rivalry*, p. 86.
36 Ibid., p. 155.
37 G.J. Resink, *Indonesia's History between the Myths*, The Hague: Van Hoeve, 1968, p. 110.
38 Ibid., p. 128.
39 G.J. Resink, 'The significance of the history of international law in Indonesia', in Soedjatmoko et al., eds, *An Introduction to Indonesian Historiography*, Ithaca, NY: Cornell University Press, 1965, p. 366.
40 E. Locher Scholten, *Sumatran Sultanate and Colonial State*, Ithaca, NY: Cornell SEAP, 2003, pp. 33–4.
41 P. Borschberg, *Hugo Grotius, the Portuguese and Free Trade in the East Indies*, Singapore: NUS Press, 2011, p. 154.
42 Quoted in ibid., p. 137.
43 Edward Keene, *Beyond the Anarchical Society*, Cambridge: Cambridge University Press, 2002, pp. 107–8.

44 Castlereagh/Clancarty, 13.8.1819. FO 37/107.
45 Jan M. Somer, *De korte verklarung*, Breda, Corona, 1934, pp. 277, 362–3.
46 M. Leifer, *The Foreign Relations of the New States*, Camberwell: Longmans, 1974, p. 4.
47 Keeton, pp. 303–4, 317–18.
48 Quoted in Nguyen The Anh, *The Withering Days of the Nguyen Dynasty*, Singapore: ISEAS, 1978, pp. 26–7.
49 Bruce Lockhart, *The End of the Vietnamese Monarchy*, New Haven, CT: Yale Center for International and Asian Studies, 1993, p. 193.
50 Peter Burroughs in *Oxford History of the British Empire*, Oxford: Oxford University Press, 1999, III, p. 190.
51 C. Newbury, '"Treaty, grant, usage and sufferance": the origins of British colonial protectorates', in G.A. Wood and P.S. O'Connor, *W.P. Morrell: A Tribute*, Dundein: Otago University Press, 1973, p. 70.
52 Ibid., p. 71.
53 Quoted in W. Ross Johnston, *Sovereignty and Protection*, Durham, NC: Duke University Press, 1973, p. 177.
54 Ibid., p. 179.
55 Quoted in K.J. Bade, 'The German colonial movement', in S. Forster, W. J. Mommsen and R. Robinson, eds, *Bismarck, Europe and Africa*, Oxford: Oxford University Press, 1988, p. 163.
56 Johnston, pp. 194, 201.
57 Johnston, pp. 178–9.
58 Quoted in Newbury, p. 79.
59 Newbury, pp. 80–1. Leopold II's campaign against slavery in his Congo state took the form of conquest. E.H. Kossmann, *The Low Countries*, Oxford: Clarendon Press, 1978, p. 386.
60 Johnston, pp. 236–8.
61 Newbury, pp. 81–2.
62 Johnston, p. 261. See also A. Rubin, *Piracy Paramountcy and Protectorates*, Kuala Lumpur: Penerbit Universiti Malaya, 1974, pp. 7.
63 Johnston, p. 263.
64 Minute by Clubley, 16.9.1823. Straits Settlements Factory Records 91, British Library.
65 Cavenagh/Secretary, 16.12.1861, 213. Collection No. 6 to No. 94 of 1862, Collections to Political Despatches to India 63, British Library.
66 Cavenagh/Secretary, 31.12.63, no. 243/1732. Collection 6 to No. 33 of 1864. Collections to Political Despatches 72.
67 Viceroy/Wood, 8.2.1864, 23. Collection 2 to No. 33 of 1864. Ibid.
68 C.D. Cowan, *Nineteenth-Century Malaya: the Origins of British Political Control*, Oxford: Oxford University Press, 1961, p. 163.
69 Ibid., pp. 167–8.
70 Minute, 31 August 1873, q. Cowan, p. 165.
71 Ibid., pp. 165–6.
72 Q. ibid., p. 169.
73 Q. Cowan, p. 160.
74 Smith/CO, 1 October 1884, quoted in Eunice Thio, *British Policy in the Malay Peninsula 1880–1910*, Kuala Lumpur: University of Malaya Press, 1969, p. 67.
75 Quoted in Thio, pp. 68, 69.
76 Thio, pp. 78–81.
77 Nesasamalar Nadarajah, *Johore and the Origins of British Control*, KL: arenabuku, 2000, pp. 31–2.
78 Smith/CO, 3 July 1888, and minute, q. Thio, *Malay Peninsula,* pp. 89, 90.

79 Ibid., pp. 94, 129, 131.
80 Q. ibid., p. 134.
81 Q. ibid., p. 126.
82 Q. ibid., pp. 144–5.
83 Ibid., p. 159.
84 Q. ibid., p. 166.
85 A. Lau, *The Malayan Union Controversy*, Singapore: Oxford University Press, 1991, p. 11.
86 Opinion, 26 January 1855. Parliamentary Papers 1854/5 XXIX [1976], pp. 4ff.
87 Memorandum on the Position of Sir James Brooke at Sarawak. ibid., pp. 12ff.
88 Memorandum, 20 February 1856. FO 12/23.
89 Brooke/Charles Grant, 15 August 1856. MSSPac.s 90 vol. 4, Rhodes House Library.
90 Minutes on Brooke/Russell, 26 November 1859. FO 12/35.
91 Brooke/Brooke Brooke, 6 December 1859. MSS Pac.s 90 vol. 2B.
92 Brooke Brooke/Brooke, 18 December 1859. Ibid., vol 5.
93 Etienne Denis, *Bordeaux et la Cochinchine,* Bordeaux: Delmas, 1965, pp. 138–9.
94 Quoted in Tarling, *The Burthen*, p. 340.
95 Report upon the Settlement of Sarawak, 20 November 1862. Secret Letters Received from Bengal, second series, 19, British Library. See also his *Reminiscences of An Indian Official,* London, 1884, pp. 330–1.
96 Elgin/Russell, 8 January 1863. Mss Eur F. 83 vol. 25, India Office Records.
97 Russell/Ricketts, 27.2.64, 2. FO 12/32A.
98 Treacher/Derby, 2.1.1878, Cons 1. FO 12/53.
99 Minute in CO 144/51 [3242], National Archives, Kew.
100 Memorandum, 11.10.1879. FO 12/54.
101 LO/FO, 17.9.1880. FO 12/55.
102 N. Tarling, *Sulu and Sabah*, Kuala Lumpur: Oxford University Press, 1978, pp. 236–7.
103 A. Dent/W.H. Read, 21.4.1882. CO 874/113.
104 R. Oliver and G. Mathew, eds, *History of East Africa,* Oxford: Clarendon Press, 1963, pp. 360–1, 379–80.
105 Minute, 14.1.1885. CO 144/58 [22442].
106 Memorandum in FO 12/68.
107 Memorandum, 26.8.1886. FO 12/72.
108 Memorandum, 27.1.1887. FO 12/76.
109 Minute in FO 12/75.
110 Minute, 18.5.1896. CO 144/70 [10680].
111 Minute, 6.12.1906. CO 531/1 [34640].
112 Quoted in John D. Blanco, *Frontier Constitutions*, Berkeley, Los Angeles, CA, and London: University of California Press, 2009, p. 49.
113 Quoted in Peter A. Jackson in Rachel V. Harrison and Jackson, eds, *The Ambiguous Allure of the West*, Singapore: Hong Kong University Press/Cornell SEAP, 2010, p. 45.
114 Quoted in ibid., pp. 45, 49.
115 Sarasin Viraphol, *Tribute and Profit Sino-Siamese Trade 1652–1853*, Cambridge, MA, and London: Harvard University Press, 1977, pp. 236–7.
116 Kobkua Suwannathat-Pian, *Thai-Malay Relations*, Singapore: Oxford University Press, 1988, p. 211.
117 Wu Xiao An, *Chinese Business in the Making of a Malay State*, Singapore: NUS Press, 2010, p. 115.
118 *Report on the Condition of the Philippines in 1842*, Manila: Historical Conservation Sciety, 1963, pp. 191–2, 194.

119 Tobin/State Department, 23.11.1925, quoted in N.A. Bootsma, *Buren in de koloniale tijd*, Dordrecht: Foris, 1986, p. 70.
120 K.S. Mathew in V. Suryanarayan and V. Sudarsen, eds, *Andaman and Nicobar Islands*, Delhi: Konark, 1994, p. 55.
121 Ibid., pp. 55–6; R. Singh in ibid., p. 158.

5 The Co-Prosperity Sphere

1 Niall Ferguson, *The War of the World*, London: Penguin, 2007, p. 160.
2 Quoted in Paul Dukes, *October and the World*, London: Macmillan, 1974, p. 96.
3 E.H. Carr, *The Bolshevik Revolution 1917–1923*, London: Penguin, 1966, I, p. 433.
4 Terry Martin, *The Affirmative Action Empire*, Ithaca, NY: Cornell University Press, 2001, p. 3.
5 Quoted in J. Chen, *Mao and the Chinese Revolution*, London: OUP, 1965, p. 60.
6 Quoted in A. Zimmern, *The Third British Empire*, London: OUP, 1934, p. 44.
7 Percival Spear, *India*, Ann Arbor, MI: University of Michigan Press, 1961, pp. 342–3.
8 S. Hell, *Siam and the League of Nations*, Bangkok: River Books, 2010, p. 35.
9 Zhang Yongjin, *China in the International System, 1918–20*, Basingstoke: Macmillan, 1991, p. 196.
10 Quoted in Iwata Masakazu, *Okubo Toshimichi,* Berkeley and Los Angeles, CA: University of California Press, 1964, p. 156.
11 Ibid., p. 190.
12 Quoted in George Hicks, *Japan's War Memories,* Aldershot: Ashgate, 1997, p. 8.
13 J.M. Saniel, *Japan and the Philippines,* Quezon City: University of the Philippines, 1962, p. 182.
14 Usha Mahajani, *Philippine Nationalism,* St Lucia: University of Queensland Press, 1971, p. 405.
15 Quibuyen in Fujiwara Kiichi and Nagano Yoshiko, eds, *The Philippines and Japan in America's Shadow*, Singapore: NUS Press, 2011, p. 117.
16 Quoted in Saniel, p. 232.
17 Quoted in P. Oblas in Chaivat Khamchoo and E.B. Reynolds, eds, *Thai-Japanese Relations in Historical Perspective,* Bangkok: Innomedia, 1988, p. 53.
18 Quoted in Shimazu Naoko, *Japan, Race and Equality,* London, New York: Routledge, 1998, p. 102.
19 Quoted in Jerome Chen, *Yuan Shih-kai,* Palo Alto, CA: Stanford University Press, 1972, p. 156.
20 Quoted in Roger Hackett, *Yamagata Aritomo and the Rise of Modern Japan*, Cambridge, MA: Harvard University Press, 1971, p. 285.
21 Kimitada Miwa, 'Japanese policies and concepts for a regional order in Asia, 1938–40', in James W. White, Michio Umegaki and Thomas R.H. Havens, eds, *The Ambivalence of Nationalism*, Lanham, MD: University Press of America, 1990, p. 137.
22 Quoted in Akira Iriye, *Pacific Estrangement*, Cambridge, MA: Harvard University Press, 1972, p. 232.
23 Quoted in C. Thorne, *The Limits of Foreign Policy,* London: Hamilton, 1972, p. 35.
24 Quoted in ibid., pp. 182–3.
25 Tsai in Liao Ping-hui and David Der-wei Wang, eds, *Taiwan under Japanese Colonial Rule*, New York: Columbia University Press, 2006, p. 98.
26 Carter J. Eckart et al., *Korea Old and New*, Seoul: Ilchohak, 1990, p. 281.

27 Yamamuro Shin'ichi, *Manchuria under Japanese Dominion*, Philadelphia, PA: University of Pennsylvania Press, 2006, p. 32.
28 Ibid., pp. 36–7.
29 Ibid., pp. 38, 52.
30 Ibid., pp. 84–7.
31 Ibid., pp. 97, 103–4, 115.
32 Quoted in ibid., p. 117.
33 Quoted in ibid., p. 146.
34 Quoted in ibid., p. 147.
35 Ibid., pp. 236–7.
36 Ibid., p. 123, 186, 187.
37 Hui-yu Carline Ts'ai, *Taiwan in Japan's Empire-Building*, London, New York: Routledge, 2009, p. 170.
38 J.H. Boyle, *China and Japan at War*, Palo Alto, CA: Stanford University Press, 1972, pp. 192–3.
39 David P. Barrett and Larry N. Shyu, *Chinese Collaboration with Japan, 1932–1945*, Palo Alto, CA: Stanford University Press, 2000, p. 9.
40 Quoted in Kimitada, 'Japanese policies', p. 148.
41 Ibid., p. 148.
42 Kimitada Miwa in Sven Saaler and J. Victor Koschmann, eds, *Pan-Asianism in Modern Japanese History*, London, New York: Routledge, 2007, p. 24.
43 Quoted in Akira Nagazumi, *The Dawn of Indonesian Nationalism*, Tokyo: Institute of Developing Economies, 1972, p. 129.
44 P. Baudouin, *The Private Diaries*, London: Eyre and Spottiswoode, 1948, pp. 199, 203.
45 Ikehata Setsuho and Lydia N. Jose, *Philippines-Japan Relations*, Ateneo de Manila University Press, 2003, 59.
46 M. Peattie in P. Duus et al., eds, *The Japanese Wartime Empire*, Princeton, NJ: Princeton University Press, 1996, p. 211.
47 Quoted in Nagaoka Shinjuro in James W. Morley, *The Fateful Choice*, New York: Columbia University Press, 1980, p. 128.
48 Quoted in N. Tarling, *Britain, Southeast Asia and the Onset of the Pacific War*, Cambridge: Cambridge University Press, 1996, pp. 72–3.
49 Quoted in Kimitada, 'Japanese policies', p. 150.
50 Quoted in Akira Iriye, *Power and Culture*, Cambridge, MA: Harvard University Press, 1981, p. 64.
51 Quoted in J.B. Crowley, 'A new Asian order. Some notes on prewar Japanese nationalism', in B. Silberman and H.D. Harootunian, eds, *Japan in Crisis*, Princeton, NJ: Princeton University Press, 1974, pp. 293, 294.
52 Quoted in J. Victor Koschmann in Sven Saaler and J. Victor Koschmann, eds, *Pan-Asianism in Modern Japanese History*, London, New York: Routledge, 2007, p. 197.
53 Quoted in Tarling, *Pacific War*, p. 283.
54 Quoted in Tsunoda Ryusaku et al., comp, *Sources of Japanese Tradition*, New York: Columbia University Press, 1958, II, pp. 294ff.
55 Quoted in Joyce C. Lebra, *Japan's Greater East Asia Co-Prosperity Sphere in World War II,* Kuala Lumpur: Oxford University Press, 1975, pp. 79–80.
56 Ibid., pp. 69–70.
57 Togo Shigenori, *The Cause of Japan*, New York: Simon and Schuster, 1956, pp. 250–1.
58 Quoted in Harry S. Benda et al., *Japanese Military Administration in Indonesia*, New Haven, CT: Yale University Press, 1965, p. 48.
59 Quoted in Iriye, *Power*, p. 115.
60 Quoted in Duus et al., p. xxvi.

61 Shigemitsu Mamoru, *Japan and her Destiny,* trans. O. White, London: Hutchinson, 1958, pp. 289–90.
62 Q. Lebra, *Sphere,* pp. 88ff.
63 Quoted Iriye, *Power,* p. 119; also Lebra, *Sphere,* p. 93.
64 Iriye, *Power,* p. 121.
65 Ibid., p. 170.
66 Quoted in Benda et al., pp. 240–3.
67 L.D. Meo, *Japan's Radio War on Australia 1941–1945*, Melbourne: Melbourne University Press, 1968, p. 189.
68 Iriye, *Power,* p. 241.
69 Ileto in Fujiwara and Nagano, p. 41.
70 Iritani Toshio, *Group Psychology of the Japanese in Wartime,* London and New York: Kegan Paul, 1991, p. 129.
71 Louise Young, *Japan's Total Empire,* Berkeley and Los Angeles, CA: University of California Press, 1998, p. 49.
72 Quoted in Frank N. Trager, ed., *Burma: Japanese Military Administration*, Philadelphia, PA: University of Pennsylvania Press, 1971, pp. 145–8.
73 Quoted in H. Benda and John A. Larkin, *The World of Southeast Asia,* New York: Harper, 1967, p. 228.
74 Ba Maw, *Breakthrough in Burma*, New Haven, CT: Yale University Press, 1968, pp. 312–14.
75 Quoted in Trager, p. 158.
76 Quoted in ibid., pp. 164–8; Benda and Larkin, pp. 230–4.
77 Trager, pp. 168–70.
78 Iriye, *Power,* p. 114.
79 U Nu, *Burma under the Japanese,* London: Macmillan, 1954, p. 87.
80 Ba Maw, p. 335.
81 The minutes of the meetings held at Yulo's house from 6 January onwards, kept in Spanish, are printed in M. Garcia, ed., *Documents on the Japanese Occupation of the Philippines,* Manila: Philippine Historical Association, 1965.
82 A.J. Malay, *Occupied Philippines: the Role of Jorge B. Vargas*, Manila: Filipiniana Book Guild, 1967, pp. 6, 10, 16–17. T. Friend, *Between Two Empires,* New Haven, CT: Yale University Press, 1965, pp. 212–14.
83 Malay, pp. 31–2, 19.
84 Ibid., pp. 60–4.
85 Quoted in Mahajani, p. 426.
86 Manuel L. Quezon, *The Good Fight*, New York: Appleton-Century, 1946, p. 270.
87 Q. Friend, p. 222.
88 Q. Malay, p. 186.
89 Rafaelita H. Soriano, 'Japanese Occupation of the Philippines', PhD thesis, University of Michigan, 1948, p. 232.
90 Quoted in A.V.H. Hartendorp, *The Japanese Occupation of the Philippines,* Manila: Bookmark, 1967, p. 620.
91 Quoted in ibid., p. 636.
92 Quoted in ibid., p. 650.
93 Li Yuk-wai, 'The Chinese Resistance Movement in the Philippines during the Japanese Occupation', *Journal of Southeast Asian Studies*, 23, 2 (September 1992), p. 313.
94 Ibid., pp. 243–4.
95 T. A. Agoncillo, *The Fateful Years,* Quezon City: Garcia, 1965, pp. 829, 831.
96 Ibid., p. 237.
97 Quoted in M.P. Onorato, ed., *Origins of the Philippine Republic,* Ithaca, NY: Cornell University, 1974, p. 207.

98 Friend, p. 237.
99 Mahajani, pp. 442, 443.
100 Quoted in J.M. Lee and M. Petter, *The Colonial Office, War and Development Policy*, London: Temple Smith, 1982, p. 163.
101 Minute, 20.9.1943. Burma Records R/8/13, British Library.
102 Quoted in Goto Ken'ichi, *Tensions of Empire*, Athens, OH and Singapore: Ohio and Singapore University Presses, 2003, p. 62.
103 Kobkua Suwannathat-Pian, *Palace, Political Party and Power*, Singapore: NUS Press, 2011, pp. 105, 107.
104 Quoted in Anthony Reid, *To Nation by Revolution*, Singapore: NUS Press, 2011, p. 159.
105 Quoted in Benda et al., pp. 257–9.
106 Ba Maw, pp. 185–6.
107 Quoted in Goto, p. 215.
108 Quoted in David Scott, *China and the International System 1840–1949*, Albany, NY: SUNY Press, 2008, p. 266.

6 Independence

1 N. Ferguson, *The War of the World*, London: Penguin, 2007, pp. 612, 615.
2 In *Caesarinus Furstenerius*, 1677. Torbjorn Knutsen, *A History of International Relations Theory*, Manchester: Manchester University Press, 1992, p. 77.
3 Memorandum by Byrnes, 18.4.1946. *Foreign Relations of the United States* [FRUS], VIII, p. 874.
4 Walsh to Foreign Secretary, 26 March 1942. FO 371/31751 [F4969/90/61].
5 FE (O) (46) 52, 16.4.1946. CAB 134/280, National Archives, Kew.
6 Telegram, 8.5.1947, 108. FO 371/63591 [F6393/45/62].
7 Minute, 21.7.1947. FO 371/63605 [F9759/45/62].
8 Minute, 13.12.1947. FO 371/63628 [F16032/45/62].
9 Minute, 22.12.1947. FO 371/63630 [F16846/45/62].
10 Minute, n.d. FO 371/69764 [F7623/5/62].
11 Bevin/Jebb, 29.7.1950, 195. FO 371/83705 [FH 1022/62].
12 Quoted in N. Tarling, *Britain and the West New Guinea Dispute*, Lewiston, Queenston, Lampeter: Mellen, 2008, p. 123.
13 Quoted in ibid., p. 212.
14 Minute, 1.6.1960. FO 371/152513 [DJ 1015/13].
15 Minute, 21.7.60. FO 371/152512 [DJ 1015/10].
16 Memorandum, sent to Canberra, 17.9.1960. FO 371/152514 [DJ 1015/33].
17 Note of meeting, Wellington, 16.9.1960. DO 169/187, National Archives, Kew.
18 Minute, 11.1.1961. FO 371/159993 [DJ 1015/12].
19 The Future of the Netherlands New Guinea in the context of a possible 'Melanesian Federation', 9.1.1961. Ibid.
20 Andrew Linklater, 'Rationalism', in Scott Burchill et al., *Theories of International Relations*, Basingstoke, New York: Palgrave, 2001, p. 117.
21 Quoted in ibid., p. 118.
22 D. Vital, *The Inequality of States*, Oxford: Clarendon Press, 1967/72, p. 184.
23 Ramesh Thakur, 'The elusive issue of size: Australia, New Zealand and small states in international relations', in R. Higgott and S.L. Richardson, eds, *International Relations: Global and Australian Perspectives on an Evolving Discipline*, Canberra: RSPacS, ANU, 1991, p. 281.
24 Minute by P. Dean, 9.3.1956. FO 371/123212 [D 1052/4].
25 Record of Conversation, 3.3.1960. FO 371/152145 [D 1061/1].
26 Matthew Jones, *Conflict and Confrontation in South East Asia, 1961–1965*, Cambridge: Cambridge University Press, 2002, p. 62. Tan Tai Yong, 'The

"Grand Design" ...', in Marc Frey, Ronald Pruessen and Tan Tai Yong, *The Transformation of Southeast Asia*, Armonk, NY, and London: Sage, 2003, p. 158.
27 Minute, 24.6.1960. FO 371/152141 [D 1022/21].
28 David Easter, *Britain and the Confrontation with Indonesia,* London, New York: Tauris, 2004, pp. 10–13.
29 Record of Meeting at Quai, 7.8.1961. FO 371/159727 [D 2231/26].
30 Quoted in Ashraf Ghani and Clare Lockhart, *Fixing Failed States*, New York: Oxford University Press, 2009, p. 36.
31 Cablegram, 11.8.1965, 940. Moreen Dee, ed., *Australia and the Formation of Malaysia*, Canberra: DFAT, 2005, p. 475.
32 Brief for Conservative MPs, 28.5.1963. FO 169678 [D1015/8].
33 Henry Chung, *Korea and the United States through War and Peace 1943–1960*, Seoul: Yonsei University Press, 2000, p. 251.
34 Record of a meeting, 26.5.1952. FO 371/101058 [FF10317/78].
35 Telegram, 30.3.1954, 548. FO 371/112049 [DF 1071/107].
36 Telegram, 26.4.1954, 7. FO 371/112055 [DF1071/309].
37 Conversation, 25.4.1954. FO 371/112059 [DF1071/408].
38 Conversation, 27.4.1954. FRUS VI, pp. 577–8.
39 Quoted in Ronald H. Spector, *United States Army in Vietnam Advice and Support: The Early Years 1941–1960,* Washington, DC: Center of Military History United States Army, 1985, p. 229.
40 Michael I. Handel, *Weak States in the International System*, London: Cass, 1990, p. 133.
41 Ibid., p. 131.
42 Chung, pp. 420–1.
43 Seth Jacobs, *America's Miracle Man in Vietnam*, Durham, NC: Duke University Press, 2004, p. 181.
44 Quoted in ibid., p. 181.
45 Quoted in ibid., p. 184.
46 Quoted in ibid., p. 185.
47 Quoted in Seth Jacobs, *Cold War Mandarin*, Lanham, MD: Rowman and Littlefield, 2006, p. 79.
48 Quoted in Jacobs, *Miracle*, p. 211.
49 Philip Catton, *Diem's Final Failure*, Lawrence, KS: University Press of Kansas, 2002, pp. 11, 12.
50 Quoted in Jacobs, *Miracle*, p. 225.
51 Quoted in ibid., p. 216.
52 Quoted in ibid., p. 228.
53 Quoted in Catton, p. 26.
54 Jacobs, *Mandarin*, pp. 10, 97–8.
55 Ibid., p. 124.
56 Ibid., p. 124.
57 Telegram, Young/State Department, 20.5.1961. FRUS 1961–63, pp. 143–6.
58 Memorandum, 20.10.61, in McConaughy/Nolting, 21.10.61. Ibid., pp. 408–11.
59 Quoted in Mark Moyar, *Triumph Forsaken*, Cambridge: Cambridge University Press, 2006, p. 143.
60 Catton, p. 84.
61 Quoted in Marianna P. Sullivan, *France's Vietnam Policy*, Westport, London: Greenwood, 1978, p. 67.
62 Jacobs, *Mandarin*, p. 151.
63 Ibid., p. 153.
64 Quoted in ibid., p. 158.
65 Ibid., pp. 161–2.

66 Ibid., pp. 162–3.
67 Quoted in ibid., p. 163.
68 Ibid., pp. 167–8.
69 Ibid., pp. 170–2.
70 Quoted in ibid., p. 180.
71 Quoted in Moyar, p. 286.
72 Jacobs, *Mandarin*, p. 188.
73 Quoted in ibid., p. 188.
74 Quoted in David W.P. Elliott, 'Official history, revisionist history and world history', in Mark Philip Bradley and Marilyn B. Young, eds, *Making Sense of the Vietnam Wars*, New York: OUP, 2008, p. 293.
75 Quoted in Jacobs, *Miracle*, p. 274.
76 Quoted in Lloyd C. Gardner, *Pay Any Price*, Chicago, IL: Dee, 1995, p. 121.
77 Quoted in ibid., p. 225.
78 Addis/Cable, 26.2.64. FO 371/175066 [D1051/21].
79 See N. Tarling, *Britain and the Neutralisation of Laos*, Singapore: NUS Press, 2011.
80 Arthur S. Dommen, *Conflict in Laos*, London: Pall Mall, 1964, pp. 97–9.
81 Martin E. Goltstein, *American Policy towards Laos*, Rutherford, NJ: Fairleigh Dickinson University Press, 1973, p. 166.
82 Dommen, *Conflict*, p. 90.
83 Roger Hilsman, *To Move a Nation*, Garden City, NY: Doubleday, 1967, p. 113.
84 Stuart Simmonds, 'Independence and political rivalry in Laos 1945–61', in S. Rose, *Politics in Southern Asia*, London: Macmillan, 1963, p. 182.
85 Editorial. Ibid., pp. 274–5.
86 Memorandum of Conversation, 29.6.1961. Ibid., pp. 276–82.
87 Memorandum of Conversation, 30.6.1961. Ibid., pp. 283–6.
88 David Kaiser, *American Tragedy: Kennedy, Johnson, and the Origins of the Vietnam War*, Cambridge, MA, and London: Belknap Press, 2000, p. 79.
89 Telegram, 3.7.1961, 878. FO 371/159857 [DF 1015/918].
90 Hilsman, p. 137.
91 Telegram, 26.10.1961, 729. FO 371/159876 [DF 1015/1299].
92 Telegram, 26.9.1961, 445. PM 479/4/1, Pt. 36, National Archives, Wellington.
93 Telegram, 6.11.1961, Confe 823. FRUS XXIV, pp. 500–1.
94 Telegram, 12.11.1961, 450. Ibid., pp. 507–9.
95 Telegram, 16.11.1961, 718. Ibid., pp. 514–16.
96 Telegram, 9.12.1961, 1378. FO 371/159884 [DF 1015/1449].
97 Australian Telegram, 4.12.1961, 2992. PM 479/4/1 Pt. 37.
98 Telegram, 31.12.1961, 916. FRUS XXIV, pp. 551–2.
99 Telegram, 3.1.1962, 932. Ibid., pp. 553–4.
100 Telegram, 4.1.1962, 937. Ibid., p. 555.
101 Telegram, 19.1.1962, 63. FO 371/166427 [DF 1015/56].
102 Telegram, 18.1.62, Confe 1055. FRUS XXIV,p. 588–90.
103 McLintock/Bowie, 21.5.57. FRUS 1955/57 XXI, p. 563.
104 Telegram, 14.5.62, 1375. FO 371/166458 [DF 103145/34].
105 Tarling, *Laos*, p. 412.
106 Memorandum for Foreign Secretary, 24.5.1962. PREM 11/3740, National Archives, Kew.
107 FRUS XXIV, p. 560n.
108 Ang Cheng Guan, *Vietnamese Communists' Relations with China and the Second Indochina Conflict, 1956–1962*, Jefferson, NC, and London: McFarland, 1997, p. 223.

109 Cyril E. Black, Richard A. Falk, Klaus Knorr and Oran R. Young, *Neutralization and World Politics*, Princeton, NJ: Princeton University Press, 1968, p. v.
110 Telegram, 26.11.63, 11568. FO 371/170062 [DU 1022/71].
111 Cable/Marshall, 20.12.1963. FO 371/170078 [DU 1072/39].
112 Andrew T.H. Tan, *Security Perspectives of the Malay Archipelago*, Cheltenham: Elgar, 2004, p. 93.
113 Telegram, 5.9.1975, 333 FCO 15/1705[100], National Archives, Kew.
114 Ford/Squire, 15.9.1975 FCO 15/1705[115].
115 Telegram, 10.12.1975, 441. FCO 15/1707[250].
116 Tan, *Security Perspectives*, p. 93.
117 M. Leifer, *Singapore's Foreign Policy*, London: Routledge, 2000, p. 88.
118 M. Leifer, *ASEAN and the Security of South-East Asia*, London: Routledge, 1989, p. 46.
119 M. Antolik, *ASEAN and the Diplomacy of Accommodation*, Armonk, NY: Sharpe, 1990, p. 87.
120 Leifer, *ASEAN*, p. 46.
121 Leifer, *Singapore*, pp. 88–9.
122 H. Indorf, *Impediments to Regionalism in Southeast Asia,* Singapore: ISEAS, 1984, p. 45.
123 *Far Eastern Economic Review*, 26.1.84.
124 Indorf, p. 13.

7 Regionalism

1 Coral Bell, *Survey of International Affairs 1954*, New York: Oxford University Press, 1957, p. 245.
2 Ibid., p. 244.
3 Chen Jian, 'Bridging revolution and decolonization: the "Bandung Discourse" in China's early Cold War experience', in Christopher E. Goscha and Christian F. Ostermann, eds, *Connecting Histories: Decolonization and the Cold War in Southeast Asia, 1945–1962*, Washington, DC: Woodrow Wilson Center Press; Palo Alto, CA: Stanford University Press, 2009, p. 153.
4 Quoted in ibid., p. 159.
5 Laking/Sy EA, 28.4.55. FO 371/116884 [D2231/343].
6 Barry Buzan, 'Security architecture in Asia: the interplay of regional and global levels', *The Pacific Review*, 16, 2 (2003), p. 150.
7 Cradock/Newsam, 21.2.58. DO 35/9913 [1].
8 Canadian Embassy Jakarta/Ottawa, 15.1.59, 33. PM 434/10/1 Pt 2 [hereinafter Pt 2].
9 Quoted in J. Saravanamuttu, *The Dilemma of Independence*, Penang: Penerbit USM, 1983, p. 42.
10 Menzies/Ottawa, 18.3.59, 172. IPt 2.
11 Observations, Malayan Proposals for Closer Economic and Cultural Cooperation in South East Asia. Ibid.
12 Hunt/Smith, 8.5.59. DO 35/9913 [53].
13 Peren/Wellington, 13.9.59. Pt 2.
14 Craw/Wellington, 7.8.59. Ibid.
15 Telegram, 18.11.59, 182S. DO 35/9913 [65].
16 Cradock/Ormerod, 28.12.59. Ibid.
17 Garner/Lloyd, 1.2.60, 6. FO 371/152140 [D 1022/3].
18 Crombie/Smith, 3.3.60. DO 35/9913 [83].
19 Telegram, 28.4.60, 258. DO 35/9913 [94].
20 Telegram ex KL, 5.8.60, 165S. FO 371/152141 [D 1022/30].

21 Arnfinn Jorgensen-Dahl, *Regional Organization in South-East Asia,* New York: St Martin's, 1982, pp. 21–2.
22 Chapman for HC/Secretary, 18.4.63. PM 434/10/1.
23 B.K. Gordon, *The Dimensions of Conflict in Southeast Asia,* Englewood Cliffs, NJ: Prentice-Hall, 1966, p. 23.
24 J.A.C. Mackie, *Konfrontasi,* Kuala Lumpur: Oxford University Press, 1974, p. 148.
25 Gordon, pp. 70–1.
26 Jorgensen-Dahl, p. 26.
27 Quoted in Gordon, p. 102.
28 Quoted in ibid., pp. 104, 102n.
29 Ibid., p. 107n.
30 Ibid., p. 71. Matthew Jones, *Conflict and Cooperation in South East Asia*, Cambridge: Cambridge University Press, 2002, pp. 195–6.
31 Ibid., p. 40.
32 Mackie, p. 318.
33 Walker/J.O. Moreton CRO, 6.5.1966. FO 371/185931 [D 1121/13].
34 Hunn for HC/Secretary, 1.7.1966. PM 434/10/1. Partly quoted in Johan Saravanamuttu, *The Dilemma of Independence. Two Decades of Malaysia Foreign Policy 1957–1977*, Penang: Penerbit Universiti Sains Malaysia, 1983, p. 73.
35 Telegram ex Rumbold, 3.6.1966, 410. FO 371/185931 [D1121/15].
36 Phillips/Murray, 16.8.1966. FO 371/185931 [D1121/31].
37 Enclosure A in ibid.
38 Quoted in Jorgensen-Dahl, p. 33.
39 Telegram, 22.5.1967, 496. FCO 24/16[40].
40 Roger Irvine, 'The Formative Years of ASEAN: 1967–75', in A. Broinowski, ed., *Understanding ASEAN,* New York: St Martin's; Australian IIA, 1982, p. 13.
41 Zohrab/Secretary, 15.8.1967. PM 434/12/1.
42 Aust DEA/all posts, 5.9.1967. PM 434/12/1.
43 Laking/all posts, Regional Cooperation in South East Asia, 6.11.1967. PM 434/12/1.
44 Q. H. Heiner, *ASEAN and the ZOPFAN Concept,* Singapore: ISEAS, 1991, p. 13.
45 Speech, 12.3.71, in Clift/Le Breton, 17.3.1971. FCO 24/967 [10].
46 'The neutralisation of Southeast Asia', *Pacific Community,* 3, 1 (October 1971), pp. 110–17.
47 Ibid., pp. 115–16.
48 Quoted in D. Wilson, *The Neutralization of Southeast Asia*, New York, Washington, London: Praeger, 1975, p. 11.
49 Ibid., p. 13.
50 Quoted in M. Leifer, *ASEAN and the Security of South-East Asia*, London: Routledge, 1989, pp. 57–8.
51 Telegram, 25.11.1971, 769. FCO 24/967[32].
52 Leifer, *ASEAN*, p. 58.
53 Heiner Hänggi, *ASEAN and the ZOPFAN Project*, Singapore: ISEAS, 1991, pp. 59–60.
54 Memo, N.Haffey/Ottawa, 26.6.1972, 148, ibid., Pt 3.
55 Middlebrook/Slatcher, 30.1.1973. FCO 24/1529 [13].
56 Tel, 21.4.1973, 387. PM 343/12/1 Pt 4.
57 *Straits Times,* 23.6.73.
58 Quoted in J.L.S. Girling, 'A neutral Southeast Asia?', *Australian Outlook*, 27, 2 (August 1973), p. 130n.

59 Regionalism and Neutralisation, Notes for Opening Remarks, ?15.10.1973. FCO 24/1530[59].
60 Cyril E. Black et al., *Neutralization and World Politics*, Princeton, NJ: Princeton University Press, 1968, pp. 191–5.
61 Memorandum, 20.7.1966. FRUS 1964–68 XXVII, Document 77.
62 Quoted in Noordin Sopiee, 'The neutralization of South East Asia', in Hedley Bull, ed., *Asia and the Western Pacific*, Melbourne: Nelson/AIIA, 1975, p. 139.
63 Girling, p. 123.
64 D. Weatherbee et al., *International Relations in Southeast Asia*, Lanham, MD: Rowman and Littlefield, 2005, p. 15.
65 Warner/Butler, 12.4.1961, and enclosure. FO 371/159835 [DF 1015/477].
66 Aust. Tel, 10.5.74, 1965. PM 434/12/1 Pt 5.
67 Simcock/SyFA, 20.5.1974. Pt 5.
68 Quoted in Irvine, p. 32.
69 *Times,* 14.5.75.
70 Quoted in Jorgensen-Dahl, p. 84.
71 Irvine, p. 35.
72 Ibid.
73 Aust Tel ex KL, 13.2.1976, 7573. FCO 15/2173.
74 NZ Tel ex KL, 19.2.1976, 199. Pt. 7.
75 Copy in Hänggi, pp. 65–8.
76 Leifer, *ASEAN*, p. 67.
77 D. Irvine, 'Making haste less slowly: ASEAN from 1975', in Alison J. Broinowski, *Understanding ASEAN*, New York: St Martin's, 1981, p. 49.
78 Aust Tel ex KL, ?3.1976, 8147. FCO 15/2174 [45].
79 For example by Z. Brzezinski, Carter's National Security Adviser. C. Brady, *United States Foreign Policy towards Cambodia*, Basingstoke: Macmillan, 1991, p. 28; Cécile Méhetry-Monchau, 'The changing post-war strategy in Indochina', in Odd Arne Westad and Sophie Quinn-Judge, eds, *The Third Indochina War*, London, New York: Routledge, 2006, p. 76.
80 Pavin Chachavalpongpun, *A Plastic Nation: the Curse of Thainess in Tai-Burmese Relations*, Lanham, MD: University Press of America, 2005, p. 141.
81 Hiro Katsumata, 'Reconstruction of diplomatic norms in Southeast Asia', *Contemporary Southeast Asia*, 25, 1 (April 2003), p. 105.
82 Quoted in Jeannie Henderson, *Reassessing ASEAN*, Adelphi Paper 328, Oxford: Oxford University Press, 1999, p. 71.
83 M. Stuart-Fox, *A Short History of China and Southeast Asia*, Crows Nest, NSW: Allen and Unwin, 2003, p. 155.
84 Ibid., pp. 236, 239.
85 Ibid., pp. 241, 244.
86 Wayne Bert, *The United States, China and Southeast Asian Security*, Basingstoke: Palgrave, 2003, p. 94.
87 Aust Tel, 26.2.1976, 7717. Pt 7.

Epilogue

1 Quoted in Robin Ramcharan, 'ASEAN and Non-interference', *Contemporary Southeast Asia*, 22, 1 (April 2000), p. 64.
2 Reviewing M. Moore, *A World without Walls*, in TLS, 26.9.2003.
3 Quoted in Thomas J. Christensen, *Useful Adversaries*, Princeton, NJ: Princeton University Press, 1996, pp. 178–9.
4 Gholamali Khoshroo, 'The experience of the Islamic Republic of Iran', in V. Hooker and Amin Siakal, eds, *Islamic Perspectives on the New Millennium*, Singapore: ISEAS, 2004, p. 155.

5 Ibid., p. 152.
6 Nur Ahmad Fadhil Lubis, 'Financial activism among Indonesian Muslims', in Hooker and Siakal, p. 94.
7 Azyumardi Azra, 'Political Islam in post-Soeharto Indonesia', in Hooker and Siakal, p. 137.

Bibliographical note

Historians are bound to make what Herbert Butterfield called 'abridgments': to set down the results of their research, if not in the first place to pursue it, they must define an area and select a period. Yet at the same time they recognize, with greater or less perspicacity and greater or less humility, that what they produce is part of a larger whole, a 'contribution', if not a reinterpretation or redefinition. Historians of Southeast Asia have written of peoples and countries within the area during different periods. They have also attempted histories of what has come to be seen as a region, though selecting different periods for emphasis. At the same time, they have lamented that neither countries, peoples nor region have generally been given a due place in more general histories and regretted the absence from them not only of the varieties of human experience they provide but also of the comparisons and contrasts for which they offer such potential.

The first attempt at a history of Southeast Asia was provided in 1955 by D.G.E. Hall, the first Professor of Southeast Asian History at the School of Oriental and African Studies in London. Going into several editions, it has never really been superseded. Most more recent substantial histories have been multi-author works, such as *The Cambridge History of Southeast Asia*. Other authors have studied the region in particular periods, most famously Anthony Reid in *The Age of Commerce* and Vic Lieberman in *Strange Parallels*.

The present work limits its range by topic rather than by area or by period. But the author takes on the risk of attempting to integrate with his historical approach some of the theories of specialists in the discipline of International Relations. They are diverse. Accounts may be found in the works of Torborn Knutsen, Scott Burchell and others. The reader may also want to tackle some of the works themselves, those of Kenneth Waltz or Hedley Bull, for example.

For his chapter on early Southeast Asia the author drew with particular profit on essays in the collection edited by Jeya Kathirithamby-Wells and John Villiers. No one can pursue this topic without reading the works of the late Oliver Wolters, whose essays have been conveniently put together in two collections, *History, Culture and Region in Southeast Asian Perspectives*, published in a revised edition in 1999 (Ithaca, NY: SEAP; Singapore: ISEAS), and in *Early Southeast Asia Selected Essays*, edited by Craig Reynolds, published in 2008 (Ithaca, NY: SEAP).

The role of China cannot be discussed without reading the works of Wang Gungwu. Derek Heng's *Sino-Malay Trade and Diplomacy from the Tenth through the Fourteenth Century* (Athens, OH: Ohio University Center for International Studies, 2009) offers the most up-to-date survey.

The author's chapter on the 'early modern' period is greatly indebted to the recent work on Grotius and the Dutch by M.J. Ittersum, *Profit and Principle* (Leiden: Brill, 2006) and Peter Borschberg, *Hugo Grotius, the Portuguese and Free Trade in the East Indies* (Singapore: NUS Press, 2011). But the author was glad to recognize the relevance of Palmira Brummett's *Ottoman Seapower and Levantine Diplomacy in the Age of Discovery* (Albany, NY: SUNY Press, 1994), and James J. Boyajian's *Portuguese Trade in Asia under the Habsburgs* (Johns Hopkins University Press, 1993). For the examples he was able to use he was often grateful to the work of his former colleagues, Barbara Watson Andaya and Leonard Y. Andaya, particularly the former's *Perak, The Abode of Grace* (Kuala Lumpur: OUP, 1979) and the latter's *The Kingdom of Johor* (Kuala Lumpur: OUP, 1975).

In writing on the colonial period the author was at once on more familiar ground and encompassed by a more copious literature. No work, so far as he is aware, discusses the nature of the 'colonial state' in our region or elsewhere, but the processes by which it was created in Southeast Asia, largely under the aegis of the British, have been quite fully investigated. More novel, perhaps, is the consideration of its various formats. The author found particular interest in the discussion of 'protectorates' offered in other contexts in W. Ross Johnston's *Sovereignty and Protection* (Durham, NC: Duke University Press, 1973) and in the article on British colonial protectorates C.W. Newbury contributed to the tribute to W.P. Morrell edited by G.A. Wood and P.S. O'Connor (Dunedin: Otago University Press, 1973).

The origins of the Japanese incursion into Southeast Asia and the nature of the empire they created there have been studied both from Japanese and English language sources. The chapter in the present book seeks to put them more fully into the changing context of Japan's earlier imperial ventures. It has been assisted by recent works, such as Hui-yu Caroline Ts'ai, *Taiwan in Japan's Empire-Building* (London, New York: Routledge, 2009) and Yamamuro Shin'ichi's *Manchuria under Japanese Dominion* (Philadephia, PA: University of Pennsylvania Press, 2006).

'Puppets' was a word used to denounce the semi-independence afforded political entities within the Japanese Co-Prosperity Sphere. But it was also an accusation deployed by the rivals in the Cold War as Southeast Asian states gained a purported independence. In the sixth chapter the relation of 'puppets' and 'puppeteers' is examined both in theory and practice, in particular in the case of Vietnam and Laos. In the former case the author draws substantially on the work of Seth Jacobs, *America's Miracle Man in Vietnam* (Durham, NC: Duke University Press, 2004) and *Cold War Mandarin* (Lanham, MD: Rowman and Littlefield, 2006). In the latter case, the author draws in part on his own recent book *Britain and the Neutralisation of Laos* (Singapore: NUS Press, 2011).

Part of the post-war problem was seen in terms of the emergence of 'weak states' that seemed unlikely to meet the security or indeed the other needs of their citizens. Yet it was more and more mandated by the world-wide adoption of the 'Westphalia' concept of the state system of which in some sense the book is an account. Regionalism, it might be said, has proved a better answer than federation, though Southeast Asia has witnessed both. It exists, of course, in several forms. The final chapter of the book is devoted to ASEAN. Particularly worth reading are the two collections edited by Alison Broinowski, *Understanding ASEAN* (New York: St Martin's, 1982), and *ASEAN into the 1990s* (Basingstoke: Macmillan, 1990), the late Michael Leifer's *ASEAN and the Security of South-East Asia* (London: Routledge, 1989), and Amitav Acharya's *Constructing a Security Community in Southeast Asia* (London, New York: Routledge, 2001). But ASEAN – like its historiography – is a work in progress.

Index

Made in the USA
Las Vegas, NV
31 October 2024

9dcb4599-0a78-486f-b209-e2fb43924ed1R01